# Process Assessment and Improvement
## *A Practical Guide*
### *Second Edition*

T0135137

# Process Assessment and Improvement

## A Practical Guide
### Second Edition

by

Han van Loon
*Leistungs Consult GmbH*
*Visiting Professor – Nottingham Trent University, UK*
*Visiting Professor – University of Business and*
*International Studies in Geneva*

Contributors:
Juan Maria Carranza, *ESA*
Katsutoshi Shintani, Masa Katahira, Hiroshi Koizumi, Yasushi Ishigai
and Satoshi Fushimi, *Japan*
Ju Anhua and Li Wenying, *NEC-CAS China*
Christ Vriens, Philips
Jon Theuerkauf and Zachery R. Brice, *Credit Suisse*

 Springer

Han van Loon
Sagenstrasse 35
CH-6318 Walchwil
Switzerland
Telephone & Fax: +41 41 7580826
email: welcome@lc-stars.com

Process Assessment and Improvement
*A Practical Guide, Second Edition*
by Han van Loon

ISBN 978-1-4899-9330-4                    ISBN 978-0-387-38163-3 (eBook)


Printed on acid-free paper.

9 8 7 6 5 4 3 2 1

springer.com

## Dedication and Acknowledgements

This book is dedicated to the many professionals committed to improving their organizations through process assessment and quality improvement.

Many people who have contributed to the development of the standards described herein, and I would like to acknowledge their collective contribution. I would also like to thank contributors from around the world who have provided information about the use of process assessment and improvement methods. Naturally my thanks extend to the contributors to the first edition, much of which remains relevant in the second edition. Input was used from the European Space Agency Research and Technology Centre, European Aerospace and Defence Systems Astrium, the Software Engineering Institute, the Software Quality Institute, the OOSPICE consortium, Rational, Audi and the Automotive SPICE group, the United States Federal Aviation Administration, the Swiss Federal Strategic Committee for Information Technology, Philips NV, HM&S, Credit Suisse, NEC-CAS, and Process Improvement Task Force, Ministry of Economics, Trade and Industry, and Software Engineering Center, Information-Technology Promotion Agency, Japan.

For the second edition I specifically wish to thank Juan Maria Carranza from ESA for risk based target profiles, Christ Vriens for input on agile software development for consumer electronics, Ju Anhua and Li Wenying from NEC-CAS, Jon Theuerkauf and Zachery R. Brice for information on Credit Suisse Operational Excellence, and Katsutoshi Shintani, Masa Katahira, Hiroshi Koizumi, Yasushi Ishigai and Satoshi Fushimi on ISO/IEC 15504 in Japan.

Han van Loon                                                    2007

Leistungs Consult GmbH
Web site: www.lc-stars.com
Email: welcome@lc-stars.com

# Table of Contents

# List of Figures

# List of Tables

xvi

# Introduction to the Practical Guide

## Practical Guide Overview

In this book, we look at the practical aspects of process assessments and their use. It is a companion book to: **Process Assessment and ISO/IEC 15504. A Reference Book.**

In chapter 1, I start by describing a model framework, the "People-Process-Product" model in which the importance of processes is explained. I describe the status of Software and Information Technology projects, which reveals the scope of ongoing problems and the economic impact of poor quality. The final part of the introduction provides a user-centric view of the standard.

In chapter 2, the user view is expanded to cover the three major business reasons for process assessment. These are setting Target Profiles, Process Capability Determination and Process Improvement.

In chapter 3, the user view of Target Profiles is explained in detail. A specific and advanced example of using risk to set target profiles for safety critical software is covered.

In chapter 4, the user view of Process Capability Determination is explained.

In chapter 5, the user view of Process Improvement is explained with a model derived from the standard. I introduce a more agile improvement cycle. I expand upon the topic of improvement to cover culture.

In chapter 6, I provide a method using teams that has proven to be highly effective, called Team Based Business Design Improvement, which is used with Business Process Mapping. The combination of these methods has been successfully used in high capability organisations.

In chapter 7, I introduce the major agile methods, including Evolutionary Development, Extreme Programming, SCRUM, Crystal and Feature Driven Development. I describe how to apply process assessment and improvement to agile methods.

In chapter 8, I describe a standard method for performing assessments; based upon ISO/IEC 15504 and the European Space Agency sponsored SPiCE for SPACE variant.

In a new chapter 9, I explore the role of the assessor as a guide and coach.

In chapter 10, I provide an overview of what the assessment results may look like, using the SPICE 1-2-1 tool, together with some interpretation.

In chapter 11, I summarize industry experience in using the standard, both in general from the SPICE trials and with particular industry examples. This section has extensive additions covering more industry applications of process assessment and improvement.

Annex 1 provides some templates. Annex 2 covers assessment tools. Annex 3 provides some additional improvement information.

## Reader Guidance

The following table suggests the most useful chapters for readers of the Practical guide and the Reference book.

There is a natural amount of overlap in the general descriptions between the Practical guide and the Reference book. However, the majority of the content of both books is complementary, and reinforces aspects of the other.

**Table 1. Reader Guidance to Books.**

| Reader | Reader's interests and expected benefits | Reference Book | Practical Guide |
|---|---|---|---|
| Manager | Benefit from the use of process assessment and process improvement | 1 | 1, 2, 5, 4, 10 |
| Quality Professional | General quality system and process management. Comparing assessment models, and the uses of process assessment. | 1, 2, 3, 4, 5, 7, 9, 10, Annex 1 | 1, 2, 3, 4, 5, 8, 9, 10 |
| Assessors | Conducting a conformant assessment, developing the skills and competencies needed to perform an assessment. In-depth capability rating guidance. | 3, 4, 6, 8, 9, Annex 2, Annex 3 | 2, 6, 7, 8, 9, 10, Annex 1, Annex 2 |
| Assessment Sponsor | How an assessment is conducted, what tools and other support are required, how to initiate an assessment. Various types of uses of assessments, Interpreting the results. | 1, 3, 4, 8, Annex 3 | 1, 2, 3, 4, 5, 6, 8, 11 |
| Process Owner | Design and implementation of processes. Improving processes. | 1, 5, 7 | 1, 5 |
| Process Expert | Provide expertise on process design and applicability of the standard to design and improvement of processes. | 2, 4, 5, 6, 7 | 5, 7, 8 |
| Process Practitioner | Implement a process; participate in design and assessment of processes. | | 1, 2, 4, 5 |
| Process Improvement Sponsor | Initiating an improvement programme, defining assessment inputs for an assessment for improvement purposes, using assessment results for improvement. | 1, 3 | 1, 2, 5, 8, 9, 10, 11 |
| Process Capability Determination Sponsor | Initiating a programme for the determination of supplier capability, defining a target capability profile, verifying and using assessment results in a capability determination exercise. | 1, 3 | 1, 2, 4, 8, 10, 3 (optional) |
| Developers of Process Assessment Models | Developing Process Assessment Models for performing assessments against a compliant Process Reference Model and measurement framework of ISO/IEC 15504-2. | 1, 2, 3, 4, 5, 6, 7 Annex 2, Annex 5 | |
| Developers of Methods | Developing a method that will support the performance of conformant assessments. | 3, 5, 6 | |
| Tool Developers | Developing tools that support assessors by collecting, recording and classifying evidence in assessments. | 3 | Annex 1, Annex 2 |

| Improvement Team Facilitator | Help teams in a Team Based Business Design Improvement process. | | 2, 5 |
|---|---|---|---|
| Customer | Benefits and use of process assessment from a customer perspective, particularly for setting target profiles, capability determination and improvement. | 1 | 1, 2, 3, 5, 8, 10, 11 |

Readers should read the Reference Book for a more detailed understanding of the ISO/IEC 15504 standard. It provides details on process reference models, process assessment models and process lifecycle models that are intended to help organizations implementing and assessing processes.

# Organizational Success and People-Process-Product

## People-Process-Product

Organizations rely on three major attributes: **people**, **processes**[1] and **products**. The synergy and interaction of these creates competitive advantages leading to organizational success.

However, people, processes and products interact in organizations in a variety of ways; no two organizations interact the same way. This is primarily because each organization has different people and groups of people. I call this the People-Process-Product model [1], which has a simple way to illustrate this interaction.

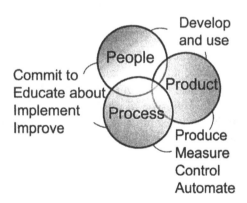

**Fig. 1. People-Process-Product model.**

---

[1] A process is a series of actions that you take in order to achieve a result. Cambridge Dictionary of American English definition.

The model indicates that:

- People develop products (goods and services) for customers.
- People invent, commit to, educate themselves and others, and implement processes in order to produce these products.
- People use products (also often referred to as technology or tools) in their organization/business.
- Processes are used to measure and control the production of products.
- People improve processes as one way to improve products.
- Products can be used to simplify and automate processes.

Each organization can decide the balance between the way people, processes and products interact and to the extent that they interact and rely on each. For example, I can decide upon various ways to achieve success:

- Do I allow people to choose the way they do something (e.g. craftsmanship)?
- Do I automate the way something is done by means of a product (e.g. an automated tool or software)?
- Do I define a standard process?

All three ways may be possible. Naturally, an organization striving for success wants to use the 'best way' (the most efficient and effective) that is available to them. This will normally require the organization to select a particular combination of people, processes and products that reflects the experience and knowledge of their people, the types of products they create and the processes they need to follow.

However, people vary in the way that they perform activities. This variation is a natural phenomenon. Different people can vary in doing the same or similar tasks, and one person can vary depending upon how they feel or think at different times. Sometimes this variation can be positive, for example finding ways to improve a product or service, sometimes this variation can be negative, for example failing to completely test a product due to time constraints.

To illustrate how processes can affect products consider the following:

*When a computer program produces an incorrect result, we do not correct the result, rather we correct the program.*

Similarly, when a process produces an incorrect (product) result, we should not correct the product, but rather correct the process (the means) we followed to produce it.

Organizations therefore *define* processes in order to minimize the negative aspects of variation in production of products and services. They educate people to follow the defined processes in order to produce consistent quality products and services.

Furthermore, to *improve* products, an organization can improve their people (through education) and/or improve the processes used. Improving the process leads to more consistent, higher quality results.

At the same time, it is important that processes do not create restrictions or impose negative unproductive overheads in activities, especially in creative activities.

Bureaucratic aspects of processes or process rigidity can undo much of the benefit of processes. It is therefore important that processes are designed to suit the size and type of organization, what products it produces and the people it employs. Processes need to be adaptable (tailorable) to suit the particular application within an organization.

Many organizations have sought to improve their efficiency and extend their capabilities by use of Information Technology and software to automate processes. Using these products to automate a process can also lead to more consistent (and quicker) results, when both the process and the tools are of high quality (both efficient and effective).

However, if the process is poor, then automating it will not improve quality. Dr Michael Hammer famously summarized this as follows: "*automating a mess yields an automated mess*" [2].

This increasing focus on process automation has created a boom in software development, which despite the economic downturns is still a major growth industry. However, the increasing complexity of systems, the lack of experienced IT people, the continued below-par performance of software projects (many are too late with too many problems), and maintenance of software has been termed the 'Software Crisis' [3]. The NATO Conference in 1968 in which this term was first expressed, suggested that the solution was a more formal, structured approach to software development. This implies the use of consistent, high quality processes that help people to produce consistent high quality products.

In summary, poor processes can lead to poor or inconsistent quality products and failure. Using appropriate processes are one of the 3 important organizational prerequisites to achieve success.

## The Software Crisis and Status of Software Projects today

In the more than 3 decades since the 'Software Crisis' term was coined, there has been much research, many methodologies and products (tools) produced to improve the way we produce software.

*So, has this meant that the software crisis is over and we no longer have a problem?*

Not according to research by the Standish Group [4] and the National Institute of Standards and Technology (NIST) [5]. The Standish Group had examined 8,380 Software Projects by 1994 and over 40,000 projects by 2003. It categorizes projects as Successful, Challenged (over-budget, late, missing capabilities in delivered products) and Cancelled. The following graphs show the results for their surveys in 1994 and 2000.

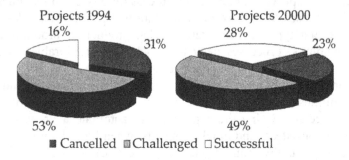

Fig. 2. Percentages of successful challenged and cancelled software projects.

The statistics show that the situation has improved, but still only 28% of projects in 2000 were considered successful. The Standish report also indicates that as projects become larger in scope and budget, they are more prone to failure. Very large projects have a very low success rate (approaching 0%).

The NIST report looks at the economic cost of software problems due to inadequate infrastructure for software testing. It estimates that in 2002 the economic impact was US $59.5 Billion and estimated that there were potential savings of US $22.2 Billion. While the report title discusses software-testing infrastructure, it also states that: *"(software) testing tools are still fairly primitive."* The report further identifies that finding problems as soon as possible, to when they are (inadvertently) created is the most cost effective means of problem resolution. It provides detailed estimates for transport and financial services sectors for specific software (including software tools such as CAD/CAE/CAM).

Cost of Software Problems - Financial Services

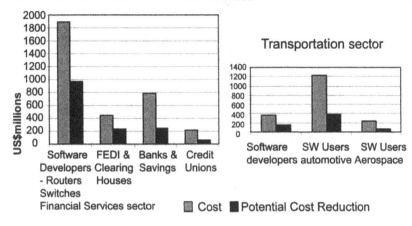

**Fig. 3. Cost of Software Problems and potential cost reductions.**

The surveyed results in just the two sectors in the figure estimate a cost of US $5.18 billion and a potential cost reduction of US $2.1 billion. The cost per employee was calculated in order to extrapolate to the total economic cost estimate of US $59.5 billion for the entire US software industry (consisting of US $21.2 billion for software developers, US $11.4 billion for users in manufacturing sectors and US $26.9 billion for users in the service sectors). So even users with of developed and pre-packaged (shrink-wrap) software are suffering the effects of the software crisis[2].

The reports estimate where the Software Errors were introduced: 9% in Installation and Commissioning, 23% in Design and Implementation and 68% in Requirements Specifications.

Furthermore, they report that early error detection and correction are very important; the cost to correct a software error multiplies during the development lifecycle by at least 2 to 2.5 times that of the previous activity/phase. So an error in requirements typically costs twice (2 times) as much to fix during the Requirements activity (as opposed to it being correct), 5 times in the Preliminary Design activity, 10 times in the Detail Design activity, 20 times in the Coding activity and 40 times in the Test activity. The incremental cost of change is subject to debate, on the one hand agile development believe the cost curve is flatter, while other studies consider the

---

[2] Life is like a box of software – you never know what you are going to get! (Apologies to Forest Gump).

above rations may even be conservative (Bazluk study in the NIST report [5][3]).

The NIST report also highlights the change in allocation of effort to earlier activities in software development [6].

**Table 2. Allocation of Effort in Software Development.**

|  | Requirements Analysis | Preliminary Design | Detailed Design | Coding and Unit testing | Integration and Test | System Test |
|---|---|---|---|---|---|---|
| 1970's | 10% | | | 80% | 10% | |
| 1980's | 20% | | | 60% | 20% | |
| 1990's | 40% | | 30% | | 30% | |

It is evident that the industry still has a long way to achieving consistent success, but that some success is being achieved as organizations focus increasingly on earlier activities.

In the latest version of the Chaos Chronicles from the Standish Group, some of the topics addressing improvement include process capability, user involvement, executive management support, experienced personnel, agile methods and formal methods.

## The need for process assessment

So given the NATO Conference perception of the software crisis, the need for better approaches to software development, and the research indicating that the crisis has yet to be solved, how does an organization know if it has consistent high quality processes that help achieve project success?

Ideally, the organization should consider its performance against its competitors and peers in its market, and against peers in related markets – in other words its overall 'business success'. It should relate this performance to the processes (and technology) it uses to determine how those processes contribute to business success. It should also consider its absolute performance (or lack of performance) and attempt to calculate the cost of failure.

It is not always possible to obtain performance data about competitors and especially about their processes. In this situation, the organization needs an independent measurement system for its processes.

Process assessment provides an accepted, independent measurement framework for assessment of processes. The ISO/IEC 15504 standard has

---

[3] A study by Bazluk in 1995 (see NIST report [5]) estimates that the cost to correct a requirements problem in operation and maintenance can be between 470

been developed as an international view of 'best practice' in process assessment. Using ISO/IEC 15504 allows organizations to assess whether their processes are capable of helping them achieve organizational success.

## Overview of Process Assessment

When an organization sets goals to achieve success, it must know how well it is performing and what it still needs to do to achieve success. Since success in our competitive world is a moving target (we need to continually be faster/ better/more cost efficient), we need to constantly re-evaluate and improve our performance against new goals and targets.

Defining and implementing processes (a set of related activities, inputs and outputs) helps an organization to achieve success[4]. However, it is not sufficient to just implement any process; the organization must know that these processes are effective (they achieve their purpose) and efficient (they provide superior cost/benefit).

Process assessment therefore fits within a value chain leading from organizational goals to success.

- The first step is to translate the organization goals into the required processes.
- The second step is implement processes to meet these goals.
- The third step is to assess whether these processes achieve the organizational goals.
- The fourth step (normally) is to decide how to improve the current processes to achieve the current goals and the desired goals in the future.
- The final step is to celebrate organizational success (and then set new goals and targets).

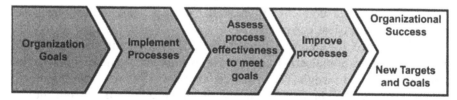

**Fig. 4. Process Assessment and Improvement value chain.**

Simple isn't it? Yes and no.

---

Organizations sometimes fail to implement successful processes, improvement efforts slow down or stop, internal organizational politics interfere with well-directed process implementation and improvement. For some more reading on organizational politics and problems, I recommend Death March by Ed Yourdon [7].

So how does an organization achieve this? They need a 'roadmap' to guide them, or in other words, objective evidence of where their processes are now, and a set of actions to take their processes to where they want to be in the future. Process assessment helps fulfils the above needs by:

✓ Determining the current state of the organizations processes (their process capability), through collecting objective evidence against defined Process Assessment Models.

✓ Providing guidance to organizations in selecting which processes to implement by referring to or containing Process Reference Models that define processes.

✓ Providing guidance to organizations to help them improve their processes through a measurement scale for processes.

Simply, the concept behind process assessment is to compare an actual, implemented process against a defined standard set of process characteristics (attributes) consisting of process descriptions and a measurement framework.

First, process assessment evaluates whether the organization performs the process with all the basic activities (Base Practices) needed to achieve the process goals by looking at evidence (Work Products such as documents or products produced).

Secondly, process assessment looks at how well a process is managed, by comparing the performance, management, definition, measurement and improvement of the process against a standard scale of good management practice. The measurement framework defines this scale for the measurement of process capability[5].

Thirdly, Process Reference Models provide a coherent framework for processes that an organization can choose to implement and/or improve to achieve the desired results. These models may cover software development, system engineering, human resources or other areas of organizational processes, and they reflect industry best practices.

Process assessment must have a set of characteristics to make it useful for an organization. These can be summarized as:

• A framework to ensure consistent assessments.

• A measurement framework that specifies a scale of performance (capability).

---

[5] Process capability relates to the organization's ability to deliver specified or

- A description of the processes the organization wishes to assess.
- A method to ensure consistent assessment performance by assessors.
- Guidance on how to tailor the assessment to suit the organization.
- Requirements on assessors to ensure they are capable and consistent in performing assessments.
- Guidance on how to apply assessment results.

To address all the above issues, the international community has embraced the need for an international standard for process assessment. This resulted in creation of the standards working group focused on process assessment, who have created the ISO/IEC 15504 process assessment standard.

The standard provides a universally applicable process assessment model and method, and is a harmonization standard – this means that it acts as an 'umbrella standard' covering multiple process assessment methods and models by setting requirements for compliance and conformance.

ISO/IEC 15504-2 specifies the requirements for process assessment using two complementary orthogonal dimensions:

- Capability dimension.
- Process dimension.

The two dimensions work together to provide complete process assessment ability.

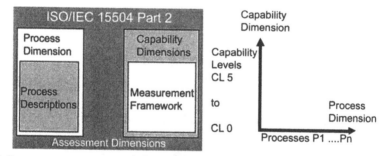

**Fig. 5. Process assessment and the continuous dimension model.**

ISO/IEC 15504-2 uses a continuous model representation for the capability and process dimensions. The advantage of this two dimensional continuous model is that it allows for any process to be assessed and rated at any Capability Level, independently of any other process.

The companion Reference Book describes these areas in detail (starting in the chapter on Conformance Requirements and in Annex 1).

**User view of the ISO/IEC 15504 document set.**

It is possible to view the ISO/IEC 15504 standard document set as consisting of 3 layers. This 3 dimensional view can guide readers to the most applicable parts of the standard (of course, they should also read these books!).

The three layers are:
- The User view layer, which specifies what you may wish to use the standard to achieve. It consists of Part 4 (ISO/IEC 15504-4).
- The Standards view layer, which consists of the normative part of the standard and how to apply it for process assessment. It consists of ISO/IEC 15504-2, ISO/IEC 15504-3 and ISO/IEC 15504-1.
- The Application detail view layer, which consists of the process assessment model and process reference model that apply to the organization. Here I specify ISO/IEC 15504 parts 5 and 6 and the externally specified process reference models. Note that this layer may comprise different models from these shown here. These are described in more detail in the Reference book.

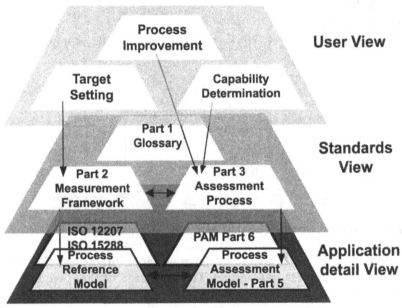

**Fig. 6. Layered view of ISO/IEC 15504 relationships.**

The Practical Guide follows this way to view the standard. The User View Chapters cover:
- The purpose of process assessment
- Defining Target capability Profiles

- Capability Determination
- Process Improvement

Standards View:

- Performing assessments

Application detail view:

- Rating a process to Capability Level 5
- What assessment results look like.

The book then provides information on industry experience with ISO/IEC 15504, including experience from the SPICE trials, space industry experience, financial, public institutions and automotive industry experience.

## Standards Reading Guide

The standard uses a different representation for reader interest. They provide a table, which identifies the principal readers for ISO/IEC 15504. It shows where their likely interests are addressed within the document set.

**Table 3. Readership of parts of ISO/IEC 15504.**

| Reader | Reader's Interests | Suggested parts |
|---|---|---|
| Assessment Sponsor | How an assessment is conducted, what tools and other support are required, how to initiate an assessment. | 1, 2, 3 |
| Process Improvement Sponsor | Initiating an improvement programme, defining assessment inputs for an assessment for improvement purposes, using assessment results for improvement. | 4 |
| Process Capability Determination Sponsor | Initiating a programme for the determination of supplier capability, defining a target capability profile, verifying and using assessment results in a capability determination exercise. | 4 |
| Assessors | Conducting a conformant assessment, developing the skills and competencies needed to perform an assessment. | 2, 3, 4, 5, 6 |
| Developers of Process Assessment Models | Developing Process Assessment Models for performing assessments based on a compliant Process Reference Model and the measurement framework as defined in ISO/IEC 15504-2 | 2, 3, 5, 6 |
| Developers of Assessment Methods | Developing a method that will support the performance of conformant assessments. | 2, 3, 5, 6 |
| Tool Developers | Developing tools that will support assessors by collecting, recording and classifying evidence in the performance of assessments. | 2, 3, 5, 6 |

Readers should use these books in conjunction with the standards when they require a detailed understanding or have to interpret the statements in the standard.

# User View – the purpose of process assessment

## User View – the purpose of process assessment

In this chapter, I look at the reasons to use process assessments. This chapter will be of interest to customers, managers, assessors, assessment sponsors, process capability determination sponsors, improvement sponsors and quality professionals.

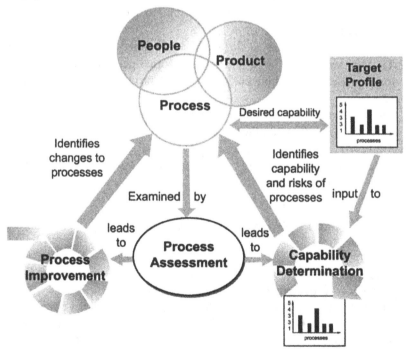

**Fig. 7. Process Assessment Purposes.**

This chapter presents the most common cases why an organization should consider process assessment. The cases are:

- Target Capability Profile definition.
- Process Capability Determination.
- Process Improvement.

The three cases are illustrated in terms of the People-Process-Product model. The diagram illustrates the main relationships and can be summarized as follows:

- Processes are examined by process assessment.
- The desired capability of processes can be set through Target Profiles.
- Target Profiles act as a major input to Capability Determination.
- Process assessment leads to Capability Determination of the actual process Capability Levels.
- Capability Determination identifies the actual capability of processes, compares it to the target capability to identify process capability gaps, and from these is able to identify process related risks.
- Process assessment leads to identification of opportunities for Process Improvement.
- Process Improvement identifies and implements changes to processes. These changes may be to improve the actual performance of processes, or to improve the desired performance of process and hence the process capability.

The People-Process-Product framework also implies that process change affects people (for example people need to be educated about a changed process), and products (for example the technology used to automate parts of a process may need changing). Therefore, process change should not be seen as an activity occurring by itself.

## Business Case – Process Improvement

The business case to perform process assessment for improvement purposes can be summarized by looking again at the cost of poor processes and products as described in the section on the Software Crisis.

The NIST report [8] estimates that the economic impact of poor software was US $59.5 Billion with potential savings of US $22.2 Billion for the US software industry. They estimate this economic impact consisted of US $21.2 billion for software developers, US $11.4 billion for users in manufacturing sectors and US $26.9 billion for users in the service sectors. The NIST report estimates where software errors were introduced as being:

✗   9% in Installation and Commissioning,

✗   23% in Design and Implementation, and

✖ 68% in Requirements Specifications.

In other words, most errors occur early in the process value chain. The report further identifies that finding problems as soon as possible after they are (inadvertently) created is the most cost effective means of problem resolution.

The report cites that the cost to correct a software error multiplies during the development lifecycle by at least 2 to 2.5 times that of the previous activity/phase. An error in requirements typically:

✖ costs twice (2 times) as much to fix during the Requirements activity (as opposed to it being correct),

✖ costs 5 times as much to fix in the Preliminary Design activity,

✖ costs 10 times as much to fix in the Detail Design activity,

✖ costs 20 times as much to fix in the Coding activity and

✖ costs 40 times as much to fix in the Test activity

The above cost estimate may even by conservative. A study by Bazluk in 1995 (see NIST report) estimates that the cost to correct a requirements problem in operation and maintenance can be between 470 and 2900 times as high!

It is evident that the industry still has a long way to achieving consistent success, and that process improvement activities based upon process assessment can be an important means to reduce the poor cost of software quality. While the magnitude of the problems facing the software industry is still large, process improvement efforts are showing clear benefits.

There have been several studies highlighting improvement benefits. The Software Engineering Institute and the Defence Information Analysis Center have provided a range of evidence of improvement benefits. The National Research Council of Canada has also analysed improvement efforts based upon ISO/IEC 15504 and CMM®. I present some of the results here.

The Department of Defence Information Analysis Center has prepared a State Of the Art Report describing the benefits of software process improvements including secondary benefits [9].

The report analyses whether software process assessment and improvement can significantly:

• Reduce the amount of time and effort required to develop software.

• Reduce the number of defects induced into a system.

• Reduce the costs and time to find defects that are introduced.

• Reduce maintenance costs on software products.

• Improve productivity of the development team.

The report looks at total development costs, total rework costs, average schedule length and post release defects (delivered defects). It also looks at secondary benefits including the effect of project sales, penalties and bonuses, yearly turnover costs (staff, etc.), repeat business, SPI risks and the cost of improvements. The overall result is shown in the following table.

**Table 4. Comparison of process improvement metrics.**

| Metric | Without Improvement | With Software Process Improvement | Benefit |
|---|---|---|---|
| Primary Benefits | | | |
| Total Development Costs | $ 2,886,543 | $ 780, 174 | $ 2,106,370 |
| Total Rework costs | $ 619, 369 | $ 26,080 | $ 593,288 |
| Average Schedule length | 27 calendar months | 17 calendar months | 10 months |
| Post Release Defects | 15% of Total Defects | < 5% of Total Defects | 80% |
| Secondary Benefits | | | |
| Projected sales | $ 10,000,000 | $ 10,500,000 | $ 500,000 |
| Penalties/Bonuses | ($ 50,000) | $ 50,000 | $ 100,000 |
| Yearly Turnover Costs | $ 615,000 | $102, 500 | $ 512,000 |
| Repeat Business | $ 1,000,000 | $ 5,000,000 | $ 4,000,000 |
| Cost of the Improvement | | $ 373,000 | ($ 373,000) |
| Weighted Risks | | | |
| High | $ 412,500 | $ 0 | $ 412,500 |
| Medium | $ 1,678, 125 | $ 0 | $ 1,678,125 |
| Low | $ 0 | $ 175,000 | ($ 175,000) |

The report concludes that process improvement can have a significant bottom line cost savings to a software development organization (as much as a 67% reduction in development and rework costs). In summary, it states that process improvement:

✓ Reduces Development and Maintenance Costs.

✓ Improves Customer Satisfaction. Reduces delivered defects from 15% to less than 5% (in some cases near to zero). Improving customer satisfaction is shown to result in repeat customer business and an improved company image.

✓ Reduces Cycle Time. Improvement efforts can reduce typical schedule lengths by 30% to 40%. This result can be higher profit, being more competitive, or receiving schedule related bonuses for early delivery.

✓ Combining improved schedules with higher quality - getting better products out sooner -is a winning combination as far as our customers are concerned.

✓ Improves professional staff morale and confidence of developers. It results in less overtime, less crisis, less employee turnover, and an improved competitive edge. The reduction in employee turnover costs and retraining costs could pay for the improvement costs alone.

✓ Increases Profitability. There is a significant Return on Investment (many organizations have reported a 7:1 ROI). This high return on investment is achieved by reducing development costs; rework costs, and turnover costs. Product sales increase from higher quality software; penalties turn into bonuses, and repeat business increases. Furthermore, a risk analysis of doing software improvements versus not performing the improvements highly favours performing the improvements.

The Software Engineering Institute at Carnegie Mellon University in Pittsburgh is the leading US institution studying software process assessment and improvement. Mark Paulk has prepared several reports on the benefits of software process improvement [10] and there are also reports by Dennis Goldenson and Diane Gibbon [11].

The results are for organizations improving process capability through use of the Capability Maturity Models (SW CMM$^{SM}$ and CMMI$^{SM}$).

The results achieved are generally considered applicable to sustained forms of process improvement leading to higher capability processes.

The reports display results of participating organisations including Boeing, Motorola and Advanced Information Systems.

First, the estimation and control of the cost performance index of project improves as maturity improves. Data is drawn from a study by Clark [12].

This study used a sample of 161 software projects from different companies to analyse the impact that process maturity has on the COCOMO cost estimation model (impact of higher maturity on effort). The effect of changes in process maturity levels is summarised in the following figures.

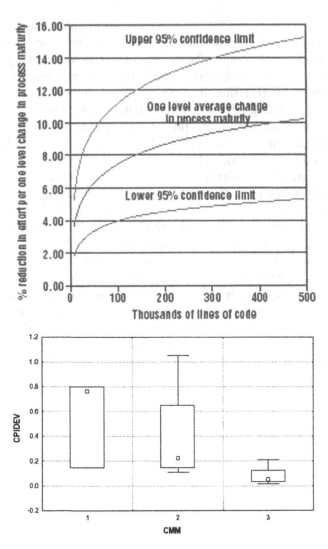

**Fig. 8. Reduction in effort for process maturity and estimation accuracy.**

This study shows that higher process capability leads to better estimation of effort (and hence cost). This is represented by the height of the box for each estimate in the graph on the right. Higher capability also lowers the effort needed to develop software (the mean value represented by the small mark inside each box). The reduction is higher for larger software projects.

Carnegie Mellon University
Software Engineering Institute

## "Trends" in Quality Results

| Maturity Level | Design Faults / KSLOC (Keene) | Delivered Defects / FP (Jones) | Shipped Defects / KSLOC (Krasner) | Relative Defect Density (Williams) | Shipped Defects (Rifkin) |
|---|---|---|---|---|---|
| 5 | 0.5 | 0.05 | 0.5 | 0.05 | 1 |
| 4 | 1 | 0.14 | 2.5 | 0.1 | 5 |
| 3 | 2 | 0.27 | 3.5 | 0.2 | 7 |
| 2 | 3 | 0.44 | 6 | 0.4 | 12 |
| 1 | 5-6 | 0.75 | 30 | 1.0 | 61 |

Samuel Keene, "Modeling Software R&M Characteristics." Unpublished report.
Capers Jones, "Software Benchmarking," IEEE Computer. October 1995, pp. 102-103.
Herb Krasner, "Self-Assessment Experience at Lockheed." Third Annual SEPG Workshop, 7 November 1990.
Karl D. Williams, "The Value of Software Improvement... Results! Results! Results!" SPIRE97, 4 June 1997.
Stan Rifkin, "The Business Case for Software Process Improvement." Fifth SEPG National Meeting, 26-29 April 1993.

October 2002          33          Trends

**Fig. 9. Effect of software process improvement by CMM maturity level.**

The above two slides from the SEI shows the improvements achieved, both in product defect rates and in process metrics such as cycle time and productivity.

The following figures quoted for companies are collated from the Goldenson and Gibbon report.

✓ 33% decrease in average cost to fix a defect (Boeing Australia).

✓ 20% reduction in units' software costs and 15% decrease in defect find and fix costs (Lockheed Martin M&DS).

✓ 60% reduction in cost of customer acceptance (Thales Research and Technology).

✓ 60% reduction in work and outstanding actions following pre-test and post-test audits (Boeing Australia).

✓ Percentage of milestones met increased from 50% to 95% (General Motors).

✓ 15% improvement in internal on-time delivery and 10% improvement in first pass yield which reduces rework (Bosch Gasoline Systems).

✓ Reduction of all defects found in fielded systems to 2% (Norththrop Grumman ITI).

✓ Reduction in error cases in the factory by one order of magnitude (Bosch Gasoline Systems).

✓ Most of $2 million savings resulted from early detection and removal of defects (Sanchez Computer Associates).

✓ Increased customer satisfaction quantified by 55% increase in award fees (Lockheed Martin M&DS).

✓ Received 98% of possible customer award fees and a rating of "exceptional" in customer performance survey (Norththrop Grumman ITI).

Mark Paulk makes the following comments/conclusions about process improvement. Software projects must deal with both known and unknown factors.

- The known factors are process capability, specifically repeatability through use of disciplined processes and statistical process control.

    ✓ The ability to estimate and manage a project (encompassing the planned acquisition, development, product assurance, operations and management activities) at a budgeted cost means that the planned activities are more likely to be performed.

    ✓ When the planned activities follow processes that are designed to assure product quality, then the delivered product quality will be improved. The report shows the effect of this higher process capability (maturity) in terms of lower defect rates for the delivered product.

- The unknown factors are commonly the focus of risk management, covering aspects such as requirements change, identifying, tracking and mitigating risks.

    - If software projects improve control of the known factors (the processes followed and the costs involved) through higher process capability, then they are able to focus on the unknown factors better, for example the risks associated with changing requirements. Risk reduction is a necessary activity as software criticality increases.

✗ Paulk also warns against the risk of dysfunctional behaviour, focused upon receiving a good maturity rating. He emphasizes to focus on improvement to realize business value.

✓ Benefits of model and standards based improvement include ability to build upon a broad set of processes and practices from a community of interest; a framework for prioritising actions, performing assessments and comparing them to industry 'benchmarks'.

Specific study of ISO/IEC 15504 based process improvement had been performed by the National research Council of Canada [13]. The report concludes:

- The results of more methodologically defensible predictive validity studies of capability tend to demonstrate an association between increased process capability and increased performance, and no studies showed the opposite. The report has a table that summarises the predictive validity of process capability levels leading to improved performance.

**Table 5. Predictive validity study on effects of higher process capability.**

| Performance Measure | Processes in a large IT organizations | Processes in a small IT organizations |
|---|---|---|
| Ability to meet budget constraints | Develop Software Design Implement Software Design | |
| Ability to meet schedule constraints | Develop Software Design | Develop Software Design |
| Ability to achieve customer satisfaction | Develop Software Design | |
| Ability to satisfy specified requirements | Develop Software Design | |
| Staff productivity | Develop Software Requirements Integrate and Test Software | |
| Staff morale/job satisfaction | Develop Software Design | |

This predictive validity analysis shows that there is a correlation between the increase in process capability of the process and an improvement in an ability to meet the performance measures on the left for large IT organizations (more than 50 IT Staff).

One of its clear conclusions is:

*"There is ample evidence that higher process capability is associated with improved performance."*


## Business Case – Target Capability Profile definition

There are two reasons to consider definition of Target Capability Profiles. First, organizations may wish to define or use a target capability profile that minimizes process risk to a successful implementation of a specified requirement.

Secondly, a customer organization may wish to set a target capability profile for supplier selection. This may be related to criteria for a particular class or criticality of software (for example mission or safety critical software). In this way the customer organization can reduce effort required to assess offers from organizations that are unsuited to the development of the desired products. In both business cases, the focus is upon actively using process capability as a way to reduce risk. The detailed reasons for Target Capability Profile include:

- Specify the supplier's level of competence, in other words the required process capability for the processes of relevance to the customer.
- Reduce uncertainties in selecting suppliers of systems by enabling risks associated with the process capability to be identified before contract award.
- Enable appropriate controls for risk mitigation.
- Provide a quantified basis for choice in balancing business needs, requirements and estimated project cost against the capability of competing suppliers.
- Force the supplier to achieve an explicitly stated level of capability and demonstrate this capability as part of a supply contract.
- Differentiate between suppliers based on their process capability, for example when assessing potential suppliers as part of a pre-contract acquisition evaluation.

To reduce risk, the organization must determine what processes are important (key processes), and to what Capability Level the key processes have to be performed to avoid/mitigate the risks. The importance of processes will vary according to project/product needs. Different processes are important if a product is developed from requirements or being maintained. If only a service is being provided, then other processes are more important.

The division of work between organizations causes another variation. If a system has safety critical and non-safety critical software, the organization developing the safety critical software needs better processes. Normally the setting of Target Capability Profiles will be followed by:

- Process assessment for Capability Determination of the proposed supplier(s); or
- Responses from the suppliers who have already been assessed.

## Business Case – Process Capability Determination

One of the earliest reasons to promote process assessment was because larger organizations (especially in the Defence and Telecommunications industries) wished to assess the competence and capability of their suppliers. The United States Department of Defence sponsored the Software Engineering Institute to produce the SW CMM[SM] for just this purpose. The reasons to assess the capability of a supplier are many:

- Determine the supplier's areas of competence from a process perspective.
- Determine the supplier's level of competence, in other words their current process capability for the processes of relevance to the customer.

- Reduce uncertainties in selecting suppliers of systems by identifying risks associated with the contractor's process capability before contract award.
- Enable appropriate risk mitigation.
- Provide assurance to the customer that the supplier has the desired level of process capability.
- Provide assurance that the specific organizational instance(s) assessed, for example specific projects, are performing at the desired level of process capability.
- Identify any shortcomings in a supplier's processes or process capability.
- Investigate the process capability of a supplier in greater detail and in a more differentiated manner than normally possible through 3$^{rd}$ party quality audit to ISO 9000. In ISO 9000 compliance rather than capability is more often the norm.

Organizations may also seek to determine their own process capability for the following reasons:
- Differentiate themselves from less capable competitors.
- Achieve the process capability of competitors so that differentiation is not based on process capability.
- Set internal goals for their level of process capability in order to motivate the organization.
- Provide summary information on the process capability of various organizational units to management.
- Provide summary information on the differences in process capability of various organizational units.
- Provide information on changes in levels of process capability of an organizational unit over time (especially in conjunction with improvement activities).
- Highlight particular organizational process strengths and weaknesses to management.

Organizations that achieve higher levels of process capability should be better able to:
✓ Maximize their responsiveness to customer and market requirements.
✓ Minimize the full life-cycle costs of their products.
✓ Maximize end-user satisfaction.

In general, the most useful result of Capability Determination is an agreed capability between the organization (e.g. the supplier) and the sponsor (e.g. the customer).

This provides confidence to the customer that the supplier is using processes that are capable to deliver the desired level of process performance, while helping the supplier to focus on which processes deliver business value to the customer.

# User View - Defining Target Capability Profiles

## Defining Target Capability Profiles

In this chapter, I look at the reasons to consider why an organization would set target capability profiles. I then describe how this is done and what a profile should look like, and summarize the risk and process related aspects of this activity.

This section is based largely upon the technical report version of the standard: ISO/IEC TR 15504 part 8 [14]. In addition, I describe a novel technique I used for the European Space Agency that uses risk to determine target process capability for software required to meet various levels of system safety criticality. This chapter will be of interest to customers, assessment sponsors, process capability determination sponsors and quality professionals.

Organizations may wish to define or use a target capability profile that minimizes process risk to a successful implementation of a specified requirement.

There are two dimensions to setting a target capability profile, the processes to be assessed (process dimension) and the Capability Levels of each process (capability dimension). The target capability is usually expressed within a target capability statement which lists the most important (i.e. key) processes required to meet the specified requirements and for each required process, the required achievement of each Process Attribute. For each key process, the organization identifies which Process Attributes are required, and the desired degree of achievement for each Process Attribute (this should either be Fully achieved, Largely achieved or Not achieved).

The simplest way to set Process Attribute achievement is to set all Process Attributes to a certain Capability Level, for example to Capability Level 2 or 3. However, this is not recommended as it fails to consider the specific requirements that normally exist in each instance or set of instances. An instance may be a particular project, or the work of a specific group (or department). The following simple examples illustrate why setting one Capability Level and associated Process Attribute levels is unwise. The 3 examples illustrate different business needs as well as project needs.

## Target Capability Profile for Projects

### Project A.

Project A requires design and development of a safety critical software application in the aerospace domain within a critical, defined time period meeting Aviation Administration certification.

In this case, the engineering processes will require *at least* Capability Level 3 (established) to meet the safety critical regulatory aspects (such as documented processes). If part of the certification proof requires generation, collection and analysis of metrics to manage the process, then the process will require Capability Level 4 (predictable).

There will be a requirement for a Capability Level 3 process for an independent verification and validation. The support processes such as configuration management and problem tracking will require a minimum of Capability Level 3. The management processes such as project management, risk management and quality management will also require at least Capability Level 3. If risk and project management also require metrics to manage the overall process, then they will also require to Largely achieve Capability Level 4.

### Project B.

Project B requires *design* of a database within a critically short time period. In this case, not all engineering processes may be required (for example coding and unit testing is probably not needed). If the organization has a small experienced development team (or even one person) to do the work, the Capability Level may be level 2.

On the other hand, if the time period is short and there are many projects competing for resources, then project management will have to be at a higher capability level. This is especially true if management or the client requires tracking of schedule, cost and resources, and they require adjustment to the project based on feedback from the metrics for these. In this case the project management process should largely achieve Capability Level 4.

## Project C.

Project C requires design and development of a database within the same critically short time period, but the actual database work will be subcontracted.

In this case, the required processes need to include acquisition and supply processes, and the project management process for the organization. The organization would not need to have any process capability for the engineering processes if the work is subcontracted (but the subcontractor/supplier would!).

### Project target capability overview

As illustrated in the examples, it is therefore recommended that the Capability Level and the associated Process Attributes achievement are set based upon the business and project needs. The following presents a suggested way to perform target capability profile setting based upon the method described in ISO/IEC TR 15504-8:1998:

- Identify the business needs (this sets the broad terms of reference).
- Identify the project needs, including whether the organization performs the work or it is subcontracted (and the related processes to be assessed).
- Create sets of similar business needs/project needs.
- Identify whether the target profile will cover all organizations involved, or only some of them (for example, suppliers).
- Identify the set of key processes for the defined need (or set of needs).
- Review the value chain that the processes should achieve to ensure that the selected processes constitute a viable process set.
- Optionally set a general guidance capability target when the business need dictates this (for instance in the Aviation example project above, a guidance capability target of level 3 is more sensible than one at level 1).
- Look at project, product and process risks, and relate the risks to processes that mitigate these risks (optional)[6].
- Set individual Capability Levels for each key process and document in a capability statement.
- Set individual Process Attribute achievement targets for each key process (this determines whether the Capability Level is fully or largely achieved).
- Review the Capability Level and Process Attribute achievement targets to ensure that:

---

[6] A specific risk management approach should be selected, using a standard risk based taxonomy when possible. This risk-based approach is beyond the scope of the present text but offers strong advantages when correctly implemented.

- processes that *strongly* interface to and rely on each other do not have totally dissimilar targets (this is especially important for processes that form a value chain);
- whether the Process Attribute achievement targets sufficiently mitigate the identified risks (optional);
- identify the effect of not achieving the target, in other words, the effect of any capability or Process Attribute gap;
- check that implementing the processes to the target profile is practical for the organization to do (involve the managers/process implementation personnel); and
- adjust the Capability Level and Process Attribute targets as necessary.
- Repeat the target setting for additional processes, and set achievement targets for the additional processes.

**Table 6. Example target capability statement.**[7]

| Key Process | Process Attributes | Process attribute ratings required | Capability Level |
|---|---|---|---|
| ENG.1 Requirements elicitation | PA1.1, PA2.1, PA2.2 (i.e. all up to and including the *Managed* Capability Level) | Fully Achieved | Level 2 |
| ENG.5 Software design | PA1.1, PA2.1, PA2.2, PA3.1, PA3.2 (i.e. all up to and including the *Established* Capability Level) | Fully Achieved | Level 3 |
| ENG.6 Software construction | PA1.1, PA2.1, PA2.2, PA3.1, PA3.2, PA4.1, PA4.2 (i.e. all up to and including the *Predictable* Capability Level) | Fully Achieved | Level 4 |
| ENG.8 Software testing | PA1.1, PA2.1, PA2.2, PA3.1, PA3.2 | Fully Achieved | |
| | PA4.1, PA4.2 | Largely Achieved | Level 4 |
| MAN.3 Project management | PA1.1, PA2.1, PA2.2 | Fully Achieved | |
| | PA3.1, PA3.2 | Largely Achieved | Level 3 |
| SUP.8 Configuration management | PA1.1, PA2.1, PA2.2 | Fully Achieved | |
| | PA3.1, PA3.2 | Largely Achieved | Level 3 |

In the example target capability statement, there are 5 different Process Attribute target levels, but only 3 different Capability Level targets.

For rating purposes, ISO/IEC 15504 specifies that when the Process Attributes for a specific Capability Level are largely achieved, then that

---

[7] Example based on ISO/IEC TR 15504-8:1998

Capability Level be considered achieved (assuming all lower levels are fully achieved).

In the example, software testing has a target of *Largely Achieved* for the Process Attributes (PA4.1 and PA4.2) for Capability Level 4, but this is not the same as *fully achieving* PA4.1 and PA4.2. Software construction has a target of *Fully Achieved* for PA4.1 and PA4.2. The Process Attribute target for software construction is therefore higher than for software testing.

One valid explanation may be that software construction requires metrics that monitor each of several software teams' performance and support changing the process and training the teams, while testing may only collect metrics on faults found and managing completion of testing.

Not all the components of the Process Attribute (for example, the associated management practices/practice performance indicators) may be required to achieve the desired performance. In addition, there may be a significant difference in the effort required to fully achieve PA4.1 and PA4.2 that does not enhance the end result and so should not be specified as mandatory.

In general, the failure to achieve the target Process Attributes and by implication the Capability Levels affects the probability of not meeting the business need(s), it increases risk. This failure to achieve the target Process Attributes is called the Process Attribute gap. Similarly, a failure to achieve the target Capability Level is called the Capability Level gap.

**Table 7. Process Attribute gaps.**

| Target rating | Assessed rating | Process attribute gap |
|---|---|---|
| Fully Achieved | Fully Achieved | None |
| | Largely Achieved | Minor |
| | Partially Achieved | Major |
| | Not Achieved | Major |
| Largely Achieved | Fully Achieved | None |
| | Largely Achieved | None |
| | Partially Achieved | Major |
| | Not Achieved | Major |

When the target rating for a Process Attribute is assessed as achieved or exceeded, there is no Process Attribute gap.

## Process Capability Gaps and Risk

The relationship between a gap in Process Attribute(s) and its related Capability Level gap is summarized in the Process Attribute to Capability Level gap table in terms of the probability a risk will eventuate.

**Table 8. Process Attribute to Capability Level gap relationship.**

| Number of Process Attribute gaps within Capability Level | Capability level gap |
|---|---|
| No major or minor gaps | None |
| Minor gaps only | Slight (unlikely) |
| A single major gap at Levels 2 - 5 | Significant (moderately likely) |
| A single major gap at Level 1 or more than one major gap at Levels 2 - 5 | Substantial (highly likely) |

The table also shows the potential *probability (or risk likelihood)* that a Process Attribute gap and Capability Level gap will affect the ability to meet the business need(s).

The potential *severity and type of impact* of a Process Attribute or Capability Level gap depends upon the Capability Level in which the gap occurs.

The type of impact is deduced from the statements of the Capability Level and the Process Attributes. The table below shows the explicit risk/impact of a gap at each Capability Level (first two risk statements per level) as well as the risks associated with the higher Capability Levels that are also not mitigated if that Capability Level is not achieved. The severity will be greatest at the lower Capability Levels.

Not performing a required process (at Capability Level 1) naturally has the greatest impact as the work is not or is inadequately performed!

**Table 9. Impact of Capability Level gaps.**

| Gap at Capability Level | Risk severity and type of impact | Notes |
|---|---|---|
| Performed | • **Reduction in ability to produce acceptable quality.**<br>• **Work products not produced.**<br>• Reduction in ability to prevent time or cost overruns.<br>• Missing or inadequate work products.<br>• Reduction in cost effectiveness.<br>• Reduction in uniformity of performance over time or in different organizational instances (e.g. different projects).<br>• Reduction in ability to predict performance.<br>• Reduction in ability to detect problems in time.<br>• Reduction in cost/time/resource optimisation.<br>• Reduction in ability to cope with changes in technology. | Quality and work products are the fundamental outcomes of a Performed process. Note: Each Capability Level gap brings specific risks, and infers that all risks associated with higher Capability Levels apply when the target is set for the higher Capability Level. |
| Managed | • **Reduction in ability to prevent time or cost overruns.**<br>• **Missing or inadequate work products.**<br>• Reduction in cost effectiveness.<br>• Reduction in uniformity of performance over time or in different organizational instances (e.g. different projects).<br>• Reduction in ability to predict performance.<br>• Reduction in ability to detect problems in time.<br>• Reduction in cost/time/resource optimisation.<br>• Reduction in ability to cope with changes in technology. | Managing the time and cost to achieve the process, and managing work products are outcomes of a Managed process. |
| Established | • **Reduction in cost effectiveness.**<br>• **Reduction in uniformity of performance over time or in different organizational instances (e.g. different projects).**<br>• Reduction in ability to predict performance.<br>• Reduction in ability to detect problems in time.<br>• Reduction in cost/time/resource optimisation.<br>• Reduction in ability to cope with changes in technology. | Use of defined process based upon a tailored standard process, and the deployment including proper resource allocation are outcomes of the Established process. |

| Predictable | • **Reduction in ability to predict performance.** <br> • **Reduction in ability to detect problems in time.** <br> • Reduction in cost/time/resource optimisation. <br> • Reduction in ability to cope with changes in technology. | Operation of a process within defined limits using measurement to manage and change the process performance is outcomes of the Predictable process. |
|---|---|---|
| Optimising | • **Reduction in cost/time/resource optimisation.** <br> • **Reduction in ability to cope with changes in technology.** | Continuous improvement and process innovation are outcomes of the Optimising process. |

The next step in assessing the overall risk is to combine the probability with the severity of the risk. The risks caused by capability gaps can then be grouped as High risk, Medium risk, Low risk or no identifiable risk. This is summarized in the Capability gap process-oriented risk table [15].

**Table 10. Capability gap process-oriented risk.**

*Extent of Capability Level Gap (probability, likelihood)*

| *Capability Level Gap (severity, impact)* | None | Slight (unlikely) | Significant (moderately likely) | Substantial (highly likely) |
|---|---|---|---|---|
| Performed | No Identifiable Risk | Medium Risk | **High Risk** | **High Risk** |
| Managed | No Identifiable Risk | Medium Risk | Medium Risk | **High Risk** |
| Established | No Identifiable Risk | Low risk | Medium risk | Medium Risk |
| Predictable | No Identifiable Risk | Low Risk | Low Risk | Medium Risk |
| Optimising | No Identifiable Risk | Low Risk | Low Risk | Low Risk |

When setting the target capability profiles, consider each key process in turn (either in value chain order, or in order of priority of the key processes). For each process, consider each Process Attribute and Capability Level. It is possible to either work upwards (from the lowest Capability Level) or downwards (from the highest Capability Level). The main activities are:

- Categorize any Process Attribute gaps using the 'Process Attribute gap' table.
- Determine the Capability Level gap using the 'Process Attribute to Capability level gap relationship 'table.
- Determine whether the severity and impact from the 'Impact of Capability Level gaps' table are relevant.

- Finally map the probability and the severity within the 'Capability gap process-oriented risk' table to categorize the overall risk. This table assumes that the Process Attributes for a particular Capability Level are required; otherwise they are not a basis for a Process Attribute gap.
- The highest risk is used to determine the desired Capability Level and extent of achievement required at that Capability Level.
- The risk level is subject to expert review.

For example, a substantial gap within the Managed level implies a high probability of problems arising, which would impact upon budget and schedule. According to the 'Capability gap process-oriented risk' table, this constitutes a high risk.

Note: the approach is generalized and may be complemented by use of an appropriate risk methodology and taxonomy.

## The European Space Agency Target Capability Profile

In a project for the European Space Agency, I led a team creating a Target Capability Profile for a specific purpose. The purpose was to define profiles for software meeting various levels of system safety criticality. In space projects, the safety criticality is defined at system level in a variety of space standards. The European Space Agency Technical Authority has created a space industry variant of ISO/IEC 15504 called SPiCE for SPACE, which has many additional practices and recommendations (see Reference book). The agency wanted to:

- Define a practical approach to setting target profiles for SPiCE for SPACE, and

- Propose target profiles for use in the space industry.

There are two specific approaches found to reduce risk and to improve quality when setting target capability levels related to safety and software criticality. The first consisted of an approach suggested in the United Stated Federal Aviation Administration document describing a Safety and Security Application Area [16]. This defines an Application Area to handle safety and security issues in software products with an aim to reduce risk. Four goals are defined; each has associated Application Practices and processes. An organisation achieves more goals as they implement more Application Practices and related processes.

The second approach is described in a study by O. Benediktsson, R.B. Hunter, and A.D. McGettrick. [17]. It provides a viable hypothesis that product quality as expressed by Safety Integrity Levels in ISO/IEC 61508 [18]. The probability of failure at system level can be effectively related to

SW criticality levels, which are expressed as the severity of the consequence of a failure and hence to software quality. The paper addresses the relationship between process capability and Safety Integrity Levels. The main issue is how to relate Safety Integrity Levels (which are expressed as the probability of failure of a safety function at system level) to Software criticality levels, which are expressed as the severity of the consequence of a failure. These types of consequences (and hence their implied severity) may be safety consequences, mission consequences and environmental consequences. It may also have programme consequences (e.g. effect on a project). The concepts of probability and severity are orthogonal.

Rather than looking for a relationship between them, it suggests that they be combined in a risk-based approach, as risk is often depicted as the product of probability and severity. They proposed a relationship based upon the capability levels as defined earlier in this chapter. This therefore suggested target capability levels against safety requirements for a product by using a risk-based analysis. Based upon these two approaches, further clarification of a proposed approach was derived.

- A categorisation scheme for the types of products developed must be used, the primary attributes being safety and product criticality.
- A risk based approach covering both product and process risk, and encompassing probability and severity dimensions is required.
- The setting of target profiles must take into account the ability to select the processes.
- For safety and mission critical systems, specific processes need to be included in the target profiles, including hazard analysis, risk analysis and management, and software verification and validation.

I therefore proposed an initial idea to use a method to categorise and evaluate risk and then derive process capability. This approach was further evolved using an approach to risk classification proposed by team partner EADS Astrium [19]. EADS Astrium is a large prime contractor for space projects and provided industry experience in identifying and managing risk. They proposed a differentiation between Mission related risks (i.e. the risk of the inability of the product to achieve its mission) and programmatic risk (risk of not achieving the project goals, e.g. on time, within budget). Mission risks are considered to have a greater impact (risk severity) than programmatic risk. The scheme used allows differentiation between mission and programmatic risks, and assigns each different importance.

### The ESA Target Profile Approach

The following presents the overall approach used to perform target capability profile setting.

First, identify the business needs. In this case it is space software development for systems of various system safety criticalities.

Next, create a list of risk descriptions relevant to the space industry for software. This list was based upon both standard risk taxonomies and practical industry experience of actual risks. EADS Astrium maintains risk lists so it was relatively easy to filter their existing lists.

Create a risk categorisation approach that addresses mission risk and programmatic risk. Group the list of risks into the two categories. There were 3 groups per risk category:

• Product needs
• Product meeting requirements.
• Cost and schedule risks.
• Communication risks.
• Industrial efficiency risks.
• Maintainability risks.

Create a Risk Index (RI) that captures both likelihood and severity for each type of risk. It is important to note that risk likelihood and risk severity are orthogonal dimensions. Processes can reduce the likelihood of a risk occurring but not its specific severity. Risk severity depends on the context of the project and on the usage of the product (e.g. the safety criticality).

• After iteration, we simplified the risk index to be the product of likelihood and severity. Each dimension was on a scale of 0 to 3. Therefore the risk index can have values from 9 (highest), to 1 (lowest).
• Check using expert opinion on whether severity alone provided a different result to the use of the risk index; this was used to set the risk index levels chosen during the analysis phase.
• Identify a criticality scheme to categorise the major software criticality groups against which risks can be assessed. The resultant categorisation consisted of four categories from very critical to non-essential.

Identify the organisational entities that produce or use software that meets each type of software criticality (e.g. projects, departments). Interview people from each organisational entity to obtain a comprehensive risk picture that is representative of all the likely risks. The interview participants covered all software criticality categories, and various roles including technical customers, operators, project managers, system designers, etc. They had a wide range of experience in both developing and supporting space systems and software.

In each interview, the participant selected their list of project, product and process risks. Each participant highlighted his or her most important risks. Each participant classified the most important risks according to likelihood and severity, for both mission risk and programmatic risk. Each participant related the risks to processes that mitigate these risks (the processes from the process model).

The results of each interview were captured in a form that allowed further multivariate analysis. In the data synthesis phase of the study, the following data sets were created:

- Individual risk categorisation per interview
- Grouping for all interviews
- Uncovered risks (not selected)
- Number of risks covered by a process
- Grouping for each risk category (i.e. [A], [B], [C], [D] )
- Grouping by process for Mission risk
- Grouping by process for Programmatic risk
- Number processes for a risk
- Number of process citations for a risk

One result of the analysis was the conclusion that the bigger the difference between number of processes per risk and number of process citations per risk, the more likely that one or few key processes mitigate the risk.

Some general conclusions from data obtained in the interviews and synthesized were:

- More processes per risk indicates it is less likely that there is one specific process to mitigate the risk (i.e. no key process),
- If a process covers a high number of risks but is not the key process for any risk, then its importance may be low,
- All risks are covered by at least one process.

Based upon analysis of the graphical risk-process synthesis, it was possible to make several pattern matching conclusions:

- Program risks lead to acquisition and management process focus.
- Mission Risks lead to engineering and operations process focus.
- Configuration, quality and infrastructure processes affect both Mission and Program risks.
- When programme (project) complexity is higher, a higher Capability Level is indicated for project management and risk management.
- When product complexity (software) is higher, a higher Capability Level is indicated for engineering processes (especially System Requirements Analysis and Software Requirements Analysis), the project management process, quality assurance and configuration management processes.
- When product criticality is higher, a higher Capability Level is indicated on risk management.
- There are definite processes to risks patterns based upon their lifecycle occurrence.

Next followed a more detailed analysis phase, focused on the mitigation of mission risk. New groups focusing on the mission risk index were created and iteratively analysed in order to determine specific process to risk relationships. We used categories of 'Key', 'Major', 'Important' to represent various risk indices.

Most risks exist whatever the criticality of the software. Nevertheless, we considered in general that only Mission risks with the higher risk index have to be mitigated in lowest criticality category [D].

The severity of the risk is higher as we move from category [D] to category [A]. That is a natural consequence of the classification system adopted. Therefore we analysed risks iteratively for each category.

- It was found that there was a distinct differentiation between criticality category [D] on and the other criticality categories as a group.
- Consequently, we paid a special attention to risks considered as major for mission risks, and for higher programmatic risk indices for the criticality categories [A], [B] and [C].

We considered the overall severity of the risk due to the criticality category and made an adjustment in our analysis. We also took other factors into account when setting capability levels:

- System level processes will be at the same capability level as software processes for the highest criticality category of software managed. Since a system may contain software at various categories of criticality, the highest criticality category is used for system level.
- Having a high capability level on the risk management process is not enough to mitigate all risks. This process identifies and tracks actions in a right way but the capability to implement these actions in the other processes still have to be demonstrated.
- If we have a high capability level on earlier processes in the lifecycle (e.g. requirements elicitation), then we reduce the likelihood of not having enough time/resources to perform later lifecycle processes (e.g. system testing).
- Higher criticality software increases the need for higher capability processes that occur earlier in the lifecycle.
- When the criticality of the software has no impact on what could be required for a process, then generally the capability level does not depend on the criticality category.
- When the work product associated to the process is a part of the final product, there is a direct relationship between the capability level and the criticality category.

We set the individual capability levels for each process in a capability statement. This reflects the following questions:

- What are the Key Mission risks?
- What are the Key Programmatic risks?
- What are the Major Mission risks?
- What are the Major Programmatic risks?
- What is the percentage of risks in each of the six risk groups that the process mitigates?
- Does the most process mitigate key risk(s) and /or major risk(s)?
- How do one or more Generic Process Indicators help to mitigate the risk(s) resulting in a need to have a higher Capability Level?
- Are all the Generic Process Indicators required or are only some required?
- What is the effect of increasing criticality categories?

We set individual capability level achievement targets for each process. We reviewed the Capability Level and process attribute achievement targets to ensure that:

- Processes that strongly interface to and rely on each other do not have totally dissimilar targets (this is especially important for processes that form a process value chain).
- Identified the effect of not achieving the target, in other words, the effect of any capability or process attribute gap, by risk (this followed the guidance described in the earlier sections of this chapter).
- Checked that implementing the processes to the target profile is practical for the organization to do (involve the managers/process implementation personnel in the study workshop and external reviewers to critically review the study results.
- List any complementary techniques required (mainly safety related).

The target setting approach provides usable capability target profiles based upon analysis of real industry risks. The target capability profile consists of a set of processes for each criticality, together with their capability levels. For the agency, this specifically addressed categories based upon four levels of system safety criticality. The profiles highlight specific processes required for each of four different criticality categories for space systems and software.

### Industry relevant conclusions

At lower criticality categories, there are fewer processes required than previous theoretical approaches dictated. This means that it may be possible to use agile software development approaches for low critically projects.

As criticality increases some additional processes are required, but more importantly the target profiles specify which key processes should be at higher capability levels. Therefore, the target profiles derive better and more practical profiles than the theoretical approaches used so far.

Depending upon the particular products being developed, it is possible to select fewer processes with specific capability levels to mitigate risk, rather than have to apply more processes. This also applies at higher critically categories, where it is possible to select a few higher capability processes to mitigate most risks.

The approach improves upon the approach described in ISO/IEC 15504 by providing a practical basis for target setting in additional to the theoretical basis described in the standard.

If a specific programme/project performs a risk analysis, it can select the best processes to mitigate these risks. The target setting approach can be used for any type of product, organisation or industry. I foresee a distinct benefit to use the approach in large organisations or in other industry sectors.

The approach leads to a better method for selecting processes for improvement. I describe this method in a new section to the Team Based Business Design Improvement chapter, called TBBDI Risk.

# User View - Process Capability Determination

## Process Capability Determination

In this chapter, I describe how to perform process capability determination. The entire process is described, including the target definition stage, the assessment and response stage, and the verification and risk analysis stage.

I then look at process-oriented risk analysis and analysis of capability gaps, and the activities to agree on Capability Level/Process Attribute achievement targets.

This section uses input from ISO/IEC TR 15504-8:1998. I expanded the approach here to improve interactivity in the determination, analysis and agreement of capability profiles. Activities are indicated as either essential or optional. This chapter will be of interest to assessment sponsors, process capability determination sponsors, process practitioners and quality professionals.

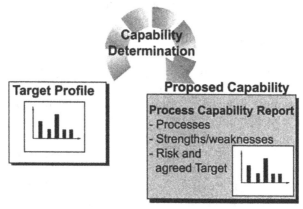

**Fig. 10. Capability Determination.**

## Performing process capability determination

The party who is interested in performing a process capability determination is referred to in this chapter as the Process Capability Determination Sponsor (PCD sponsor or sponsor). The sponsor is an organization or person wishing to determine the process capability of his or her own organization or a supplier (or group of suppliers). The sponsor may have specific requirements that may require a different method to that proposed in the standard. The sponsor and the responding organization will in general follow a three-stage process:

- Target capability profile definition – what processes and Capability Levels the sponsor desires.
- Performing assessment or requiring a response from the organization on their proposed capability.
- Verification and risk analysis of the proposed capability and achieving agreement on a proposed capability and actions for any capability gaps (or rejecting the proposed capability).
- The proposed capability consists of several aspects:
  - The organization(s) involved;
  - The processes they deploy; and
  - The Capability Level of the processes.

In some situations, the proposed capability may be a simple response from an existing organization indicating compliance with the target profile. In other situations the sponsor may need to perform assessment of the organization's capability. If this is the situation, it normally requires substantial resources from both the sponsor and organization being assessed, and therefore should only be performed when the aim is to achieve agreement on a proposed capability. The proposed capability may be iterated more than once to achieve agreement.

Note that the specified requirement may be for a general assessment of process capability in an organization, rather than for a specific product or service. An example may be a specified requirement to establish a strong configuration management process as an end in itself, and the key process set would then include just this single process. This class of specified requirement would arise from an organization's business goals and priorities.

In the diagram, there are two optional activities – Self Assessment and Independent Assessment Review. A sponsor may accept a self assessment result as input to the Assessment and Response stage.

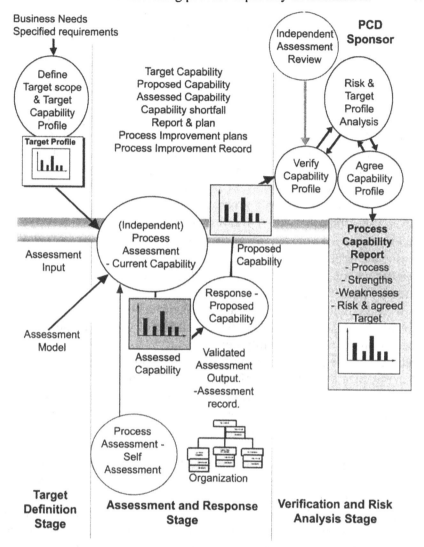

**Fig. 11. Process Capability Determination activities.**

The sponsor will go through a process of review and agree on a proposed capability profile, using a risk and target profile analysis to determine the effect on any gaps between the original target capability profile, the proposed capability profile and the assessed capability profile. The result will be a process capability report and agreed target capability profile. When there is a one-to-one relationship between customer sponsor and the organization, the activities may be simplified, when there are multiple suppliers in a proposed organization, the sponsor will need to decide which process apply to which suppliers and at what Capability Level.

## The target definition stage

When a sponsor wishes to perform process capability determination, they will normally set target capability profiles in a target definition stage (see previous section for more details). The target profile will be part of the sponsor's assessment input. The target capability profile may:

- Cover one organization or several organizations working together.
- Be for a new or existing task/project/product/service.
- Cover a specific contract or cover a set/class of contracts.
- Be for an internal or external (e.g. supplier) organization.
- During the target definition stage, the sponsor:
- Decides whether a core process capability determination is needed, or an extended process capability determination[8].
- Plans and initiates the target capability determination.
- Creates the target capability profile consisting of which key processes are needed, and at what Capability Level.
- Decide whether the target capability profile applies in whole or in part to each organization in the case of multiple organizations being involved.
- Defines the target scope of each process assessment, including which key (and perhaps extended) processes should be assessed to represent the overall organizational capability (the assessment may not assess all key processes).
- Decides whether to perform independent (2nd party or 3rd party) process assessment (either full assessment or a sample), allow self assessment, and/or accept existing assessment results.
- Decides what are the assessment constraints and responsibilities and any additional information to be collected. This may include additional information on similar projects, and their prior or current process assessment results (if any).

---

[8] **Core process capability determination** is a minimum, streamlined set of activities applicable whenever a single organization proposes to meet a specified requirement by deploying its current process capability, without any partners or sub-contractors being involved.

**Extended process capability determination** is applicable when an enhanced capability is proposed, or when consortia or sub-contractors are involved.

- Provides the target scope and the target capability profile to the assessors, and optionally to the organization to be assessed (generally it is better to provide this information).

Many Process Attributes for the higher Capability Levels are related to processes within the Management, Support and Organization process categories. For example, if the *Performance Management* attribute (PA2.1) has been included for a process within the Engineering process category, then the *Project Management* process within the Management process category should also be included as a key process.

The target capability for processes in the Management, Support and Organization process categories is determined by the extent to which they support Process Attributes applying to the initial set of key processes. Other processes from the Support, Management and Organization process categories may also be included in the target capability statement where they are relevant to the specified requirement.

In a two-party contractual situation, a procurer may wish to invite potential suppliers to provide a self-assessment profile - produced from an assessment using conformant models and mapped to the reference model - when submitting a proposal for a contract. Such an approach offers the benefit of sharing both the cost and the benefit of the process assessment, since suppliers may also use the assessment results within their own process improvement programmes.

## The assessment and response stage

The involved organization(s) will plan a response. This will include which organizations are involved (if multiple entities involved), what allocation of processes and assessments is needed, and the involvement of assessors.

It is becoming common for a team to consist of several organizations in larger projects. Therefore, it is not enough to just assess the main contractor, but necessary to create a proposed capability that handles the multiple organizations. This is given the term 'constructed capability'. Where only a single organization is involved, there is no need for this step in a response, readers can skip to: Assessing capability and responding.

### Constructed Capability

A constructed capability consists of several aspects:
- The organizations and organizational units involved.
- The processes each organization will use for the contract/project.
- The capability of each process within each organization.

The constructed capability covering a number of organizations can be created in two modes.

**Unique mode**: Each key process is deployed <u>uniquely</u> by one organization and the proposed constructed capability consists of the accumulated set of the processes of the involved organizations.

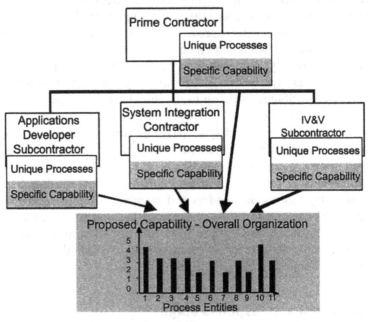

**Fig. 12. Unique mode constructed capability.**

**Concurrent mode**: Within the overall organization, each organization deploys the same or shared processes. For example, the Applications Developer and the Independent Verification and Validation (IV&V) subcontractor both perform software testing. Alternately, the organizations deploy processes concurrently that strongly interact with each other. For example, the IV&V subcontractor deploys a validation process that strongly interacts with the Application Developer's software testing process.

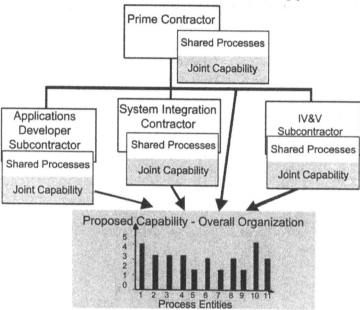

**Fig. 13. Concurrent mode constructed capability.**

Organizations may need to consider in large or complex contracts a mixture of both Unique and Concurrent modes, depending upon the degree of interaction of the various capabilities of the specific organizational entities.

In general, the author advises that the Unique mode of capability determination is the most suitable to use, unless the organization has many shared resources and strong dependencies that create complex interactions between the organizations. For example, in a project has clear contractual, organizational and technical interfaces between the participants, performing unique mode capability determination of each participant separately will normally be sufficient to provide a manageable result.

### Unique mode example

Unique mode is used to construct a proposed capability by combining two or more **key processes** (processes from the Acquisition-Supply and Engineering process areas in ISO/IEC 12207) to meet a proposed target. Each process is performed by a separate organization with supporting processes. The proposed constructed capability is illustrated in the following example diagram, which shows some typical key processes that may apply[9].

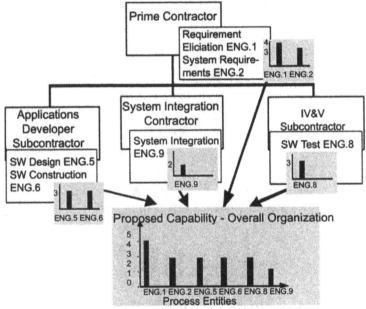

**Fig. 14. Example Unique mode capability construction.**

In Unique mode, it is assumed that each key process is operating in its own environment, independently of the other processes in the organization and the other organizations. It is also assumed that the other processes employed (for example, project management, configuration management) should not affect the ability of each key process to perform to its assessed capability. Therefore, within the two stated constraints, the constructed capability becomes a simple accumulation of the capabilities of each key process as illustrated in the above diagram.

Care should be taken when looking at the management, support and organizational processes.

---

[9] This figure illustrates constructing a capability profile in Unique mode and does not intend to imply the processes and Capability Levels will always be those illustrated.

The Unique mode applicability can vary depending upon the level of central management of processes. If the organization has standard processes with tailored defined processes (Capability Level 3) for its business units and project, then the Unique mode is applicable.

If participating organizations (e.g. different companies) have widely varying management and organizational processes, then the interfaces between the participating organizations must be clearly specified, in order for the Unique mode to apply.

## *Concurrent mode example*

Concurrent mode covers the more complex situation where two or more organizations are deploying the same key processes in parallel and/or the processes have strong interactions or dependencies.

In this case, it is unlikely that averaging the Process Attribute ratings across different organizations is valid, especially when the process capability varies by more than one Capability Level. Possible capability determinations may use:

- Worst case process capability - representing the weakest link in the chain (although as a supplier you are unlikely to want to use this approach!).
- A combination of the minimum, maximum and median process capability ratings – representing the overall range of capability.
- Where the relative importance of each process by each organization is possible, a weighting could be given to each process - organization pair to provide a weighted mean or median together with minimum and maximum. This would acknowledge that some parts of the customer need may be more important than other parts and also allow organizations to optimise the use of the highest capability processes between the team.

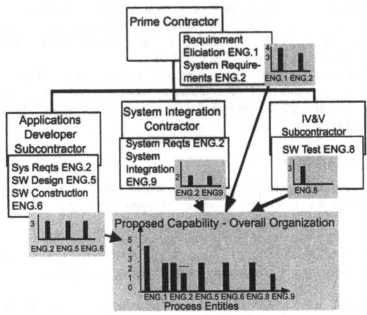

**Fig. 15. Concurrent mode example – multiple ENG.1.5 rating.**

In the example, the summary constructed capability shows the median for the 3 instances of System Requirements (ENG.2 in ISO/IEC 15504-5). Note however that the constructed capability should be representative of the capability of each process in isolation.

Because several organizations are involved, the organizational interface issues must be addressed. The organization proposing the constructed capability and the sponsor should ensure that suitable interface mechanisms have been identified to address these issues (for example specified technical, communications and management interfaces).

If the constructed capability reflects anticipated complexity in the way the organizations will work, it is more probable that interfacing problems will occur.

Many of these interface problems can be addressed by Management, Support and Organization processes, which therefore should focus on supporting the Process Attributes of individual key processes. However, there are practical technical solutions for some of the interface issues. One possible solution is the use of a shared development environment that encapsulated several processes such as configuration management, testing and problem reporting.

If the constructed capability is focused on the key processes and specific focused Management, Support and Organization processes, the information will support the proposed capability (rather than bury it in needless detail).

There may be many ways of combining various processes within various organizations into a constructed capability, especially when weighting is used. Therefore, the organization and the sponsor should cooperate and the sponsor will have to apply professional judgment in determining how best to carry out the capability determination in such cases. The proposed constructed capability is most likely to be best depicted by showing the individual capability profiles in addition to a summary profile and describing the interface mechanisms proposed.

## Assessing capability and responding

The assessors assess the organization's current capability with respect to the target scope. In some cases this will require an assessment to be performed, in other cases existing conformant assessment results may be aggregated and analysed.

A key feature of ISO/IEC 15504 is that process assessment results are meant to be re-useable. Organizations with higher process capability may already have a repository of process assessment outputs available. These may have been generated as part of a process improvement or earlier capability determination programmes. If the organization believes a number of suitable process assessments are available, then they may use the results as the basis to respond with their capability. The assessors will have to judge whether these earlier assessment results are suitable. This includes judging the applicability of the processes assessed and the assessed instances (types of projects and products).

If the assessors are not satisfied with the available assessment results, they will be required to perform an assessment.

The organization's assessed capability may meet or exceed the target capability profile. In this case, the organization will respond with a statement of compliance to the target Capability Levels and their capability profile. The sponsor will review these in the next stage.

However, the organization may not meet the sponsor's target profile for a number of reasons. This includes the possibility that the organization or parts of it may not yet exist, or may have to be constructed from existing organizational elements plus sub-contractors, consultants, partners etc.

If the organization does not meet the target capability profile, it may wish to offer a proposed capability. The proposed capability may be somewhere between the assessed capability and the target capability.

The proposed capability may be derived by examining the gap between the current assessed capability and the target capability, plus planned actions/results in a process improvement process.

The assessors need to review planned improvements against those necessary to close the gap between the assessed and target capabilities. However, not all the gaps may be closed due to constraints with available resources. The following figure illustrates a simple example of the 3 capabilities and the resultant capability gaps.

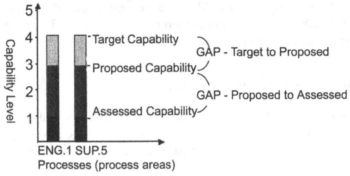

**Fig. 16. Target, proposed and assessed capabilities.**

When the organization wishes to create a proposed capability profile, it must create this from assessments of a number of current or recent projects, aggregating the results as described in ISO/IEC 15504-3. This profile:

• should be based on a number of ISO/IEC 15504 conformant process assessments;
• should correspond to the target scope; and
• should be a truly representative of the organization's current process capability;

It is likely that the result is based upon self-assessment, but it could also have been produced by a previous independent assessment. Since the sponsor's specified requirement relates to work to be undertaken in the future, the organization may wish to propose to meet a capability higher than its currently assessed capability. This is shown in the above figure as a 'Proposed to Assessed' capability gap.

This enhanced capability would consist of the currently assessed capability and a process improvement plan. In this situation, the organization (and sponsor) should ensure that records of process improvement support the process improvement plan. This includes evidence of improvements that have occurred in an existing process improvement programme ('track record').

In the situation that there is a 'Target to Proposed' capability gap, the organization may wish to submit a shortfall plan, addressing each area where process capability is lower than the target capability. The organization should assess the gap for each key process, associated risks, and propose mitigation actions. The organization may therefore wish to pass to the sponsor a proposed capability, justified by:

- an assessed capability;
- a process improvement plan;
- a process improvement track record; and
- a capability shortfall plan.

## The verification and risk analysis stage

### Verify Proposed Capability

The sponsor reviews the proposed capability to verify:

- Whether the proposed capability (consisting of assessed capability and a capability shortfall plan if prepared) is credible and to what extent it represents the organization's processes. The factors in assessing credibility include:
  - checking that the context of the proposed capability matches the target scope;
  - checking that the assessed capability is the result of a conformant assessment;
  - the sponsor's previous experience of the reliability of the capabilities proposed by the organization in question;
  - the sponsor's previous experience of the reliability of the capability determination assessment method;
  - the number and size of the supplier's assessment teams (one team for all organizations involved or several, one assessor or several in each team); and
  - previous experience of the reliability and experience of the assessors involved especially the competent assessor(s) involved.
- Whether any associated process improvement plans are credible when a 'Proposed to Assessed' capability gap exists (check the existing process improvement track record).

The sponsor decides whether any further action is needed to establish confidence in the proposed capability, including any need to carry out an independent assessment of processes (particularly key processes).

An advantage of having carried out the independent assessment is that the sponsor will be able to compare this independent output with the proposed capability of the organization, and record the level of confidence as shown in table 5. A disadvantage is that this requires extra effort on the part of the sponsor and the organization.

If the process capability determination involves a number of competing suppliers, then sponsors may wish - if it is practical to do so - to employ the same assessment team, using the same assessment method, to verify each supplier's proposed capability. This should not only provide the sponsor with greater confidence in the consistency with which each supplier is assessed, but also provide the suppliers with enhanced confidence in the fairness of the sponsor's selection process.

**Table 11. Terminology for expressing confidence in proposed capability.**

| Correspondence of independent assessment to proposed capability | Degree of confidence |
|---|---|
| The sponsor has no reason to doubt the proposed capability, or The results of an independent assessment confirm the organization's self-assessed capability. | Fully confident |
| The results of an independent assessment have varied slightly from the organization's self-assessed capability | Largely confident |
| The results of an independent assessment have varied significantly from the organization's self-assessed capability | Partially confident |
| The results of an independent assessment have varied substantially from the organization's self-assessed capability | Not confident |

The terms *slightly, significantly* and *substantially* are defined in the 'Process Attribute to Capability level gap relationship' table in the section on defining Target Capability Profiles.

Following appropriate verification, the proposed capability becomes an input to risk analysis.

## Process-oriented risk analysis and capability gaps

The sponsor assesses the process-oriented risk for each key process within the target capability statement as follows:
- examine the Process Attribute rating for each Process Attribute within the target capability statement, and designate any individual Process Attribute gaps;
- consider each Capability Level and designate any Capability Level gaps;
- identify the risk corresponding to each Capability Level gap; and
- record this risk in the process capability report.

### Process-oriented risk

Process-oriented risks are those risks associated with incomplete/incorrect/poorly-managed implementation of processes. Process-oriented risks do not address all aspects of risk, which may include strategic, organizational, financial, personnel and product related risks. During the process capability determination, the organization's processes are assessed and the results analysed to identify process strengths, weaknesses and risks. The output should be fed into the wider risk analysis.

The types of process-oriented risk are derived from the process reference model. The process reference model describes process purpose and outcomes. The purpose is expanded into good base process and process management practices, which are translated into the Process Attributes for assessment purposes. The process outcomes illustrate the benefits that arise from deploying these practices. Process-oriented risk arises from inappropriate process management, including:

- not deploying base practices; or
- inappropriate management practices; or
- inappropriate deployment in the particular context, resulting in not achieving the required Process Attributes.

In ISO/IEC 15504, the process architecture is referred to in the Process Reference Model – which is defined in a separate standard or document. For software, a commonly applied model exists in ISO/IEC 12207. See the Reference Book chapter: Process Reference Models for more process models. ISO/IEC 15504 defines the nine Process Attributes, which apply to all processes (see the Reference Book chapter: The Measurement Framework).

During a conformant assessment, the competent assessors rate the processes to form its process profile. Process attribute ratings for several processes are collected into a process capability profile that indicates, for each process and organizational instance assessed, which Process Attributes are being achieved.

### Process-oriented risk analysis and capability gaps

The sponsor needs to assess the risks from the 'Target to Proposed' capability gap and the 'Proposed to Assessed' capability gap. Initially the sponsor should focus on the risks associated with the key processes in the *Customer-Supplier* and *Engineering* process categories. Depending upon the risks exposed, more processes in other categories may be added later in the analysis.

The process-oriented risk analysis firstly assesses for the *probability* of a particular problem occurring, and secondly its potential *impact/severity*, should it occur. The relationship between a gap in Process Attribute(s) and its related Capability Level gap is summarized in the Process Attribute to Capability level gap table in terms of the probability a risk will eventuate.

**Table 12. Process Attribute to Capability level gap relationship.**

| Number of Process Attribute gaps within Capability Level | Capability level gap |
|---|---|
| No major or minor gaps | None |
| Minor gaps only | Slight (unlikely) |
| A single major gap at Levels 2 - 5 | Significant (moderately likely) |
| A single major gap at Level 1 or more than one major gap at Levels 2 - 5 | Substantial (highly likely) |

The table also shows the potential *probability (or risk likelihood)* that a Process Attribute gap and Capability Level gap will affect the ability to meet the business need(s).

The potential *severity and type of impact* of a Process Attribute or Capability Level gap depends upon the Capability Level in which the gap occurs.

The severity will be greatest at the lower Capability Levels. Not performing a required process at Capability Level 1 naturally has the greatest impact as the work is not or is inadequately performed!

The type of impact is deduced from the statements of the Capability Level and the Process Attributes. The types of impact are limited at the highest capability level and increase as the capability level is lower. Hence gaps at lower levels expose more impacts, while retaining the impacts from the higher levels. In general, the specific type of impact at the lower level has a higher severity or effect. Thus the main impacts are highlighted in bold, and the impacts due to gaps with the higher levels are shown in grey text. The impacts are summarized in the following table.

**Table 13. Impact of Capability Level gaps.**

| Gap at Target Capability level | Risk severity and type of impact | Notes |
|---|---|---|
| Performed | • **Reduction in ability to produce acceptable quality.**<br>• **Work products not produced.**<br>• Reduction in ability to prevent time or cost overruns.<br>• Missing or inadequate work products.<br>• Reduction in cost effectiveness.<br>• Reduction in uniformity of performance over time or in different organizational instances (e.g. different projects).<br>• Reduction in ability to predict performance.<br>• Reduction in ability to detect problems in time.<br>• Reduction in cost/time/resource optimisation.<br>• Reduction in ability to cope with changes in technology. | Quality and work products are the fundamental outcomes of a Performed process. Note: Each Capability Level gap brings specific risks, and infers that all risks associated with higher Capability Levels apply. |
| Managed | • **Reduction in ability to prevent time or cost overruns.**<br>• **Missing or inadequate work products.**<br>• Reduction in cost effectiveness.<br>• Reduction in uniformity of performance over time or in different organizational instances (e.g. different projects).<br>• Reduction in ability to predict performance.<br>• Reduction in ability to detect problems in time.<br>• Reduction in cost/time/resource optimisation.<br>• Reduction in ability to cope with changes in technology. | Managing the time and cost to achieve the process, and managing work products are outcomes of a Managed process. |
| Established | • **Reduction in cost effectiveness.**<br>• **Reduction in uniformity of performance over time or in different organizational instances (e.g. different projects).**<br>• Reduction in ability to predict performance.<br>• Reduction in ability to detect problems in time.<br>• Reduction in cost/time/resource optimisation.<br>• Reduction in ability to cope with changes in technology. | Use of defined process based upon a tailored, standard process, and deployment including proper resource allocation are outcomes of the Established process. |
| Predictable | • **Reduction in ability to predict performance.**<br>• **Reduction in ability to detect problems in time.**<br>• Reduction in cost/time/resource optimisation.<br>• Reduction in ability to cope with changes in technology. | Operation of a process within defined limits using measurement to manage and |

| | | | change the process performance are outcomes of the Predictable process. |
|---|---|---|---|
| Optimising | • **Reduction in cost/time/resource optimisation.**<br>• **Reduction in ability to cope with changes in technology.** | | Continuous improvement and process innovation are outcomes of the Optimising process. |

Many Process Attributes are related to processes within the Management, Support and Organization process categories, so the sponsor may add processes from these categories when risk pertaining to these attributes is exposed. For example, if the *Performance Management* attribute (PA2.1) has been included for a process within the Engineering process category, then the *Project Management* process within the Management process category should also be included as a key process.

The sponsor should include processes in the Management, Support and Organization process categories when they support Process Attributes applying to the initial set of key processes. Further processes may be included when they help achieve the specified requirement.

In some cases, the specified requirement may be for an organizational capability. One example may be a requirement for a high capability in a customer support process. This would address risks associated with this process (customer dissatisfaction, failure to respond to customer problem reports, failure to fix product problems in future releases, etc.). Another example could be high capability for an Independent Verification and Validation. In this situation, the organization may be interested in use of this capability internally and externally as a service. In either situation, this may address risks associated with safety critical or high criticality product development.

The sponsor combines the probability with the severity of the risk. The risks caused by capability gaps can then be grouped as High risk, Medium risk, Low risk or no identifiable risk. This is summarized in the Capability gap process-oriented risk table [20].

**Table 14. Capability gap process-oriented risk.**

| Capability Level Gap (severity, impact) | Extent of Capability Level Gap (probability, likelihood) | | | |
| --- | --- | --- | --- | --- |
| | None | Slight (unlikely) | Significant (moderately likely) | Substantial (highly likely) |
| Performed | No Identifiable Risk | Medium Risk | High Risk | High Risk |
| Managed | No Identifiable Risk | Medium Risk | Medium Risk | High Risk |
| Established | No Identifiable Risk | Low risk | Medium risk | Medium Risk |
| Predictable | No Identifiable Risk | Low Risk | Low Risk | Medium Risk |
| Optimising | No Identifiable Risk | Low Risk | Low Risk | Low Risk |

When assessing the proposed capability profiles, the sponsor should consider each key process in turn (either in value chain order, or in order of priority of the key processes). For each process, the sponsor considers each Process Attribute and Capability Level.

It is possible to either work upwards (from the lowest Capability Level) or downwards (from the highest Capability Level). For example, a substantial gap within the Managed level implies a high probability of problems that would impact upon budget and schedule. According to the 'Capability gap process-oriented risk' table, this constitutes a high risk. In summary, the activities include:

- Categorize any Process Attribute gaps using the 'Process Attribute gap' table.
- Determine the Capability Level gap using the 'Process Attribute to Capability level gap relationship 'table.
- Determine whether the severity and impact from the 'Impact of Capability Level gaps' table are relevant.
- Finally map the probability and the severity within the 'Capability gap process-oriented risk' table to categorize the overall risk. This table assumes that the Process Attributes for a particular Capability Level are required; otherwise they are not a basis for a Process Attribute gap.
- The highest risk is used to determine the desired Capability Level and extent of achievement required at that Capability Level.
- The risk level is subject to expert review.

## Agree Process Attribute achievement targets

After assessing the proposed process capability target, the capability gaps and associated risks, the sponsor needs to decide whether the proposed capability profile is adequate or requires revision. When the sponsor does not agree with the proposed capability profile, they may either:

- request a new proposed constructed capability, for example by addition or removal of some parts of the organization;  or
- request a revised capability profile, for example some processes to be at a higher Capability Level or level of achievement of Process Attributes/Capability Levels; or
- request an improvement plan or an updated improvement plan; or
- reject the organization's proposed constructed capability.

The sponsor and the organization decide upon the amount of iteration of the constructed capability. When the sponsor agrees with the proposed capability profile, it is documented in a Process Capability Report.

**Table 15. Example Process Capability Summary Report.**

| PROCESS CAPABILITY SUMMARY REPORT | | |
|---|---|---|
| Confidence in Proposed Capability | | |
| | Confidence that proposed capability is realistic | Largely confident |
| **Process-Oriented Risk** | | |

| Key Process | Strength/Weakness | Process-oriented risk |
|---|---|---|
| ENG.6 | Assessed capability falls slightly short of target capability at the Established Capability Level. | Low risk |
| ACQ.2 | Assessed capability falls slightly short of target capability at the Performed level, substantially short at the Managed level, and substantially short at the Established level. | High risk |
| SUP.2 | Assessed capability falls slightly short of target capability at the Managed level, and significantly short of target capability at the Established level. | Medium risk |
| MAN.3 | Assessed capability meets or exceeds target capability in all respects. | No identifiable risk |

The Process Capability Summary Report consists of three parts:

- an introduction that describes the context of the process capability determination, who carried it out, and where, when and why it took place;

- the sponsor's statement of confidence that the proposed capability is realistic and likely to be applied to the specified requirement; and
- a report for each key process, of any gap between target capability and proposed capability, and of the process-oriented risk arising from this gap.

The summary report should be supported by a detailed report, showing for each process within the target capability statement:

- The target and proposed achievement of every Process Attribute.
- Listing individual Process Attribute gaps.
- Summarizing Capability Level gaps
  - Target to Proposed Capability gap.
  - Proposed to Assessed Capability gap.

# User View - Process Improvement

## Process Improvement

In this chapter, I describe the reasons to perform process improvement. I then describe a general process improvement cycle, specifically describing a 9 Step process improvement cycle based upon ISO/IEC 15504 and a space industry variant. Some explanation of how to tailor the cycle to various organizations is covered.

I also describe a more agile 5 Stage process improvement cycle for smaller or less formal organizations (or for those that want to start actions sooner).

I then look at the wider cultural issues to achieve sustainable improvement and propose a Team Based Business Design Improvement (TBBDI) method that together with Business Process Mapping provides an improved way to perform and sustain improvement in an organization. This is further extended with a risk dimension – TBBDI Risk. TBBDI provides active risk mitigation through process capability increase.

People who may wish to read this chapter include:

- Senior managers leading software organizations.
- Improvement sponsors
- Members of improvement teams, particularly leaders and facilitators.
- Software engineers that are performing the processes to be improved.

This chapter will also be of interest to customers, process owners and practitioners, process experts, quality professionals and improvement consultants.

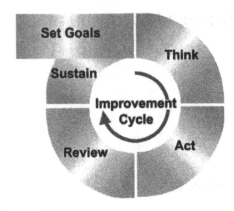

**Fig. 17. Improvement Cycle.**

## Improvement

An organization is judged by the results it achieves (whether measured by profit, quality, customer satisfaction, workplace desirability, corporate prestige, etc.). The reason that an organization should embrace improvement is to be more effective and efficient at achieving these results. The more effective and efficient the organization becomes, the more competitive it is. Organizations can compete in several ways:

- Differentiation – the product or service is different to those of competitors; it impacts on the customer's perception of value (e.g. physical characteristics, service attributes, uniqueness-value perception).
- Responsiveness – the organization provides its customers with products/services that meet its particular needs; it is flexible, reliable and quick.
- Cost – the organization provides a superior value proposition (cost/benefit) in the perception of its customers compared to its competitors.

In general, competing on cost/price is considered the least profitable alternative for commercial organizations (if price wars develop then the competing organizations lose profitability). Commercial organizations that have been most successful are noted for differentiation or responsiveness. To do this, the organization often provides new or enhanced products. Dell and FedEx are classic examples of responsiveness. Hilton hotels, Rado and Harley Davidson use differentiation to target their clients.

Even organizations that traditionally do not perceive themselves as competitive (for example government or charitable institutions) have increasing restrictions on funding. This means they need to be more efficient. This efficiency will show sponsors that funding the organizational initiatives and operations will provide superior value. These organizations are therefore likely to be better funded (ignoring other political aspects, of course).

Organizations can improve the three fundamental aspects of their operations and what they offer: their people, their products and their processes. Each area has particular benefits and limitations in terms of improvement, but in general, it is important to improve all three.

Starting a process improvement initiative should lead to product improvement, and provide a means to help people improve. Improvement can occur through continuous (or better phrased continual[10]) improvement or through innovation. A well-planned process improvement programme should use both continual and innovative improvement. It will create improvement synergies in the people, process and products that lead to organizational success and competitiveness.

**The principle value for an organization to use ISO/IEC 15504 is to provide input to process improvement.**

It is important that process improvement aims to achieve the business goals (effectiveness) with the least possible resources (efficiency) and the minimum possibility of failure (risk). To efficiently deliver new and enhanced products and services, organizations are increasingly making use of automated processes. One way to automate a process is by use of software implementing an appropriate process model. Automating processes can reduce unwanted process variability (invoked by people) and hence reduce associated risks. Some resultant products may be:

- Information Systems, including enterprise resource planning systems, customer relationship management, etc.
- Embedded software (for example in communication networks, automated bank teller and point of sale machines, or medical diagnostic products).
- Specific types of tools (for example, test software, integrated circuit layout software, or engine diagnostic tools).

However, the increasing reliance upon software is often creating greater complexity in the product and the process needed to create it. Hence, there is a greater risk of failure to deliver the required software products (see the

---

[10] I use the term continual improvement to indicate that generally organizations improve in a series of improvement actions with some pauses between them, rather than a continuous non-stop improvement effort.

introductory chapter on the software crisis if you want a reminder of the costs of failure)[11].

Risk of failure to deliver the desired software products can increase overall organizational risk.

*So, are organizations in a vicious risk cycle?*

Not necessarily.

The organization must balance their approach to managing risk[12].

This means that the organization must look not only at process automation, but also at process improvement and helping their people improve.

It is possible to reduce risk of failure by using higher capability processes. For a reminder on process risks, readers should look at the chapter on Capability Determination. Process improvement leading to higher capability processes can reduce process related risk.

When process improvement goals are based upon the organization's goals, it can also reduce organizational risk. For many organizations, their organization's business goals are directly centred on:

✓  The need to achieve enhanced customer satisfaction.

✓  Operate with greater competitiveness, efficiency and effectiveness.

✓  Provide improved business value through delivery of products and services using software or Information Systems.

At the same time, industry evolves further in the direction of lower budget projects with shared risk between customer and supplier. This forces the supplier to face the challenge of streamlining costs and reducing risk further, while having fewer resources to do so.

For organizations with a dependence on software, these business goals are key management drivers for software process improvement with the aim to:

✓  Achieve higher software quality.

✓  Reduce their development and maintenance costs.

✓  Shorten their time to market and/or meeting critical schedule deadlines.

✓  Increase predictability and controllability of software products and processes.

Therefore, the organization should consider software process improvement as part of a general process improvement programme.

---

[11] It is apparent that the industry concerned most with automating processes, has the highest need for high capability processes.

[12] There is an old expression: "Don't put all your eggs in one basket". Roughly translated, don't tackle risk in only one way.

Process improvement itself may be a vulnerable and risky process. Many process improvement programmes fail because these risks have not been properly addressed.

The number one cause for failure of process improvement programmes is the general lack of business orientation of the program and the people participating (reflected by a missing link with business strategy, goals and organisation culture).

Therefore, process improvement should be based upon the overall organization's business goals expanded by the goals of the organizational units. These goals are then related to the processes that deliver the outcomes meeting these goals. Process assessment using ISO/IEC 15504 can determine how well the processes deliver these outcomes; at the same time, process assessments can provide suggestions for improvement based upon sound management practice.

For sustainable improvement, avoid improving just to reach an 'ideal' capability profile. An 'ideal' capability profile could be that a set of processes attain Capability Level 4. If a customer requires achievement of a capability profile, look at the business implications first. This should make the capability profile reflect the business goals, rather than some 'ideal'. If some processes meet current business goals at Capability Level 2 or 3, then it is better to invest the available resources in other processes that maximize return at Capability Level 4. Simply stated, for *process improvement purposes,* the capability profile should reflect the desired business improvements, not vice versa. For example, if the business goal was customer satisfaction, but we have the following:

✗ Software products are delivered with serious defects. Perform process assessment of software engineering processes that can reduce delivered defects (e.g. design, coding, testing).

✗ Software products are consistently delivered late. Perform process assessment of project management and scope related processes (e.g. requirements elicitation).

✗ Customers receive the wrong product versions or the wrong upgrades. Perform process assessment of configuration management, maintenance or supply processes.

Based upon the assessment results, choose to improve the processes that correct the most important problems.

### *Be pragmatic.*

There will be limited resources available for improvement.

Since there will be limited resources available for improvement, invest where the return on this investment is maximized.

Improvement in managing processes has what I call a management-multiplier effect. Better management of a selected process affects everyone using that process, thereby multiplying the benefits when the process is used in many areas. As improvements start to pay back upon the investment made, the organization can use some of this return to invest in more improvements. I describe several improvement models and associated improvement aspects.

- The 9 Step process improvement cycle.
- The 5 Stage agile improvement cycle.
- Improvement and culture
- Team Based Business Design Improvement and TBBDI Risk.

Other improvement models exist and include the IDEAL$^{SM}$ model [21] and ISO 9004-4 [22]. Readers may already be familiar with these, or wish to read more about them.

Readers interested in reading about good and bad management and improvement practices, are advised to look at: The Witch Doctors by John Micklethwait and Adrian Wooldridge [23].

## Process Improvement and ISO/IEC 15504

The process improvement guidance in this chapter has been especially developed for companies involved in the procurement, development, operation or maintenance of software, but is generally applicable to any organization.

Process improvement is best considered as a continuous endeavour, where an organization progresses around an improvement cycle. Within this cycle, improvement is accomplished in a series of steps or specific improvement phases such as introducing new or changed practices into processes or removing old ones.

At the same time, it should be possible to introduce innovations. Innovations are discontinuous improvements (they do not necessarily follow prior improvement activities). Therefore, the improvement cycle needs to handle innovations.

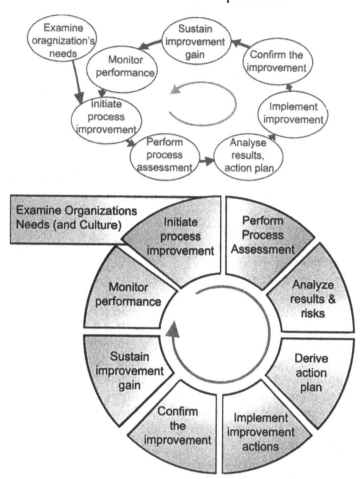

**Fig. 18. ISO/IEC 15504 + Revised Process Improvement Cycles.**

The top figure illustrates the original process improvement cycle in ISO/IEC 15504. The lower figure shows the improved, revised process improvement cycle. The revised cycle includes additional activities and orients the cycle in a logical direction. Both use these general principles:

- Process improvement is based on process assessment results and process effectiveness measures.
- Process assessment produces a current process capability profile which may be compared with a target based on the organization's needs and business goals.

- Process effectiveness measures help identify and prioritize improvement actions that support organizations in meeting their needs and business goals, and in achieving process goals.
- Process improvement is a continuous process. Improvement goals identified and agreed within the organization are realized through a process improvement programme that continues through multiple cycles of planning, implementing and monitoring activities.
- Improvement actions identified within a process improvement programme are implemented as projects.
- Metrics are used for monitoring the improvement process in order to indicate progress and to make necessary adjustments.
- Process assessment may be repeated in order to confirm that the improvements have been achieved.
- Mitigation of risk is a component of process improvement and should be addressed from two viewpoints:
  - The risk inherent in the current situation.
  - The risk of failure of the improvement initiative.

Process improvement plans and records may be used to support process capability determination (see previous chapter). This is a means to respond to a customer proposed process capability (in a contract), which exceeds the currently assessed profile. The revised cycle is a general process improvement model, based in part upon a space industry variant [24]. It has been converted to apply to improvement of all types of processes, and not just software processes. Terminology and additional analysis and descriptions have been added. It separates the Analyse Results and Derive Action Plan into 2 steps:

- Analyze Results with a risk analysis component.
- Derive Action Plan.

Another change is that the improved cycle is now depicted logically in a clockwise direction.[13] This revised model will be the basis for detailed discussion on how to implement a process improvement programme. It is described in detail in the next section of this chapter.

---

[13] I don't know why quality people show things in an anti-clockwise direction – there must be a streak of contrariness in their personality! Or maybe I've been around Swiss watchmakers too long!

## Implementing a Process Improvement Programme

For organizations wishing to start a comprehensive process improvement programme, the following 9 Step Process Improvement Cycle will provide a reliable basis to implement an ongoing improvement process.

Improvements to a process may start at any hierarchical level in the organization. Nevertheless, senior management leadership is needed to launch and sustain a change effort and to provide continuing resources and impetus, although, ultimately, everyone in the organization should be involved (creating a culture of improvement). For a process improvement programme to be effective, it:

- Demands investment, planning, dedicated people, management time and investment.
- Requires an understanding of the current process and clear goals for improvement.
- Is continuous – it involves continual learning and evolution.
- Must provide recognisable benefits to the business and people implementing it.

Process changes will not be sustained without conscious effort and periodic reinforcement. The needs and business goals of the organization determine the process improvement goals that help to identify improvement actions and their priorities. A process improvement programme particularly suits organizations requiring more formal management and control of initiatives.

## The 9 Step Process Improvement Cycle

The 9 step process improvement cycle consists of the following steps or stages[14].

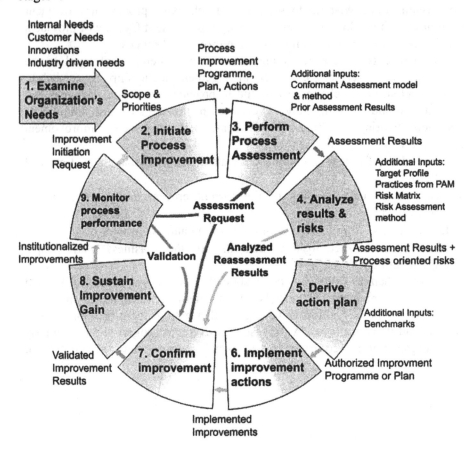

**Fig. 19. The 9-Step Process Improvement Cycle.**

The sequence of activities is shown as a cycle of 9 separate steps. The organization should decide if all these steps are always necessary. It may be that some steps may be combined or not performed in some situations.

The cycle contains a high level of formalism. It assumes that the organization wishes to plan a process improvement programme, not just one

---

[14] The 9 Step cycle is based upon the suggested approach in the ESA space industry model plus the author's additions for a longer term programme of improvement.

improvement action. For large organizations, the entire cycle provides a means to manage corporate improvement programmes across multiple departments, business units and divisions. Small organizations with few people should combine several steps.

If you have been assigned to look into starting an improvement programme, it may seem daunting at first. However, by following the steps in the improvement cycle, you will develop and implement improvements in a controlled and successful manner.

As you become more familiar with the improvement cycle activities and more confident after successful improvements are implemented, you will find that most of the activities described in the following sections become self sustaining and easier to follow. However, I recommend that you work through the sections in detail first so that you don't miss important steps that can be vital to creating a sustainable improvement programme.

It is also easier to start with smaller but worthwhile improvement actions, rather than tackle more demanding improvement actions. But remember - always base the improvements on the organization's business needs so that business benefits are visible.

## Getting Started – Examine the Organization's Needs

It is extremely important to clarify the business issues/goals of senior management at the beginning of a process improvement initiative. It is also important to have an improvement sponsor in senior management for both budgetary and motivational support. Meet with senior management to get sponsorship to start the examination of the organization's needs. Triggers for a process improvement programme may be:

- ✘ Dissatisfied customers due to late delivery of products.
- ✘ Quality problems such as defects in delivered products.
- ✘ Excessive costs.
- ➢ A supplier audit or process assessment.
- ➢ A need to respond to a Capability Determination.
- ✓ A desire to improve use of resources.
- ✓ A desire to improve efficiency and effectiveness of the organization.
- ✓ A desire to create or maintain a competitive edge.

The stimuli for improvement may be derived from a review of mission statements and strategy documents, and interviews with major stakeholders to understand problems, visions and needs.

First, establish a clear relationship between the high-level business goals (often expressed in the business' vision, strategy and business plan) and the process related goals and needs, and hence to the necessity of investing in process improvement. It is useful to make a short list of the relevant business goals and add the subsequent information collected. This information can include local business unit drivers, cultural factors, triggers and stimuli, and process related improvement activities.

Organize guided interviews/workshops with local management (business, marketing, technical and quality) to understand which business unit drivers (typically quality, cost, schedule or product issues) are of the highest priority. A high correlation has been found between lasting programs and business management involvement (and understanding) from the beginning.

Recognize and manage the human and organizational cultural factors. In particular an improvement programme must recognize and be prepared to handle issues including: management leadership and support; the cultural aspects (values, norms, attitudes and behaviours) of the people; commitment to improvement goals and targets; communications and teamwork; formal structures and reporting lines; and informal relationships within the organization. In addition, improvement requires provision of education and training.

Recognize how the recognition and rewards system will support improvement actions. If this system does not support improvement, then the organization is not ready to improve.

Where the organizational culture requires change in order to foster improvement, it will be necessary to address this with senior management before commencing the process improvement initiative. See the section on **Improvement and culture – a wider view,** in this chapter for additional guidance. If the organizational readiness is perceived as low, the process improvement initiative should be postponed. At a high level (depending upon the availability of information), you need to:

- Clarify the motivations for action.
- Develop a business case, collecting any available benchmarking information describing why the process improvement initiative should take place.
- Estimate what it will cost[15].
- Estimate how long it will take to see the benefits. Both estimates may be 'order of magnitude' figures at this stage if no prior date is available[16].

---

[15] I use a simple 3-step approach when initially trying to determine cost or schedule. First, if I have data, I use this to make an estimate. Secondly, if I have limited data but some relevant previous experience, I make a guesstimate (half guess – half estimate). Thirdly, if I have no data, I make a guess (based upon as much experience as possible). To make better guesses, get several people to guess and then use a combined judgment to derive the most likely figure plus the likely variance.

- List the expected results.
- Identify potential improvement champions (people with a motivation and commitment to implementing improvements).

With the improvement programme sponsor, establish and review the improvement initiative. Together with the improvement champions, identify ongoing and future activities as well as constraints, dependencies and external factors that may influence the initiative. Determine the readiness to start. Obtain organizational commitment from the line and project managers who will be involved, and start to manage expectations. As improvement implies change, there will be political and cultural barriers and resistance to be overcome. If you have created clear expectations and have senior management sponsorship, it will be easier to overcome barriers.

Prepare and run information collection and communication events (workshops, briefings). Review the proposal for the process improvement initiative. Explain the process improvement initiative to those affected, describe what approach is chosen and who is involved.

It is also important to avoid exceeding the capability and capacity of the organization to invest in improvement.

## Initiate Process Improvement

The initiation of process improvement should be managed in the same way as any other project in the organization. This includes definition of objectives, proper planning, allocation of resources, identification of risks, progress tracking, etc.

The Improvement processes in ISO/IEC 12207 and ISO/IEC 15504-5 provide guidance. An overall process improvement programme is developed identifying the phases of the improvement initiative and defining goals for each phase.

In the following steps, process improvement actions are assumed to be initiated based on assessment results and as described in process improvement action plans. The overall coordination of these individual actions is described in the process improvement programme plan, which covers aspects including:

- Resources required.
- Organizational structure (roles; communication, reporting and decision lines).
- Checkpoints and major milestones.

---

[16] Order of magnitude figures could be 1,000s or 10,000s (for cost), weeks, months, and years (for schedule).

In the 9 Step improvement cycle, the duration of one iteration of the process improvement cycle is defined by the time between two assessments. Since a delta-assessment (reassessment) should demonstrate measurable increase of Capability Levels, this time should not be less than 9 months. The following table provides a possible timeframe for one iteration of the cycle.

**Table 16. Example process improvement programme timeframe.**

| Step | Activity | Output Work Products | Duration |
|---|---|---|---|
| 1 | Getting started | Objectives for the process improvement initiative | 1 - 3 (Weeks) |
| 2 | Launch process improvement initiative | Process improvement plan | 1 - 3 |
| | **Milestone:** Process improvement plan review | Approved process improvement plan | |
| 3 | Process Assessment - Establish baseline | Assessment reports, process profiles | 5 - 8 |
| 4 | Analyse results and risks | Assessment results, and process oriented risk lists | 1 - 2 |
| 5 | Derive action plans | Action plans aligned with the process improvement plan | 1 - 3 |
| | **Milestone:** Process improvement plan review | Approved and updated process improvement plan | |
| 6 | Implement improvements | Improvement action progress report(s) | 15 - 30 |
| 7 | Confirm improvements | Improvement action final reports | 1 - 2 |
| | **Milestone:** Improvement actions review | Approved improvement action final reports | |
| 8 | Sustain improvement gains | Improvement deployment plans | 15 - 40 |
| 9 | Monitor performance | Process performance reports, process improvement proposals | Ongoing |
| | **Milestone:** Process performance review | Approved process performance reports, approved process improvement proposals | |

At each milestone review, the achieved results should be evaluated against the business goals of the organization, as well as the specific review criteria. In this initiation step, it is important to establish the organizational structure for the initiative so that there is an ongoing group (e.g. steering committee) to manage the programme. This steering committee gives direction, provides resources and monitors progress. The steering committee should comprise a senior management improvement sponsor, a person responsible for managing the improvement programme and sufficient organization management personnel committed to providing resources.

The steering committee appoints an Improvement Facilitation Team, to facilitate and coordinate the activities. The facilitation team should comprise the improvement program manager, personnel representing the major business units and external improvement support personnel. The facilitation team should not be too large (preferably less than 8 people) and able to meet regularly. The business unit representatives ensure their business needs remain in focus when prioritising improvements.

The team liaises with the organizational entities and functions involved. They would build internal and external networks for information exchange and dissemination. This includes organizing regular briefings, communicating messages, and making provisions for incentives, recognition and awards.

For smaller organizations, the steering committee and the Improvement Facilitation Team may be the same people. In very small organizations, they may be just one improvement person and a senior management sponsor. It is important to balance the limitations of available resources against the positive involvement of as many people as possible.

When the process improvement initiative is ready to start, there may be a kick-off event to formally acknowledge the importance of the initiative. This 'advertisement' is more important in larger organizations with dispersed business units. Otherwise, it is probably more important to acknowledge the first successful improvement.


## Perform Process Assessment – Establish Baseline

The organization should understand how processes are currently performed and how capable they are at achieving the desired result (their process capability). This then provides a baseline before changes are made.

The usual way for systematically collecting and presenting the baseline is through process assessments. The preparation and performance of a process assessment is described in the chapter on process assessment, later in this book. Most of the assessment phases (initiation, planning, briefing, data acquisition, data validation, process rating and reporting) remain as described therein.

Based upon the previously defined related goals and needs (from step 1), select the key processes[17] and desired capability. The desired capability may

---

[17] Key processes for a software-oriented organization are defined as those in the Primary Lifecycle of a Process Reference Model. These are Acquisition-Supply, Operation and Engineering processes in ISO/IEC 12207.

be the highest level that the assessment team will assess. Alternately, it may be a desired target capability profile requested by a customer.

Next, select processes that support the key processes (from management, support and organizational process areas)[18].

The scope of the assessment should cover all processes selected for improvement. Each process should be assessed at least up to its desired Capability Level.

Keep records of objective evidence used in the assessment rating. In assessments for the purpose of process improvement, it is necessary to note the *critical* process indicators (base practices, work products and management practices) that are not performed.

It is not necessary to look for all indicators and find evidence for them in order to fully achieve the corresponding Process Attribute. In particular, a process may be fully performed (level 1) although some of the base practices are not performed. The assessors judge this based on achievement of the purpose of the process with no significant weakness in performance being evident.

Similarly, not all work products (listed in the assessment model) for a given process must be produced. The assessment team, as always, must use their expert judgment based on the contractual obligations or in-house procedures to determine which base practices and work products are required for achievement of the process purpose.

However, in cases where essential base practices are not performed or required work products are not produced, these unachieved process indicators should be clearly indicated in the assessment record. In particular, anytime the assessment team rates a Process Attribute as less than 'Fully' achieved on any given process, the unachieved process indicators leading to the reduced rating should be recorded.

In addition, for unachieved or incomplete indicators, the assessment team should record at which level (or levels) in the organization improvements are needed (e.g. project level, organizational unit, business unit, etc.).

Certain base practices or management practices are applicable both to specific project environments and to the organization as a whole. The base practices of Configuration management are a good example. A 'Largely' achieved rating at level one here could be the result of a flawed project-specific configuration management scheme or of an inadequate configuration management scheme within the entire organizational unit.

Recording the organizational level helps guide future improvement suggestions.

---

[18] It is common to select project management as often work is performed in projects, supplemented by risk management, configuration management, joint review and problem resolution.

In summary, the goal is not to create an exhaustive record of unachieved indicators but to record enough detail to be able to later focus process improvement in the important areas for improving the process ratings and achieving the business goals. Each assessor must determine the degree of data recording that best suits the assessment context and meets the assessment constraints. The resultant Process Baseline will consist of:

- Assessment findings (Process Attribute ratings, specific observations)
- Strengths and weaknesses
- Improvement opportunities and recommendations.

At the end of the assessment, the assessors should make a preliminary presentation of findings to allow feedback from the assessed organizational unit(s). This is to ensure that the preliminary findings presented are considered representative and valid, or to allow further feedback and evidence to be gathered to adjust the findings before completing the assessment report.

## Analyse results and risks

In this step, the Improvement Facilitation Team analyses the assessment results in detail to derive a list of actions for process improvement. The strategy here is to identify the gap between the target capability profile and the actual process capability profile, tracing back to the unachieved critical indicators noted during the assessment. From these unachieved indicators, a list of corrective actions may be derived.

After the assessment results are complete, the gaps between the desired and the assessed capability levels are analysed for the unachieved or incomplete key process indicators. These gaps are broken down into differences in Process Attribute ratings for each process. The assessment record is used to 'trace backwards' to identify the unachieved key indicators (base practices, management practices, and work products), that resulted in the deficient ratings for each process.

For deficiencies at Capability Level 1, unachieved or incomplete base practices and work products are compiled instead of the level one management practices, as these indicators provide more specific guidance for process improvement. Of course, any Process Attributes where the assessed rating is higher than or equal to the desired level are disregarded.

The list of corrective actions should be compiled based on the unachieved key indicators.

Unachieved *Base Practices* or *Work Products* can be added directly to the corrective action list. A simple approach is to turn unachieved base practices and work products into a 'to-do' action list. In cases where the organizational unit was simply not aware that they had to perform certain activities, this approach is useful. However, in many cases, an underlying problem prevents the project or organizational unit from fully achieving the indicator(s), although project staff may be fully aware that this is undesirable. In these cases, it is more important to analyse the unachieved indicators to determine the root cause of the indicators' absence. From this root cause analysis, meaningful corrective actions may be derived.

Unachieved *Management Practices* may require some translation, as they are worded in a generic manner in the assessment model to be applicable to all processes. The analysis group therefore should exercise their expert judgment to derive improvement actions related to (each of) the key processes.

If an unachieved key indicator was noted at both project and the organizational unit level, it may be desirable to form two corrective actions from it, so that each relevant level of the organization is addressed. The selection of improvement actions can be further refined by:

- Addition of a risk analysis, as proposed in the following subsection.
- Addition of best practices and suggestions for improvement, gathered from internal and external sources.

Organizations can sometimes become 'myopic' (internally focused) when analysing their strengths and weaknesses. It is important to always include some external viewpoint into assessment, analysis and action planning. Use of external personnel in a process assessment team can broaden the range of experience available and therefore the potential range of improvement opportunities proposed.

Similarly, an experienced improvement consultant can provide valuable benefits by providing both improvement opportunities and implementation approaches that reduce overall resources needed, and speed up implementation.

### Analyse risks

Risk analysis based upon process capability gaps is a powerful addition as it not only addresses current problems but also helps managers to avoid future problems (represented by risks). While this activity is optional, it is recommended that the improvement team look at employing this activity.

A process capability gap presents a set of possible process-oriented risks[19]. For example, when a process capability gap in requirements analysis exists,

---

[19] Analysis of risks is an optional extension going beyond the process improvement cycle described in ISO/IEC TR 15504-7:1998. This step has been incorporated as part of the assessment results analysis, and the derivation of action plans has been made a separate step in the cycle.

there are several associated risks, including the risks of missing requirements, incompletely specified requirements, and requirements not matching customer needs. The following are the benefits of risk-based analysis:

- Classify risks within a process assessment framework.
- Focus recommendations on the riskiest processes/practices.
- Minimise the effort of process improvement to achieve an acceptable risk level.
- Clarify the link between process assessments and risk management.
- Serve as an input to a risk management routine or process.
- Provide a Risk to Company/Project profile for multiple comparison purposes.

It has been found that inclusion of risk analysis provides the group analysing the assessment results with another highly useful perspective (one focused on mitigation and/or prevention of future problems) and aligns well with the risk orientation of **Capability Determination** and **Defining Target Capability Profiles** chapters. There are several risk models available, the one described here is based upon work done for the European Space Agency [25]. The risk model has three main components:

- A 2 dimensional matrix showing correlation between risk and processes. Correlation $C_{31}$ links risk R3 with Process P1.

**Table 17. Risk correlation matrix.**

| Risk | | | | | |
|------|--------|--------|--------|--------|---------|
| $R_3$ | $c_{31}$ | $c_{32}$ | $c_{33}$ | $c_{34}$ | |
| $R_2$ | $c_{21}$ | $c_{22}$ | $c_{23}$ | $c_{24}$ | |
| $R_1$ | $c_{11}$ | $c_{12}$ | $c_{13}$ | $c_{14}$ | |
| | $P_1$ | $P_2$ | $P_3$ | $P_4$ | Process |

- Process Risk Factors that give weightings to risks based on what Process Attribute is affected (Capability Level achieved).
- A Risk Tree based in upon risk defined in part in the Software Engineering Institute Risk Taxonomy [26], in which the potential risks are all mapped to the processes, and directly reflect the level of performance of *base practices*. In addition the risk tree contains risks reflecting the *management practices*.

The risk approach is based on two key assumptions. The first assumption is that risks related to processes that reach the target Capability Level are acceptable. The second assumption is that processes with related risks are not considered as interdependent (in order to simplify the process risk factor correlation).The risk model and method covers the two major risk dimensions:

- Likelihood; the wider the gap between the target and assessed capabilities, the higher the likelihood of the related risk. If one of the processes is not performed or does not largely achieve the process purpose and outcomes (Capability Level 0 process), the risk likelihood is set to the maximum value; if processes achieve Largely or Fully at Capability Level 1, a calculation is made of all the Process Attributes up to the target level. Process attributes are multiplied by the Process Risk Factor for the related Capability Level. This produces a cumulative likelihood value. The following table uses a normalized scale of likelihood between 1 and 5.

**Table 18. Risk likelihood matrix.**

| | $R_1$ | $R_2$ | $R_3$ | $R_4$ |
|---|---|---|---|---|
| L=5 | | | | |
| L=4 | | | | ■ |
| L=3 | | | ■ | |
| L=2 | | | | |
| L=1 | ■ | | | |

- Severity; the severity of risk's consequences depends upon the Capability Level in which the gap occurs (for example, the severity of not performing a process is higher than a lack of a continuous improvement practice in that process). Refer to the subsection: **Process Capability Gaps and Risk** in the Capability Determination chapter. Severity is based on the expert judgment of the assessor team and the project manager(s).

**Table 19. Risk severity matrix.**

| | $R_1$ | $R_2$ | $R_3$ | $R_4$ |
|---|---|---|---|---|
| S=5 | | | | ■ |
| S=4 | | | | |
| S=3 | | ■ | | |
| S=2 | ■ | | | |
| S=1 | | | ■ | |

Finally, a risk index (RI) is calculated based upon the likelihood multiplied by the severity.

**Table 20. Risk Index – Risk Magnitude designations.**

| Risk Index | Risk Magnitude |
|---|---|
| $RI \geq 20$ | Maximum |
| $15 \leq RI < 20$ | High |
| $10 \leq RI < 15$ | Medium |
| $4 < RI < 10$ | Low |
| $RI \leq 4$ | Minimum |

**Table 21. Risk Index – Risk Magnitude Likelihood vs. Severity.**

| | S=1 | S=2 | S=3 | S=4 | S=5 |
|---|---|---|---|---|---|
| L=5 | A | | | | |
| L=4 | | A | | R4 | |
| L=3 | | A<br>R1 | A | | |
| L=2 | R3 | | A | A | |
| L=1 | | | R2 | | A |
| Cost | S=1 | S=2 | S=3 | S=4 | S=5 |

The risks within the magnitude areas with $RI \geq 10$ (darker shaded areas with dot pattern) should be selected for risk mitigation *(prevention, avoidance, reduction)*. The remaining risks in the *RI<10* areas, should be monitored.

Usually, the assessment recommends improvement actions that extend to all those processes, which are not reaching target levels. Project managers are often not inclined to follow these recommendations if they go beyond the organizational unit constraints (resources, budget, and goals) or if they don't appear vital. With the integration of the risk dimension, it is possible to select recommended actions that target the processes with unacceptable risks.

Senior managers and affected line managers should therefore be involved in this stage of the decision making process to ensure that rigorous analysis is performed. They can select improvement actions for maximum organizational benefit (and not just for a particular project). They also become aware of both immediate problems and longer-term risks.

Note that at this stage, improvement actions in this list simply specify *what* should be done and not *how* the actions should be implemented. Suggestions should be noted for future use, but the final method of implementation should be determined during subsequent steps, based on additional input from other sources.

## Derive Action Plans

Once the corrective actions have been identified in the previous step, the next step is to group actions together based on relationships and interdependencies. Meaningful sorting categories depend strongly on the organizational unit or company context. Sorting criteria that may be used include:

- Sorting actions for each organizational unit or for projects. The aim is to sort improvement actions by the level of the organization they impact (i.e. project level, management level, quality assurance team, business unit level) as they are also the likely groups of process performers and improvers.
- Grouping actions affecting a single topic. For example, if several project-level actions are related to a topic like system design, then grouping these into a single improvement project will benefit multiple projects (management-multiplier effect). This also applies to actions that affect a single work product (for example, project plans, and a project management handbook) or a group of work products in the project or organization. The base practices and work products from different processes may be similarly related.
- Sorting by generic or management practices across processes. Good examples include activities associated with the practices defined for the process definition attribute (PA3.1) or the process measurement attribute (PA4.1). Thus a set of unachieved practice indicators identified in the assessment across multiple instances can be symptoms of a single problem best improved at the organizational level.
- Sorting actions related to systematic deviations between the target and the actual state for a given Process Attribute. This implies some generic or management practices are not achieved and they may have associated processes (for example ORG 2.1 Process establishment is a generic way to fulfil MP 3.1.2 Implement and/or tailor the standard process to obtain a defined process). Therefore it would be appropriate to focus on the organizational process ORG.2.1 Process Establishment.
- Relationships between the management practices and certain processes in the process reference model are defined in Annex B2 of ISO/IEC TR 15504-5:1998. An 'X' in the grid indicates that a relationship exists between the corresponding management practice (column) and process (row).

The Improvement Facilitation Team must check that the sorted and grouped actions address the business needs and achieve business value. When the identified problems and proposed actions are clearly defined, it is essential to gain a more solid commitment from management concerning resources. Detailed cost estimates are not yet mandatory but there must be an estimate of the resources and the timeframe in which expected improvements are to occur, so that management has enough information to consider the action plan priorities.

The steering committee should meet with senior management and other affected stakeholders within the organization. The steering committee summarizes the assessment results and actions, and the agenda for future improvements action plans is outlined. The business value of the action plans should be reviewed so that management commitment to proceed is re-affirmed.

If external staff will be used to support the improvement efforts, an initial estimate of the internal versus external effort that will be allocated should be agreed. Industry experience suggests that during the planning of improvements, a minimum of one internal person-hour must be spent for every 4 external person-hours, but that, during the rollout and training phases, this ratio is reversed. External support can be used to great benefit in implementing improvements, but internal effort is critical for success.

## Classify and Prioritise Action Groups

Until this step, it is possible to perform the analysis with the Improvement Facilitation Team and affected managers (although the author recommends earlier participation of personnel, refer to Team Based Business Design Improvement in a later section of this chapter).

Once there is a list of basic grouped actions, it is necessary to involve the affected members of the organization. The wider group validates and prioritises the action groups and brainstorms ideas for their implementation. Involve the people responsible for the affected processes; this will help to ensure the selection of the most relevant improvements. Their involvement also motivates their commitment and participation when the improvements are implemented.

Proposed implementations should be evaluated according to their implementation effort and the severity of the problem they correct (or the benefit expected), in other words the cost/benefit. Through weighing these two parameters, actions can be prioritised against the organization's business goals.

Improvement actions should be classified as short, medium, and long-term. Typically, short term improvements take less than one person-week to implement, medium term take one-two person-months, and long term requires more than two person-months. These definitions should be tailored to the organization.

The timeframe for implementing the selected improvement actions can be estimated based upon the available resources and if there are any dependencies to other initiatives within the organization.

## Develop Action Plans

Improvement actions with the highest priority are selected for implementation as individual process improvement projects. An improvement action team is formed (workshop participants, if applicable) and allocated to the projects. Each improvement action team performs action planning, including:
- Define the success criteria for each action plan and determine how progress will be measured.
- Decide how to implement the improvement actions by evaluating a number of scenarios if possible.
- Produce initial estimates of costs and benefits.
- Identify the risks for the proposed actions. Prepare risk mitigation strategies if needed.
- Establish a schedule for completion of the actions.
- Identify responsibilities for the actions, and agree upon the responsibilities with those affected by the actions.
- Identify recruitment and training needs.

The action planning decisions should are summarized in the action plan, which includes the following:
- The objectives of the process improvement action.
- A description of the approach to implementation.
- The organization and responsibilities.
- The cost, time schedule and resources.
- Risk management, including assessment, monitoring and mitigation.
- Monitoring policy.
- Specification of success criteria, including process goals and improvement targets.

Note: The action plan should be as short as practicable – one to two pages covering the most important details should be sufficient, the aim is to put effort into making improvements, not in using lots of effort in producing highly polished documents.

### Obtain Management Approval of Action Plans

In order to proceed with the action plans, management approval must be obtained. Improvement action teams must be prepared to make a business case for improvements. When arguing the case for improvements, remember to include both the financial benefits provided by the improvement and the costs of **not** doing anything (the pain/problems of the status quo). In fact, it is normally easier to provide the costs of not doing anything, than it is to accurately estimate/guess potential savings.

For organizations that have used cost/benefit analysis or Return on Investment calculations, they should use historical data as a basis for estimates. This is an advantage of having capability level 4 processes, which capture this data.

The updated process improvement programme plan showing the recommended, funded actions should be distributed within the organization.

## Implement Improvement Actions

The action plans are implemented in order to improve the organization's processes. Implementation may be simple or complex depending on the contents of the action plans and the characteristics of the organization. For medium to large organizations, several process improvement projects may be simultaneously initiated, each concerned with implementing one or more process improvement action plans. Such projects will often not only cover initial implementation of improvements as described in this step, but also the subsequent actions to confirm and sustain the improvements.

Where there are alternative operational approaches to implementation, they should be evaluated and the most suitable selected. For instance, it may be possible to implement a given action either in small steps through piloting in a selected unit, or throughout the whole organization at the same time, or somewhere between these two extremes.

Among the factors to monitor during implementation are costs, time scales and risks. It is useful to employ the organizations project management process (if it exists) for longer running, more important and complex improvement projects.

The improvement action team may need to carry out a deeper analysis of improvement opportunities than that already carried out in Step 4. Where appropriate, the plan should include:

- Further collection and analysis of data to establish the underlying causes of unsatisfactory current effectiveness measurements and process profiles.
- Evaluation of alternative proposals for eliminating the root causes, including analysis of costs and benefits.
- Arrangements to capture cost and resource usage data, for instance if it is desired to carry out cost-benefit analysis.

Those implementing the actions and those affected by them should be involved or be consulted as plans evolve. This consultation can draw on their expertise and help to enlist their cooperation and support. It is critical for successful improvement that human and organizational cultural factors are managed during the actions. While the factors were recognized during the first step in deciding organizational readiness to implement an improvement programme, it is often during the action implementation that other cultural factors become apparent. It is rare that organizations are mono-cultural (commonly shared values and norms). These factors may be barriers to improvement. In particular, the following should be managed:

- How to establish and retain commitment to goals and targets.
- Changes needed in values, attitudes and behaviour.
- How to foster open communication and teamwork, including implications for organizational structures and reporting lines.
- What education and training is required.

To overcome barriers, senior management commitment, education and training, open communication and teamwork plus proper recognition and rewards will be needed. Open communication means listening effectively to any concerns expressed and actively addressing these concerns. As the action plans progress, the Improvement Facilitation Team monitors the actions against the process improvement programme plan, in order to:

- Ensure tasks progress as planned, and initiate appropriate corrective action if they do not.
- Check that achievement of the planned goals and targets continues to be both realistic and relevant to the organization's needs.
- Gather data on effort and resources expended, in order to improve estimates for future process improvement projects.
- Evaluate the impacts of the implemented improvement actions on the Process Attribute ratings and Capability Level ratings.

Records should be kept for use both to confirm the improvements and to improve the improvement process itself (refer to the *Improvement Process* in ISO/IEC 12207 and ISO/IEC 15504-5).

## Confirm the Improvements

When one or several related process improvement projects have been completed, the Improvement Facilitation Team should:

- Confirm that the planned goals and targets have been achieved and that the expected benefits have been delivered.
- Confirm that the desired organizational culture has been established.
- Re-evaluate if there are any risks associated with the improved process.

- Re-evaluate costs and benefits.

The personnel affected by the change should provide feedback on the changes. Measurements or indicators of process effectiveness should be used to confirm achievement of process effectiveness targets. If measurements show that process goals and improvement targets have not been achieved, it may be desirable to redefine the process improvement project or activity (for example, by returning to an appropriate earlier step). The possibility of having introduced desirable or undesirable side effects should be investigated and the root cause established.

When major changes have occurred to processes, a further process assessment should be used to confirm achievement of targets expressed as process Capability Levels. The scope of this re-assessment should be related to the scope of the initial assessment. The scope may cover only the processes affected by the improvement actions, particularly where these had a narrow focus. Where several actions were undertaken, however, consideration should be given to a re-assessment of wider scope to check for potential side effects arising from the parallel improvement actions.

The effect of the improvements on organizational culture should be reviewed to establish that desired changes have taken place without undesirable side effects.

The Improvement Facilitation Team should re-evaluate the risks associated with the improved processes to confirm that they are reduced and are acceptable. If the improvements were intended to reduce risk, then the risk analysis (step 4) should be reviewed and performed as necessary. If the risks are not reduced or acceptable, the team should determine what further actions are required.

The costs and benefits of the improvements may be re-evaluated and compared with earlier estimates made at Steps 4 and 5. These results are useful to support planning of subsequent improvement actions.

The steering committee should be involved both to approve the results and to evaluate whether the organization's needs have been met.

Host an appropriate celebration of success with recognition and rewards for the improvement action team.

## Sustain Improvement Gain

After improvement has been confirmed, the process needs to be sustained at the new level of performance. This requires both the steering committee and the Improvement Facilitation Team to monitor institutionalisation of the improved process and to give encouragement when necessary to those implementing it.

Responsibilities for monitoring should be defined (longer term monitoring may involve additional personnel to those making the improvement), as well as how this will be done, for instance by using appropriate effectiveness measurements.

The Improvement Facilitation Team should ensure the organization's standard process infrastructure is updated. This includes the standard process descriptions and their tailoring into defined process descriptions for each applicable project/organizational unit, plus related guidelines.

If an improved process has been piloted in a limited way (e.g. on a specific project), it should be now be deployed across all applicable parts of the organization. The Improvement Facilitation Team is involved in planning the deployment. This deployment should have the necessary resources assigned to it. The plan should be documented as part of the process improvement programme plan. Consideration should be given to:

- Who is affected?
- How to communicate both the changed process and the benefits.
- What education and training are necessary?
- When to introduce changes to the different areas, taking business needs into account.
- How to ensure that the changes have been made (for example, by review, audit or process assessment).
- How to ensure that the improved process performs as expected (for instance by monitoring Capability Levels and/or effectiveness measures).

The steering committee should review and approve the changes and the process deployment.

## Monitor Process Performance

The Improvement Facilitation Team should continually monitor the performance of the organization's processes. The effectiveness and conformance measures used for monitoring performance should be chosen to suit the organization's needs and business goals. The risks to the organization and its products from using the process should also be monitored and action taken as risks emerge or become unacceptable.

The team should also collect lessons learnt from improvement project participants and affected personnel. The collected evidence should validate that the implemented improvement actions constitute sustained improvement gains.

The team should distribute the performance monitoring and lessons learnt information on a regular basis as part of its information dissemination to the organization. It is important to inform improvement program participants and affected (or potentially affected) managers. It is also important to gather their feedback.

The Improvement Facilitation Team should select new process improvement actions and implement them as part of a continuing process improvement programme, since additional improvements are always possible. In addition, the team should regularly consider possible process innovations that could be introduced.

The steering committee should regularly review the continuing suitability of performance measures and information dissemination. The steering committee should regularly review the process improvement programme to ensure that:

- Both the improvement programme and improvement actions, including goals and targets remain appropriate to the organization's needs;
- The implemented improvement actions are validated as sustained improvement gains (or what remedial actions are triggered when the gains are not sustained);
- The improvement process is itself improved in the light of experience; and
- Further improvement actions are initiated when and where appropriate as previous improvement actions have been completed within the planned improvement programme;
- Continuous improvement (covering both process optimization and process innovation aspects) becomes and remains a feature of the organization's values, attitudes and behaviour.

Based upon the results obtained, the Improvement Facilitation Team may recommend to the steering committee to perform further process assessments in the improvement programme (step 3). This is especially important where a long-term goal is to achieve higher Capability Levels and it is approached by stages; when changing organizational needs indicate a requirement to achieve higher Capability Levels; and when there is a need to give a fresh impetus to the improvement programme.

The steering committee should consider the extent to which improved processes have been institutionalised before scheduling further process assessments. The question they need to ask is:

*Are the improvements sustained?*

It may be more cost-effective to delay assessing a process until improvements have been fully deployed, rather than expend resources assessing a process, which is in transition. Process improvements in transition can cause problems interpreting an assessment result, especially for assessments across multiple organisational units.

Depending upon the extent, suitability and degree of completion of the improvement programme, the steering committee should decide when the

Improvement Facilitation Team either re-examines the organization's needs (step 1), or revises and/or initiates a new improvement programme (step 2).

*The cycle is complete.*                    **Time to start the next iteration.**

## The 5 Stage Agile Improvement Cycle

Not all organizations need (or can afford) to follow all the activities in the 9 Step improvement cycle. The more agile 5 stage improvement cycle achieves the most important improvement aims of the more formal 9 Step improvement cycle. This cycle is especially useful for smaller or agile organizations that can perform improvements in a less formal manner. It is also useful for organizations embarking upon process improvement for the first time that want to start more quickly.

**Fig. 20. Five stage agile improvement cycle.**

In the above representation of the 5 Stage agile improvement cycle, the activities in the 9 Step improvement cycle are shown for information purposes. I have re-arranged the order of activities required in the 5 Stages.

The first two stages can often be performed together in small organizations. With proper facilitation, they can often be performed within one or two half-day workshops.

As organizations become familiar with some of the pitfalls and problems in process improvement, they may wish to improve their approach by embracing the cultural aspects described in the next section, together with Team Based Business Design Improvement.

The scope of the activities in the 5 Stages is simplified, since the aim is to start rapidly and not to develop an extensive improvement programme upfront. The 5 stages are:

- **Set Goals** - includes the organization's goals and needs, as well as the individual business unit goals, and overall improvement goals.
- **Think** - comprises all activities that lead to planning improvement actions. This includes performing data collection (and hence the potential need for process assessment) and analysing this data.
- **Act** - comprises the improvement action implementation.
- **Review** - includes progress review of the implemented actions and the longer-term review confirming improvement gains.
- **Sustain** - includes all activities that sustain the improvement programme across the organization.

This 5 Stage improvement cycle is derived from a multi-dimensional improvement and quality management model called **STARS**[20] [27] [28]. This model provides many more themes in addition to the one illustrated above. It includes personal, teamwork and cultural themes. Each theme is represented by a 5 stage cycle. They act in concert as an upward spiral – *striving towards excellence.*

Although the stages in the figure are shown separated in the model representation, they in fact overlap and flow into each other. For example, deriving action plans can occur within both the **Think** stage and the **Act** stage, and **Review** starts while improvement actions are being implemented.

This model does not assume that a process improvement programme is planned in the any iteration of the cycle. However, I recommend that the organization evolve a programme over several iterations, based upon the perceived relationships between the desired and performed improvement actions.

The model should be tailored to suit the organization. Facilitation by an experienced improvement consultant can help the organization improve more rapidly, and enhances the efforts of organization staff. The consultant can prepare information needed for workshops, capture the results and provide benefits analysis (act as a benefit-multiplier).

## Stage 1: Set Goals.

Setting Goals is best handled in a workshop. The workshop starts with brainstorming, followed by analysis and some form of voting system. A good workshop facilitator will maximize the value of a workshop by

---

[20] I developed STARS in the 1990's and have successfully used it in high capability organizations. The book on the method was first published in 2006.

managing pace, idea collation, and guiding participants in a positive and constructive manner. The workshop may be performed in a half day within smaller organizations. Goal setting includes:

⊕ Reviewing management vision, mission, policy and strategy.
⊕ Capturing high-level business goals, strategies and drivers (differentiation, responsiveness, cost, quality, efficiency).
⊕ Capturing related business unit (marketing, technical, service unit) goals and drivers (quality, cost, schedule or product issues).
⊕ Recognizing human personal, team and organizational cultural factors.
⊕ Collecting customer related goals and triggers (late delivery, defect rates).
⊕ Relating these to process goals.
⊕ Deriving high-level improvement goals.

During this stage, it is important to:

✓ Obtain management leadership and support.
✓ Seek commitment to high-level improvement goals and targets.
✓ Establish the improvement team, the formal and informal relationships needed and communication patterns.
✓ Establish recognition and rewards system.

The workshop should have participants from all major business units and senior management. Since this stage needs to cover high-level business goals, it is advisable to have as many participants representing various business units and organizational viewpoints (customer, management, technical, support, human resources, supplier) as possible.

In the situation that the goals are relatively easy to set, it is recommended that the selected people in the improvement team move immediately to the next stage.

## Stage 2: Think.

In this stage, the improvement team converts the goals into a more concrete foundation for improvement. This will require different modes of thinking to the Set Goals stage. The team must use analytical and judgmental thinking to derive and select the improvement actions.

In small organizations, the same people who set the goals may form the improvement team. The team should not be more than 6 persons (preferably 3 – 4 people). The improvement team roles should include the improvement sponsor, the improvement manager and business unit personnel (not necessarily the business unit manager but someone the manager trusts and delegates authority). External personnel such as customers and an improvement consultant can be highly beneficial participants. It is possible that one person will have multiple roles, but make sure that he/she has the necessary authority needed for each role. This stage includes the following:

- Setting objectives for first process improvement action. In the first iteration of the cycle, it is better to select one improvement objective, plan one action and get started. In subsequent iterations of the cycle, the team should select more actions and evolve an improvement programme to cover several improvement objectives and actions.
- Collecting and analyzing input data as the basis for establishing the current status of processes. This can include one or all of the following:
  - Process assessment: strengths and weakness, improvement opportunities.
  - Problem data.
  - Root Cause analysis.
  - Workshops with the organizational unit(s) to discuss problems, risks and lessons learnt about their business and its processes that have a potential for improvement.
- Identify risks, using a risk calculation method if available; otherwise run a risk workshop (preferably using the Delphi method).
  - Catalogue the process, product and people related risks.
  - Estimate risk likelihood and severity.
  - Focus on the riskiest processes/practices.
- Select the best improvement candidate actions, based upon:
  - ✓ Best return on investment (cost/benefit).
  - ✓ 'Easy wins'. These are important problems that are easier to solve and provide useful benefits (not trivial problems!).
  - ✓ Organizational units wishing to improve, with an improvement champion ready to start. Even better are units with champions and willing participants.
  - ✓ Improvement that does not require a change in culture.
  - ✓ Timeframe to complete an improvement action (start with shorter timeframes to achieve early success).
- Plan one (or more) improvement actions:
  - Think about the expected benefits.
  - Set success criteria including the desired goal, objectives and process outcomes (and related product and people outcomes).
  - Set desired process capability and related measures of success.
  - Evaluate potential scenarios and select the most promising.
  - Think about any risks (both to the action itself and what it may reduce/mitigate).
  - Estimate and allocate resources (people, budget, training, other resources needed) and schedule. It is worthwhile assessing a trade-off between the number of external resources (saving time and borrowing

experience) and the number of internal resources (taking more time but gaining experience). The use of external resources can provide an attractive cost/benefit until internal personnel gain experience.

- Set checkpoints and major milestones.
- Form the action team. The team should have an improvement champion who is respected within the organization unit(s) affected. It should also have a process expert, a process capability expert (often an ISO/IEC 15504 process assessor), someone who can handle the administrative aspects, and all willing participants who are committed to performing improvement actions (no spectators please!). Sometimes the team may be just 2 people, sometimes it may be 6 people (but should not be any larger).
- Delegate authority to the action team.
- The action team creates a short action plan.
- Obtain management approval for the improvement action plan(s) and/or programme if the sponsor is not part of the improvement team.

The timeframe for this stage depends heavily on the desired scope of improvement activities, the amount of effort dedicated to the activities (using a dedicated and experienced person can shorten the timeframe), and the ability of participants to meet. The action team will often comprise some different personnel from the improvement team. Normally the action team has more personnel from the process area or organizational unit involved in implementing the improvement.

It is important that elapsed time is kept as short as possible (after all time is money), so that momentum is not lost. This is especially true when first starting improvements. In small organizations, the elapsed time can be as short as 2 days and preferably should be no longer than a week.

While it is important to plan properly, it is just as important to move to the next stage as soon as practicable. It is better to plan one improvement action and start implementing it, than it is to plan an entire improvement program. Remember, the aim is to improve the processes of the organization, not only plan and produce polished documents. The 5 Stage improvement cycle allows (and expects) you to repeat the cycle when you are ready to take new actions.

## Stage 3: Act.

This stage should use the majority of the improvement resources[21]. The action team may be able to commence the improvement action immediately,

---

[21] If the **Act** stage doesn't use the most resources, reconsider the improvement approach.

or may need to elaborate the action plan for more complex actions. The improvement actions can include:

- Implementing existing processes (including those piloted in other parts of the organization). This could include key processes or supporting processes. It could simply involve training the people to understand and follow an existing process.
- Creation of new processes and process models/descriptions.
- Revision/improvement of existing processes.
- Increasing the capability of a process. Some possible capability improvements are:
    - ✓ Improving process management through better qualitative controls, such as improved planning methods, review, lessons learnt feedback.
    - ✓ Improving work products through improved templates and examples.
    - ✓ Controlling work products through configuration management methods and tools.
    - ✓ Improved tool support for processes.
    - ✓ Education and training of the people in the organisational unit.
    - ✓ Obtaining required people for specialist roles.
    - ✓ Obtaining and implementing additional resources and infrastructure too properly support processes.
    - ✓ Creating standard process descriptions with tailoring guidelines for projects.
    - ✓ Implementing measurement programs for one project or across multiple projects.
    - ✓ Implementing cost and schedule control methods and measures.
    - ✓ Implementing quantitative process data capture and analysis, such as trend analysis and comparative analysis across projects.
    - ✓ Using quantitative process data to improve process control through use of control charts (e.g. P charts).
    - ✓ Creating a process to continually refine and improve processes.
- Cultural change of the people in the organisational unit.
- Implementing the improvements (this may require iterative and incremental improvement activities).
- Capturing feedback, lessons learnt and measurement data on the implementation.

Depending upon the improvement actions, people with different roles/skills/competencies may need to be in the action team. The people in the team may vary over time (people joining and leaving as needed). Some people may be part-time; others may participate for the entire time the team is in action. The action team needs to also ensure it obtains any specialists it needs (internal or external).

## Stage 4: Review

The Review stage starts with progress review while the Act stage is implementing improvements. The improvement team (which may or may not be composed of the same people as the action team) review progress both informally and formally. Formal review occurs at any planned checkpoints and milestones. During progress review, the improvement team:
- Ensure tasks progress as planned or take corrective action.
- Evaluate any barriers encountered and plan/review actions to overcome them.
- Check planned goals and targets remain realistic and relevant to the organization's needs.
- Gather data on effort and resources expended, in order to improve estimates for future process improvement projects.

The personnel affected by the change should provide feedback on the changes. During the review to confirm improvements after completion of actions, the improvement team:
- ✓ Confirm that the planned goals and targets have been achieved.
- ✓ Evaluate what benefits have been delivered, and compare to the expected benefits.
- ✓ Confirm that the desired organizational culture has been established.
- ✗ Evaluate any adverse impacts of the implemented improvement actions.
- ➢ Re-evaluate risks associated with the improved process.
- ➢ Evaluate measures or indicators of process effectiveness, including qualitative and quantitative data.
  - Qualitative data includes lessons learnt, problems encountered (and solved), unexpected barriers and enablers, unit personnel feedback on cultural aspects.
  - Quantitative data includes cost and schedule benefits, product quality data and capability level achievement.

## Stage 5: Sustain

After improvement has been confirmed, the processes need to be sustained at the new level of performance. Depending upon the improvements, the following may occur:

- Update the organization's process infrastructure (process descriptions, guidelines and supporting tools).
- Plan deployment of piloted processes to applicable organizational units (which occurs in the next Act stage in the cycle).
- Distribute the performance monitoring and lessons learnt information on a regular basis.
- Inform improvement program participants and managers on improvements made and performance monitoring results.
- Gather the feedback of participants in 'Lessons Learnt'.
- Regularly review the continuing suitability of performance measures and information dissemination.
- Review improvement goals and targets remain appropriate to the organization's needs.
  - ✓ Select new process improvement actions.
  - ✓ Review and select process innovations.
- Ensure that improvement gains are sustained over time.
- Improve the improvement programme, the improvement cycle and the improvement process in the light of experience.
- Build upon the improvement cycle to create an upward spiral or personal, team and organizational learning.

☑ Reward the improving teams.

Successful deployment of improved processes with associated training leads to savings that can be used to provide budget for future cycles. When improvements are sustained, subsequent improvement activities can build upon the existing foundation of improvements. This allows an upward spiral of improvement, leading to improvement activities that could not be successfully attempted earlier.

If the cycle is followed successfully several times, then continual improvement is likely to become a feature of the organization. The ongoing success increases motivation, and successful personnel adopt positive norms, values and behaviours that influence the organizational culture.

## Improvement and culture – a wider view

In the preceding sections, I have mostly focused on process improvement. While this is an important endeavour, it should be placed within a wider context if an organizational improvement is to be consistently sustainable and successful (and maximize benefits).

Surveys of organizations show that only a small number of organizations have consistently achieved capability level 5 processes, or an equivalent maturity level [29], [30], [31]. Surveys also have found that the timeframe to consistently reach the highest process capability levels across an entire organization is about 7 years [32]. Since process improvement has been a recognized improvement activity for several decades, and there are fewer organizations with the expected process capability, it raises several questions.

*Why don't all organizations that undergo process assessment always succeed with improvements?*

Furthermore:

*Why don't many organizations successfully achieve an ongoing improvement culture with higher capability level processes?*

Simply stated: **"Process improvement alone is not enough!"**

Based on first hand experience of organizations rated at both ends of the process capability scale in Australia, Asia and Europe, I believe the reason is that successful improvement is driven more by cultural factors within the organization.

The growth of outsourcing to higher maturity organizations (combined with their lower costs in some but not all cases) shows that it is important for organizations to improve and sustain higher process capabilities in order to be competitive[22]. Therefore, it is important for organizations to recognize the barriers and enablers to achieving consistently higher process capability.

During the ISO/IEC 15504 SPICE trials, there was some analysis of the factors that enable or impede successful software process improvement [33].

---

[22] Another note of caution, if your organization has capability level 3 processes and are satisfied with that, have you considered how much you are falling behind competitors improving their process at capability levels 4 and 5?

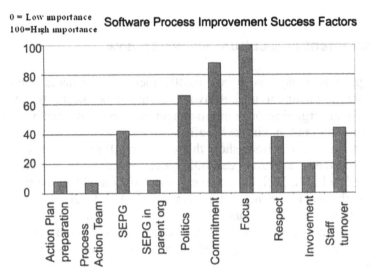

**Fig. 21. Factors that affect software process improvement success.**

It is clear from this study that the most important factors for successful process improvement are not technical factors but rather socio-cultural factors, including **politics**, **commitment** and **focus** – all of them related to **people**.

The set of factors of secondary importance includes respect, staff turnover and the formation of a SEPG (Software Engineering Process Group). These are also people factors; the Software Engineering Process Group is also a structural, organization issue.

Returning to the **People-Process-Product** model, it is therefore vital that improvement primarily recognizes and addresses people issues, and their ability to learn, affect and improve process and product.

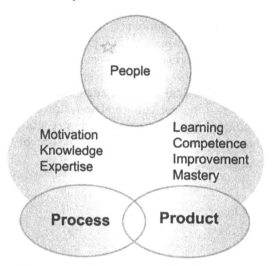

**Fig. 22. People and the process improvement knowledge domain.**

When we recognise that motivated people are the key to the knowledge needed to improve, we shape our plans to address people issues first. Any improvement programme must therefore be aligned with *'helping people to improve'*.

The organization has to recognize and actively engage its people. When we help people to improve, we increase their motivation. Motivated people are more willing to learn, gain and use their knowledge, take actions to improve further, become willing experts and lead through mastering what seemed impossible before. Motivated people will improve the processes used and products produced within their organization.

An improvement programme has to address the cultural issues that exist at personal, team, and organizational (sometimes even at regional/national societal) levels. In many organizations, the prevailing culture is against change (and improvement) or at best disinterested in improvement. People are often too busy coping with bad processes to seriously commit to improvement. The negative cultural aspects are evidenced in negative organizational politics. Therefore, we need to understand the organizational culture, in order to improve. There are many definitions of culture:

- The simple: *'the ways we do things around here'*.
- The more general: *'the way of life, especially the general customs and beliefs, of a particular group of people at a particular time'* [34]
- Temporal, humanistic and societal definitions, such as: *'the integrated platform of human knowledge, belief, and behaviour that depends upon man's capacity for learning and transmitting knowledge to succeeding*

*generations; the set of shared attitudes, values, goals, and practices that characterizes a company or corporation'* [35].

The third definition describes several cultural aspects that can be modelled. It also provides for change and improvement aspects through personal learning and transmittal of knowledge. There are nearly as many models as there are definitions of culture. The following model created by the author, depicts cultural layers as well as their strength of association and resiliency (resistance to change). The model consists of five identifiable layers:

- Explicit cultural layer.
- Behaviour layer.
- Norms and values layer.
- Basic assumptions layer.
- Core beliefs layer.

The model depicts each aspect as having two dimensions; the scope of the aspects represented by the area of coverage, and the degree of association (resilience to challenge, resistance to change) as a height of the aspect.

The model simplifies the complexity of cultural aspects (which in reality are not discretely partitioned as depicted), but still provides a useful basis to analyse and predict cultural interactions. The model is explained further in the author's book: Reach for the STARS [36]. The model should be used as an aid to classification of aspects of culture that potentially affect change, and specifically improvement.

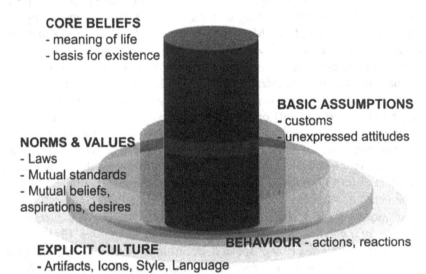

**Fig. 23. Cultural aspects and layers.**

The model attempts to show that the various layers overlap and interact. Note that the boundaries are meant to blend into each other.

Explicit cultural aspects such as artefacts, icons, style and language are superficial – they are often easily recognized, adopted, discarded and subject to change. They are also the widest in scope. Explicit cultural aspects cover many globally marketable products, for example: Coca-cola, McDonalds, Levis, Sony Discman, MP3 players, mobile phones, but also local, regional and national artefacts such as architecture, food, clothing and language.

Behaviour comprises the externally visible actions and reactions of people. External pressure can cause behaviour changes. Peer group pressure (and a willingness to conform to peers) is especially effective in prompting behavioural change.

Norms (the mutual group standards and conventions of what is usual or expected) and values (principles, qualities shared beliefs – what is 'good or 'bad') can occur at personal, team, organizational and societal levels. Real teams create shared values and norms that the team participants shape and adopt [23]. Team norms can be very powerful, both negatively and positively, and these norms may become personally adopted. The norms and values influence behaviour. However, not all the norms and values will be shared at personal, team and organizational levels, in fact when a team adopts new team values, principles and practices (for example by adopting eXtreme Programming), one important consideration may be how to nurture a new team culture that is different to that in the larger organization. External pressure is less likely to change personally held norms and values.

Basic assumptions cover cultural aspects that are normally adopted by persons without question. These include many societal customs and a person's unexpressed attitudes or opinions. Basic assumptions help people to harmoniously live in a society. External pressure rarely causes a person's basic assumptions to change. However, if there is sufficient need, evidence or self-interest, the person may perform self-examination to decide whether to change these assumptions.

Finally, there are personal core beliefs that are virtually subconscious and therefore extremely rarely questioned. These are often based upon how a society has struggled to survive in their (natural) environment, and have become an automatic way to solve challenges and problems. They are highly

---

[23] It is important to differentiate between groups and teams from a cultural perspective. For example, people waiting at a railway station can be considered a group (and can be demographically modelled), but they are not normally a team. Teams pursue common goals and share common norms and values. Real teams act in harmony and synergy to realise benefits beyond the individual contributions and efforts (I called this Synergy).

resistant to external pressure, cause much irritation if questioned, and normally change very slowly (if at all) even when a person wishes to change.

The model presents this progression from the superficial, explicit cultural aspects inwards to core beliefs, with a greater depth of association and resistance to change. To further complicate (or make more interesting) the cultural aspects of change, each person varies in what they would consider each aspect covers and their degree of association, resilience and resistance to change. The model does not require adaptation for regional and national cultures.

The effect of national and regional culture is a subject of much current research. One such directly relevant study looked at the adoption of ICT (Information and Communications Technology) within European Small and Medium Enterprises. It highlighted several national/regional cultural differences in adoption of innovative ICT, and in the way that supervision and independence of individuals affects such adoption [37].

Organizations contain sub-cultures[24]. The people in these sub-cultures share styles, languages and behaviours. Examples may include middle managers, software developers, testers, and salespeople. They have their own language, their professional 'techno-speak'[25] obscured by acronyms. This often reflects their thinking, norms and values (and can act as a barrier to 'outsiders').

As improvement implies change, we must therefore recognize that a sustainable improvement programme needs to address many of these cultural aspects. It needs to recognize the existing cultures in the team(s) and organization. This includes personal cultural aspects and sub-cultures. Improvement must consider how change affects all these cultural aspects.

Therefore, if we review the People-Process-Product model, we must now consider the relationships and interactions caused by improvement between people, process and product.

---

[24] Categorization of sub-cultures in general is a booming field of study for marketers. We have baby boomers, X-Gen, yuppies, nerds, dinks, empty nesters etc.

[25] Techno-speak is itself of course a colloquialism! It is a shortened form of technological speech or language used by a particular profession. Within most professions, the practitioners use a collection of words having particular meanings that others do not understand.

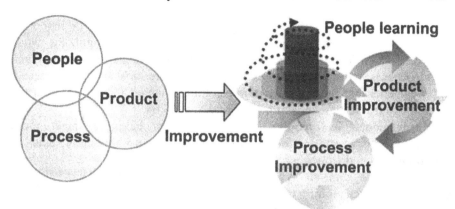

**Fig. 24. People – Process - Product Improvement.**

In the expanded model, we now have three cycles of improvement. We have the process improvement cycle, a cycle for improved products and a cycle for people improvement.

The cycle in product improvement depicts a situation that products (tools) are improved to aid people and implement part or all of an improved process. Care should be taken that tool improvement is based upon good processes adapted to suit the people who use them. Otherwise, tools will not create real improvements (adding to the scrap heap of failed software projects).

The improvement in people is shown as an upward spiral (symbolizing learning) that affects personal, team and organizational cultural aspects. Learning encompasses much more than just the ability to perform new activities or follow processes. It also encompasses new behaviours, norms and values. In the situation of continual improvement within an organization, this improvement is evident in how well people and teams 'fit' into the desired organizational culture (their degree of association with the desired culture).

In the previous improvement sections about process improvement, some cultural aspects were briefly mentioned. Unfortunately, they were handled in a subordinate manner to the mechanistic approach in improving processes.

However, people are not mechanisms. They have emotions ranging from fear of change to joy of discovery and enjoyment of challenge.

While addressing cultural aspects of change seems difficult (after all you have to deal with people), there is a need to recognize when improvement affects culture aspects and actively manage these aspects.

For another perspective on people and culture and its interaction in software development, I recommend reading Alistair Cockburn's book on Agile Software Development [38].

Some improvements affect cultural aspects that are easier or harder to change (as described in the cultural layer model). Recognizing when improvements affect these aspects is the beginning to managing their impact. Improvements that work within existing cultures are most likely to succeed. Improvements that require only minor cultural changes (for example at the explicit cultural layer) are next most likely to succeed.

Improvements that require behaviour change begin to meet more resistance. This resistance increases even more when challenging existing cultural norms and values.

Improvement is not always a linear progression; sometimes improvement must come by abandoning the existing organizational culture, processes and practices and creating a new approach and culture. This discontinuous aspect of innovation creates new ways and means to operate. Innovation in this context is framed within the organization (rather than world's best/latest practice). For example, an organization normally using System Development Life Cycle (SDLC) methodology is being innovative when it adopts eXtreme Programming.

The SEI has also recognized the need to address the people related aspects of improvement and change through the People CMM® [39].The People CMM is focused on human resource management, rather than creating and sustaining a culture of excellence. This presents one way to handle the people aspects of improvement, but there are many more.

When an improvement program is planned, the participants need to understand the existing culture(s) – at least the team cultures and the organizational as a whole, so that they can recognize the cultural factors that are a basis for the existing situation and are enablers or barriers to improvement.

To further help to recognize the existing culture and the resultant enablers and barriers, we can classify culture into various dimensions. The following dimensions are described in the book: Riding the Waves of Culture by Fons Trompenaar and Charles Hampton-Turner [40]. They describe culture in a way that is applicable to a general business context. They use 7 dimensions of culture:

1. Universalism - particularism (general rules compared to relationship based decisions).
2. Communitarianism - individualism (the power of the group compared to the individual).
3. Neutrality - emotion (the range of feelings expressed and the effect on our decisions).
4. Diffuse - specific (range of involvement we tolerate, all encompassing (diffuse) or segregated according to work, social, personal levels).

5. Achievement - ascription (how we accord status, by performance or by status).
6. Relationship to time (our past, present and future orientation and interaction).
7. Relationship to our environment (how we relate to or manage our environment, control or accommodate its forces).

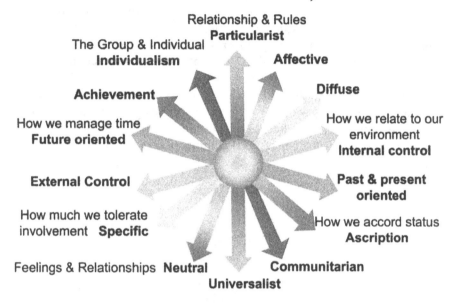

**Fig. 25. Seven Cultural Dimensions.**

The 7 dimensions provide a means of categorization of culture; each is based upon a progressive scale and not an absolute scale[26]. For example, one person may relate to their home environment differently to their work environment. In the former, they may exert control (internal control); while in the latter they may be largely subject to external control. The dimensions are used as cultural descriptors to help people understand their norms and values and how this affects their behaviour.

## Socio-cultural survey

When we perform a cultural survey, we categorize the organizational culture using the 7 dimensions. It is also important not to see the two aspects

---

[26] Very little in life is 'black or white' (right or wrong, a clear choice between two alternatives). Most issues fall within a 'grey area' (an intermediate area between various alternatives).

of each dimension as absolute opposites but as providing a progressive scale of description.

When we assess the organization's culture, we place the organization within the progressive scale. We look at the level of variation across the scale to understand how uniform the culture is. This requires graduated questions and interviews. We can also identify any particular groups or cultural cliques. These groups may be good or harmful, for example, they may be a project team with an excellent performance and improvement record. The aim is to find the good groups to use as examples and leaders within the organization. We then look at how to balance the cultural dimensions.

It is important to also determine which dimensions or particular aspects of those dimensions are within which layer (explicit, behavioural, norms, values, assumptions). This helps us determine what is easy to change and what is more difficult to change. This combination is shown in the following diagram.

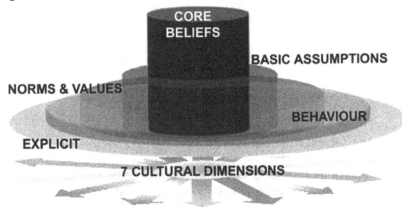

**Fig. 26. Cultural dimensions and layers.**

Combining the two models, allows the organization to:
- Determine which cultural aspects are positive and which are resistive to change.
- Use the positive cultural aspects to motivate and support people wanting to change/improve/innovate
- Change the most important cultural dimensions when negative politics prevent improvement (but be aware it takes longer!)

At the same time, we need to look at how to balance the most important aspects. When we assess the organization using the Relationship and Rules dimension, we try to reconcile the desire for universalism and practicalities of particularism. For example, if we look at the Relationship and Rules dimension, the aim is to determine how the organization balances Universalism with Particularism. We may devise central guidelines (universalism) with local adaptations and discretion (particularism) to encourage flexibility to handle a variety of situations, but not make each situation unique.

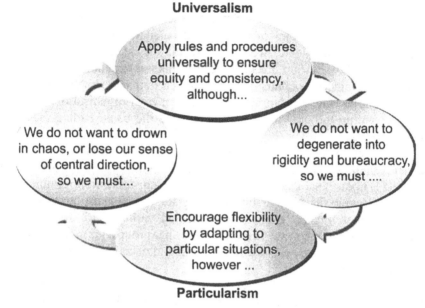

Fig. 27. Balancing Universalism and Particularism relationships

For example, if we have a standard process description and tailor it to a defined process, we have a variety of options. If the culture were strongly universalistic, we would have a well-specified standard process and very limited (if any) tailoring to suit particular projects. If the culture were very particularistic, we would have a very loosely specified standard process with extensive allowance for tailoring to suit each individual project[27]. When the culture is somewhere in between these two aspects, the best solution will also be somewhere between these examples.

In a team culture is verbally and socially oriented; the use of a process-focused methodology will require extensive adaptation. One example of this type of culture is where teams use eXtreme Programming [41].

In an ascription culture where strong supervision applies, only high status individuals are able to make decisions about improvements. If the culture is

---

[27] If the culture is extremely particularistic, there may be no standard process!

achievement oriented, then we can work more with people wishing to perform improvements, regardless of their status.

In a diffuse culture, we build relationships and involvement with suppliers based on shared interactions on many levels (personal, professional, technical), but if the culture is highly specific, we base the involvement more on contractual and technical levels.

Trompenaar and Hampden-Turner describe the application of the dimensions and the nature of the cultural balancing further in their book. They highlight the value of workshops within organizations that focus upon these issues. A workshop does not need to take an extended time, once the concepts are clearly explained, workshop participants can be led through some examples and then apply it within their own organization. Interested readers wanting to know more are encouraged the book: Riding the Waves of Culture [42].

If we recognize some of these dimensions can provide enablers and barriers, then we can guide improvement activities to avoid barriers and capitalize upon enablers. For example, in an ascription culture, it is important to gain the sponsorship of high status individuals, but this is much less important in an achievement-oriented culture. If the culture is communitarian oriented, we need to ensure that groups are more involved in improvement activities, especially planning and decision-making, than in an individualistic culture.

Cultural assessment is therefore focused on recognizing the cultural characteristics of the organization, so that they are taken into account when planning and implementing improvement programmes. Activities include:

- Assess the existing culture of the organization using the 7 cultural dimensions categorisation.
- Survey the cultural aspects of individuals and teams within the organization (by using the cultural layer model).
  - Determine past improvement performance, especially for different types of desired change.
  - Determine the general organizational enablers and barriers to change and improvement. Categorize by the cultural layer(s) affected and the specific dimensions.
  - Look at how the enablers and barriers affect the desired change.
  - Determine how willing the organization/unit/team is to change.
  - Recognise the extended effort and time needed when cultural changes are required.
- Plan improvements based upon the above information. Decide whether improvement is required to processes, to products and/or for people.
- Monitor and manage cultural factors during improvements.

If we can assess the organizational culture using these dimensions, we can also plan actions, both to address any change desired in these dimensions and/or to utilize an approach that suits the existing cultural orientation.

For example, a neutral cultural orientation is more influenced by rational statement of 'the facts', while an emotional orientation will be influenced by who presents it, how the issue is presented (spoken, body language, etc), as well as the rational aspects[28].

When we use the dimensional cultural model with the cultural layer model, we can plan actions accordingly. We can address any change desired or use an approach that suits the existing organization culture. We can decide to make improvements not requiring cultural change.

Sometimes, we need to intentionally make cultural changes, especially when the organization is very conservative and unwilling to make changes or take risks. This will require more personalized interaction with the people involved. This will be of a more general nature addressing cultural change rather than specific training associated with process or product change. This type of change takes a lot of effort, time and power in order to succeed. If management desires cultural change (top-down), it will require strong senior management involvement. If people within working teams desire cultural change (bottom-up), it will require facilitation and empowerment of these teams.

When people and teams embrace improvement, they are changing some of their cultural aspects. They display have a high degree of association with the desired result. As a minimum, they adapt their behaviour and explicit cultural aspects.

For long-term success, people must also adapt their norms and values to the team and organizational norms and values; otherwise, they will face a conflict. Cultural conflicts if left unresolved may:

✘   At a minimum cause discomfort ("I am unhappy with the way we do things here but understand I have to comply").
✘   Create varying levels of disagreement and non-adoption.
✘   Incite people to actively oppose the desired result.
✘   Cause a person to leave the organization.

Many wide-ranging improvement programmes have failed, as they have not taken the extent of desired cultural change into account. For example, Business Process Re-engineering [43] has suffered such failures. On the positive side, if we embrace cultural assessment in our improvement planning:

---

[28] This book provides a basic overview of cultural change and improvement. Readers looking for more information are encouraged to look at texts and the author's published papers covering these aspects.

✓ We recognize improvements and change that can be implemented without cultural change.

✓ We can actively manage adverse or sensitive personal aspects involved in change (for example ascription, emotion, individualism and achievement aspects).

✓ We can recognize earlier any barriers to improvement and any cultural changes required.

✓ We can use cultural approaches that suit the organization (for example, factual or emotional approaches).

✓ We can recognize and handle time-oriented aspects (past focus versus future focus) that allow us to determine how rapidly we can improve.

✓ We can motivate people.

These cultural factors should be addressed in the initial examination of the organization's needs, and when initiating improvement programmes.

By including the cultural issues at the start of an improvement programme, it is possible for process assessment to produce outcomes that better suit the organization. It can specifically lead to 'non-process' improvements, such as training and motivating people or implementation of process automation through new or enhanced products and software. By assessing cultural factors, we can motivate people to make improvements for mutual benefit, recognition and reward.

It is possible to introduce the cultural assessment into the 9 Step improvement programme. However, the benefit is amplified when used with Team Based Business Design Improvement or STARS, which recognise the importance of culture within the method.

# Team Based Business Design Improvement

## Team Based Business Design Improvement

Team Based Business Design Improvement [TBBDI][29] specifically addresses motivation of people in improvement activities. It is a specific variant of the STARS [27] methodology that suits team oriented process improvement.

The process improvement cycle of actions described under the process improvement sections of this chapter is based upon the paradigm of process assessment followed by process improvement. This can be described as an "**Assess first**" approach and naturally is highly compatible with the aims of a process assessment standard such as ISO/IEC 15504!

The Team Based Business Design Improvement approach follows a different improvement sequence. It has been successfully implemented by organizations in which the author has been involved. It makes use of the process improvement cycle, but in a different order. Team Based Business Design Improvement can be described as a "**Design first – then assess**" approach.

The approach actively involves process owners and customers, people responsible for implementing the processes and process assessors in improvement teams. The team sets the improvement goals. The approach includes addressing cultural aspects, people, process and product goals, the achievement of goals and desired value, measurement of implementation and assessment.

The process related aims are to design or re-design processes in a particular business area (for example in tendering) to achieve a desired business purpose at a desired Capability Level (disregarding the existing Capability Level) and to implement this process to achieve improved customer value.

After the process has been implemented for a sufficient time to generate evidence of the actual implementation, it is assessed to determine if it has reached the desired implementation as originally designed. In addition, it is

---

[29] © Team Based Business Design Improvement. Han van Loon. 2002

checked against the desired and designed Capability Level. The assessments may be a formal process assessment or an informal assessment.

Team Based Business Design Improvement embraces use of ISO/IEC 15504 (and the associated process models) as a source of guidance (instead of using it for process assessment). Cultural assessment of the organization is considered as a primary input, because the approach provides superior results when using motivated people in teams. This may imply some cultural change in organizations that are not team oriented (see previous chapter).

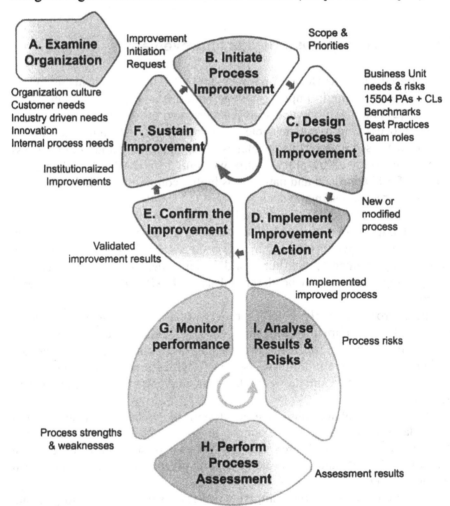

**Fig. 28. Team Based Business Design Improvement.**

The Team Based Business Design Improvement approach comprises two cycles. The main cycle initiates, designs and implements improvements. The secondary cycle monitors and/or assesses the improvement performance. Note that monitoring does not necessarily require process assessment in order to provide feedback to confirm and sustain improvement. Team Based Business Design Improvement has the following characteristics:

☑ A team oriented improvement and innovation approach. The team comprises specific roles and responsibilities:

- A process owner or champion who can sponsor the improvement.
- People with a good understanding of the selected business process purpose and objectives that they wish to design/improve.
- People with in-depth experience of process reference models and process assessment models (for example, a competent ISO/IEC 15504 assessor), with the ability to explain the relevant best practices embedded in these models (and also best practices from other sources), and how the generic practices/management practices can be applied to the selected business process. [Process Expert]
- People who will implement the process. [Process Practitioner]
- A team facilitator to handle culture and improvement facilitation aspects [Facilitator].
- The customers of the results of the process who define the desired value.

☑ The champion role leads the team oriented process design approach. She/he normally employs a facilitator. The champion must have the power to make the improvements, overcome obstacles and must be committed to:

- Achieving team consensus on the design and implementation.
- Motivating the team.
- Resolving conflicts and embracing challenges, both within and from outside the team.
- Providing the resources to ensure that the team is trained and can successfully implement the process.
- Rewarding success.

☑ The facilitator is a key role that may be filled by a person in the team or external (to the team) consultant. The facilitator should not bring any negative 'baggage' but act as a positive motivational force with high emotional intelligence. The facilitator::

- Guides the team through the Team Based Business Design Improvement process.

- Coaches the team members in how to perform the improvement activities.
- Resolving conflicts and provides positive motivation.
- Supports the champion and the team members.
- Fills in the missing skills and competencies required in the team.

☑ In the first step (Examine Organization) the team sets clearly defined goals for achieving customer value, the enterprise needs, the team/personal needs and the process capability, so that the implementation can be assessed later against these goals. The first activity in Business process mapping is similar to Value Stream Mapping (in Lean and Lean Sigma methods) as it looks at business needs (in terms of the customer value) and how they are to be met.

☑ In the second step (Initiate Process Improvement) if an existing process exists, the team studies the existing process/value stream to map the flow of work. This study covers all existing activities including value-adding, and monitoring and control activities; the speed and flow of work including work times; work in progress; work waiting for the next activity; and problems and mistakes common to the process (all forms of waste). For a team familiar with their existing processes, this activity may be performed by team review. For more complex processes across multiple teams, it may require specific mapping and analysis by the teams and a process analyst. Note that in process innovation and new business processes, the team probably does have existing processes to study and would skip this step.

☑ In the third step (Design Process Improvement), the team defines an ideal process consisting of only the value adding activities. The team specifies the value added for each activity (for example producing software code, handling a customer request). The team selects information associated with relevant base practices, generic practices/management practices and best practices, and applies the information in the design of the selected business process. I call this activity Business Process Mapping [44] as it encompasses the ability to design *completely new process descriptions* that may not exist in any documented process reference model, or to effectively modify an existing process description to include activities. Business Process Mapping can lead to business competitive advantage.

☑ In the optional step, the team determine the difference between the ideal and the existing process. The differences may consist of non-value adding activities such as control and inspection actions, excessive time taken to perform an activity or time waiting until the next activity starts or other forms of waste. This step is worth performing when the existing process creates value but is inefficient or not totally effective in delivering value to the customer (in ISO/IEC 15504 terms, its process capability is too low). This step is not needed when the team can create a desired process/value stream that is also practical to implement.

☑ The team analyse if the process can perform as desired or if they need to add non-value adding activities. These additional activities may be required to monitor and control the process, for regulatory reasons, or to ensure the required customer value is delivered. The team defines a practical desired process (as opposed to the ideal desired process in step three again aided by Business Process Mapping). By explicitly defining an ideal process and then a practical desired process, it becomes clear to the team what is value adding and what is not. For example, an inspection activity may be added to ensure that nonconforming products are not delivered to the customer. If it is possible to speed up process flow by reducing work waiting for processing (for example through use of agile methods), then it may be possible to eliminate non-value adding activities. Some directly non-value adding activities are useful as they sustain value adding activities. For example, statistical process control and measurement are directly non-value adding, but when used to better manage a value adding process can reduce waste, cost, work in progress and improve quality. Hence, the generic practices defined in a process assessment model (used to manage a process) are generally used with only minor modification. The explicit step of adding the extra required activities allows the team to look at further improvements in the value adding activities that can eliminate non-value adding activities in the future.

☑ The team specifies target time frames to perform the process activities, including any waiting period between activities. For example, an activity may require external action that is not controlled within the process. The process should set limits on acceptable delay while waiting for external action, and include a means to adjust for these delays. The team defines and applies other measurements and control requirements. These could be simple measurements or could be statistical measurement. For example, a simple measurement would be effort to prepare a plan, while a statistical measurement for the same activity may set upper and lower control limits on time and resources used to prepare a plan.

☑ The team specifies the environment required to run the process effectively and efficiently (for example, work area layout, visual workplace indicators, pull system methods and tools, use of just in time, maintaining activities, work unit sizing).

☑ The team defines and develops related products to help automate or simplify the performance of the process activities (for example, a configuration management system, Poka-yoke tools, Kanban).

☑ The team designs and provides specific training (mostly needed for non-participants in the design of the process).

☑ The team addresses the cultural aspects of change both explicitly (by design of processes, training of people and development of products) and implicitly by the fact that they are participating, cooperating, learning and sharing experience as a team while performing the improvement activities. With proper team facilitation, the team develops an improvement-oriented culture and team members align their personal cultural norms and values with the team's values.

☑ In the fourth step (Implement Improvement Action), the team now understands the purpose (and specifics) of the designed process. The team has committed to implementation of the process while designing it (motivated to succeed). Hence the team has no internal barriers to implementation and if the customer and business needs are being met, there will be little or no external barriers.

☑ In the fifth step (Confirm the Improvement), the team assess their own performance against the goals. This is both ongoing and event based. It may also comprise process assessment activities. See the section: Assessing the implementation for details.

☑ In the sixth step (Sustain Improvement), the process needs to be sustained at the new level of performance. This requires the team to monitor institutionalisation of the improved process. For cross-team or wide organizational improvements, the responsibility and requirements for monitoring should be defined. The champion or facilitator should ensure the organization's standard process infrastructure is updated. If an improved process has been piloted in a limited way (e.g. on a specific project), it should be now be deployed across all applicable parts of the organization. Consideration should be given to who is affected; how to communicate the changed process and the benefits; training needs; when to introduce changes to different enterprise areas; and how to ensure that the improved process performs as expected.

The method is most suited to motivating teams to adopt, design and implement processes to higher process capability. Results obtained by teams using the approach show that the effort to achieve Capability Level 4 or 5: is between 25 and 50% less than step wise improvement to Capability Level 3 and then to level 4 and 5. The method favours teams with a high level of experience in process design at these capabilities[30]. Hence, it is important to

---

[30] In effect, 'the strong become stronger'.

use people with this experience, whether via external consultants or from other parts of the organization who have achieved these levels.

While Six Sigma has several commonalities with the method, Team Based Business Design Improvement handles a wider variety of enterprise cultures and business needs. Importantly, the team motivation is much higher and the success and sustainability of the improvement is much better.

Team Based Business Design Improvement leads to improved business results and customer value.

## Business Process Mapping

Business Process Mapping is used during the process design activity. The team invert the existing ISO/IEC 15504 process assessment step of matching the processes to the assessment model. This means that the team match the process assessment model to the existing or a desired business processes/value stream in order to determine what elements to use in a desired process. The team takes components of a process model that suit the existing business process, and then looks at what work products are useful, and how the generic/management practices of the capability dimension apply. The team includes customer satisfaction aspects to reinforce the strength of the approach.

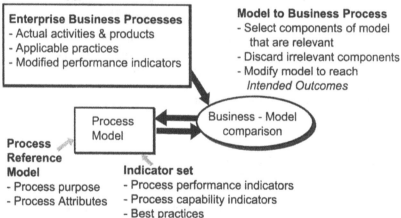

**Fig. 29. Business Process Mapping model comparison.**

In some cases, the mapping is simple and the existing process and process assessment model match quite closely. Hence the existing processes match a substantial part of the assessment model as either implemented activities in the desired process or as indicators for the management and performance of the process.

When properly applied to new business areas, Business Process Mapping can create *completely new process descriptions* not in any process assessment model. This leads to Business Process Management by ignoring outdated business processes and implementing new and appropriate business processes. Note that in effect, Business Process Mapping is allowed for in the latest revision the ISO/IEC 15504, by allowing any process reference model to be created and used for process assessment.

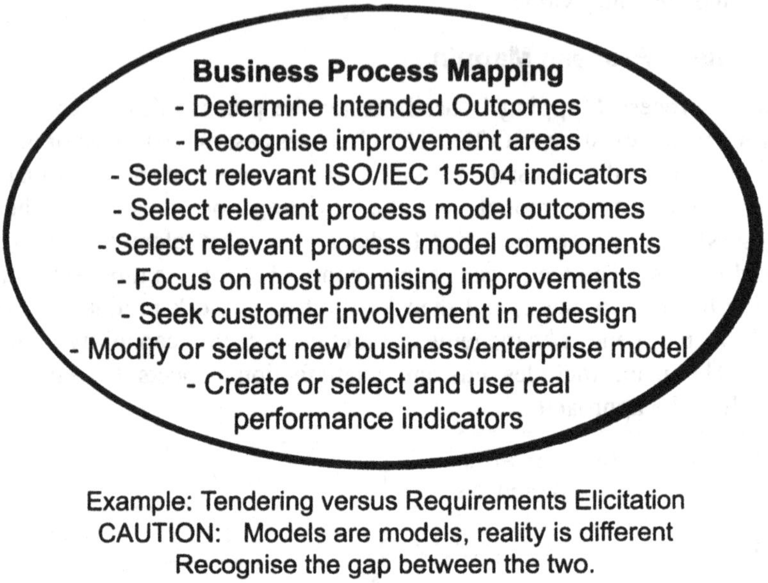

**Business Process Mapping**
- Determine Intended Outcomes
- Recognise improvement areas
- Select relevant ISO/IEC 15504 indicators
- Select relevant process model outcomes
- Select relevant process model components
- Focus on most promising improvements
- Seek customer involvement in redesign
- Modify or select new business/enterprise model
- Create or select and use real
performance indicators

Example: Tendering versus Requirements Elicitation
CAUTION:   Models are models, reality is different
Recognise the gap between the two.

**Fig. 30. Business Process Mapping actions.**

## Assessing the implementation

Assessing the implementation of processes using Team Based Business Design Improvement is relatively simple. The reason is that the team implementing the process activities is aware from the design stage what they were required to do and to produce. They also know over time what they actually achieved and produced or failed to achieve/produce.

Normally the champion and facilitator perform mid-term informal reviews and more formal milestone reviews. These milestone reviews often occur after the implemented process has been performed in its entirety (for example, for a tendering process, after submission of a tender; for a deployment process, after roll-out of a system). Mid-term reviews are used when the period of process implementation is longer than two to three months, and focus on immediate implementation difficulties. In both types of reviews, the team decides what has proven useful and should be retained, what has proven difficult and should be changed, what does not work and should be abandoned. This approach has similarities to Alistair Cockburn's approach to creating project-based methodologies as described in Agile Software Development [45]. The Team Based Business Design Improvement approach applies to more than just the software development methodology however; it can be used with any business process.

The assessor can discuss the actual implementation with the team members implementing the process who will probably be able to make self-determination whether they achieved the required process purpose, outcomes and Capability Level.

Inventing a process or a partial process assessment model using Business Process Mapping has one minor disadvantage. Business Process Mapping does not explicitly map the newly created process to a specific process in a process reference model (and hence to ISO/IEC 15504-2). This means that a process assessor must carefully map the new process to the one or more processes in the process reference model. Otherwise, they can incorrectly assess the new process against inapplicable base practices.

Business Process Mapping does have BIG advantages. Organizations that have adopted this approach have a competitive business advantage when implementing processes at Capability Levels 4 and 5. They are more often less concerned about conformant assessment and more focused on self-assessment to further facilitate internal team and business oriented improvement actions with an aim to achieve enterprise and operational excellence. It leads to Business Process Management.

When the Team Based Business Design Improvement approach is combined with Business Process Mapping, it is often possible to determine the implemented process Capability Level simply and informally.

In the case where there is a capability gap between the desired target and the actual Capability Levels, it is often due to over-ambitious goal setting by the improvement team. It may also be due to a failure to produce all the specified process measurements, or lack of measurement based process control. Sometimes this is due to a lack of time or lack of resources when performing the process, (for example, when a tendering process runs over one week instead of several months), and tailoring of the process did not take into account this shortened duration.  Having the process assessor discuss the implementation at a defined time with the team allows the assessor to judge whether failure to do some activities or produce some work products affects the process Capability Level (it may not), and is a good trigger for the next cycle of improvements.

Where the Team Based Business Design Improvement approach is used, process owners and improvement team members who design and implement the process prefer the '**design first**' approach against the '**assess first**' approach. There is a strong personal and team motivation to achieve the improvement goals and prove this to the assessor. The importance of working with people in a team to define the target process Capability Levels, to allow them to lead the process design and perform measurement is critical to greater voluntary participation, cooperation and motivation to achieve improvement success in higher capability organizations.

The approach has been successfully used to create complete process chains and value streams for new projects and business areas. In one organization, the Team Based Business Design Improvement approach created an agile project process chain in place of the former highly formalized documentation driven software engineering process. The agile project process comprised agile contracting, project management, software engineering and deployment process chains. These process chains comprised selected processes at capability level 4, which optimised the project and product goals. The people in the project were highly motivated to implement and improve the processes, and had made several improvements within 6 months of the project start.

The cooperative and participatory approach embodied in Team Based Business Design Improvement approach is psychologically better suited to motivate teams and people.

The team embraces the paradigm of '*Innovation and Improvement from WITHIN*'.

The approach reinforces a culture of *"Striving for Excellence"*.

## Risk variant

TBBDI Risk is a risk oriented extension to Team Based Business Design Improvement. It combines the ground breaking work done in creating risk based target profiles for ESA with the 'Design First' approach of Team Based Business Design Improvement. In general, managers are interested in reducing risk as it has a positive effect upon performance and reduces risk of ineffective and inefficient work and management.

The TBBDI Risk approach modified the first three steps in TBBDI. First in TBBDI it is important to identify the business needs, both at enterprise level and at the level of the value stream or process chain. This may be for one business unit or across several business units in a spanning process. The team ensure that the business unit(s) needs reflect at least part of the overall enterprise needs. If not, then the relationship to the enterprise must be re-examined.

During the second TBBDI step (Initiate Process Improvement), the team perform a SWOT analysis (Strength, Weakness, Opportunity, and Threat). This is based upon the identified needs and the enterprise goals. From the SWOT analysis, the team create a list of relevant risk descriptions. The team then create a risk categorisation approach that groups the main risks into categories. For example, there may be an enterprise risk category and a business unit risk category. Alternatively categories could be 'time to market', 'quality and low defects', 'project achievement', 'concurrent engineering' or 'competitive innovation advantage'. Group the list of risks into the chosen categories. The groups per risk category could include:

- Product needs and requirements.

- Product fulfilling stated requirements.

- Cost and schedule risks.

- Communication risks.

- Industrial efficiency risks.

- Efficiency risks.

The team define risk likelihood and severity scales and a risk index. Processes can reduce the likelihood of a risk occurring. Risk severity depends on the context of the project and product usage.

During the third TBBDI step, the team: interview people from each relevant business unit and their customers to obtain a comprehensive risk picture. The people should cover all aspects of the business where risks are valid. In each interview, the participant selects their list of risks, highlights the most important and classifies the most important risks according to likelihood and severity. Each person may also advise which processes or activities help to lower the risks from past experience. The team select the most critical risks (highest severity/likelihood) and determine which processes or activities have the best effect on reducing the risk. This is based upon data synthesis and analysis covering:

- Number of risks covered by a process/activity.
- Grouping by process for each risk category.
- Number processes/activities for a risk.
- Number of process citations for a risk.
  - The bigger the difference between number of processes per risk and number of process citations per risk, the more likely that one or few key processes mitigate the risk.

- Identify risk and process patterns, for example:
  - Early lifecycle engineering processes (requirements elicitation, design) often have greater impact on needs related risks.
  - Late lifecycle engineering processes (e.g. testing), configuration management and quality assurance processes have greater impact on risks ensuring requirements are fulfilled.
  - Schedule and cost related risks are most affected by project management, acquisition processes, problem and change processes and review processes.
  - Communication risks are most affected by engineering requirements capture and design, documentation management and project management processes.
  - Industrial efficiency risks are most affected by acquisition processes, project, quality and risk management and audit processes.

The team then design the process to include activities/practices that mitigate the most important risks. This will require management of the process (hence higher Capability Levels) to reduce certain risks. For example, if there is a high capability level on earlier processes in the lifecycle then it reduces the likelihood of not having enough time/resources to perform later lifecycle processes. The team set individual capability level achievement targets for each process and ensure that process chains/value streams have similar capability levels.

The team check that implementing the processes to the desired level is practical for the organization to do. The team involve the managers/process implementation personnel in the study workshop and external reviewers to critically review the study results.

Ideally TBBDI Risk is used with a Risk based Target Capability Profile as described in an earlier chapter. This provides an extended advantage because the Target Capability Profile for an entire enterprise or industry sector can be profiled.

TBBDI Risk extends process improvement to not only address process problems and improvement opportunities, but also address business risk. Through an active risk management approach, the number of real process and product problems is reduced.

# Agile Methods

## Agile Methods and Assessment

All process assessments require the expert judgment of an assessor. This can lead to differing interpretations depending upon the assessor's viewpoint and expertise. This is true even for assessing so-called traditional process lifecycles with well developed standard and defined processes. For agile methodologies the assessment judgment is even more critical, because agile methods have weakly defined process descriptions because agile methods rely heavily upon communication strategies to avoid formal process definitions. This section provides an overview of some of the more popular agile methods, together with some guidance on assessment.

## Agile Development Methodologies

There are several well-known agile development methodologies in use. These include eXtreme Programming (XP), Crystal methodologies (Crystal light, Crystal Orange and so on), Evolutionary and Dynamic System Development Methodology (DSDM), and Feature Driven Development.

Common aims of these methodologies are to reduce the amount of process specification, minimise process deployment and artefacts (work products). They do this in various ways, for example Alistair Cockburn describes several different weight Crystal methodologies depending mainly upon project size (workers and duration) and product type [46]. Each of these variants of Crystal is then tailored by the team at the start of the first iteration. Kent Beck describes a specific methodology for eXtreme Programming (see next section). Dynamic System Development Methodology specifies time box development tied to Joint Application Design (JAD) and Rapid Application Development (RAD). Timeboxing sets a specific (short) development iteration interval, at the end of which a running product is available. EVO (Evolutionary development) has evolved from DSDM and has a more dynamic change/improvement focus. All the agile methods emphasize people and communication with the aim to achieve a lighter weight process chain.

ISO/IEC 15504, due to its flexibility in specifying the process dimension can be effectively used with agile methodologies, when carefully adapted.

## DSDM and EVO

In one of my previous employers, where we ran several parallel projects, we originally used an incremental iterative development methodology created internally. This was specification intensive and could be considered a heavyweight methodology. Project teams were generally moderately large (40 to 140 people). Formal customer deliveries were 12 to 18 months apart. Both due to the strong (and highly effective) emphasis upon reuse of all developmental artefacts, and the type of systems produced, this methodology was very effective and successful in building large, high performance software systems.

Several of the processes (those we considered most important to successful projects) were rated at ISO/IEC TR 15504 capability level 4 and most were rated at capability level 3. Some processes were redesigned to include continual improvement aspects of capability level 5. The organizational culture was very quality focussed (evidenced firstly by high customer satisfaction, secondly by our ability to meet business goals, thirdly by our internal quality improvement programmes and finally by ISO certification and the high capability levels of our processes).

However we were asked to adopt a time to market driven approach by our customers. This necessitated introducing an agile methodology. Our approach was to introduce Dynamic Systems Development Methodology and then evolve it to suit our needs.

The project comprised a customer requirements elicitation team, a project management and contracts team, between 3 and 5 software product development teams operating in parallel, and a deployment support team. After specifying a product in a user requirements workshop, the project and contract team made an offer and if accepted by the client, created a contract for that product. This triggered a development team with fixed project duration of 6 months and two formal deliveries (with normally 4 to 6 complete internal development iterations) – a typical timebox approach. If the client wished to develop the product further, the contract could be extended or another contract created. The scope for the product development was prioritised and after the first 3-month delivery could be re-prioritised (or even another user requirements workshop could be run). As time to market was critical, scope was flexible, but as many prioritised requirements as possible were met within the contracted effort for the 6 months period.

In some cases the client was co-located with the team, in other cases, the deployment team was handed the client from the elicitation team. Depending upon client location, requirements change was 3 monthly (externally located) or monthly (when co-located and running an internal monthly development iteration).

Each of the teams required an agile process. This included an agile development process, an agile client product elicitation process, agile project management and contracting process, and agile deployment and support processes.

Due to our advanced quality culture and understanding of high capability processes, we were able to implement an agile process methodology (DSDM plus proprietary agile processes) in a very short time. Within one delivery cycle (3 months) the teams reviewed and improved the processes (Evolutionary approach) to a situation meeting our business goals, reaching our target process capability and also ensuring the desired level of process stability. Process stability makes it easier to introduce new members to the project, and is important for team understanding. Naturally, the evolutionary methods also met the client's needs in terms of time to market, and client satisfaction with the products produced against the contracted (paid) effort. With our evolutionary methods we took particular care of the following:

- All key personnel must be trained in the method's (EVO - DSDM – JAD - RAD) principles and practices and agree to follow them. This can be done during the first iteration of the work.
- There must be common and agreed understanding of roles and responsibilities of all personnel. This can sometimes be a challenge to customer personnel.
- The facilitator (and coach) is the key personal role that ensures the process is followed properly. The facilitator must have the experience and power to ensure the JAD workshop is successfully performed.
- Joint Application Design (JAD) Workshops are an intensive prototyping environment, where:
  - Users and designers produce a front-end system.
  - Prototypes are captured and users formally agree (sign off).
  - Non functional requirements are recorded (e.g. performance, capacity).
  - Key Personnel who approve and use the system attend. This includes the sponsor, workshop owner, representative users (business area, policy, legal as needed), project manager, technical coordinator, and the designer/developers, as well as the facilitator. Other practical care issues:

- Sufficient time needs to be allowed for all key personnel to indicate their attendance or to delegate their authority to someone to make all decisions on their behalf.
- The decisions of any delegate are binding on the key person who delegated them
- JAD Workshop prototypes can include:
  - Business area processes.
  - Usability / user interface.
  - Performance and Capacity.
  - Capability and techniques.
- JAD workshops and RAD increase ownership of inputs and results:
  - Users own the requirements.
  - Designers own the estimated effort for each requirement.
  - Users and designers agree to prototypes (often visual prototypes with no real functionality) during JAD workshops.
  - Regular releases create a joint sense of achievement. They allow users and developers to learn what they are capable of specifying and doing in the RAD → JAD feedback loop.
  - Regular releases create an enhanced learning environment for users and developer teams. In general teams improve performance over time.
  - Bugs and missing functionality are identified at each release, allowing early investigation and corrective actions, such as re-prioritization, correction of bugs in the next release, and running new JAD workshops.
- Rapid Application Development time boxing and prioritization is critical. The time box interval needs to balance:
  - Amount of planning – the effort/time to plan versus work planned
  - Ability to develop sufficient functionality each iteration
  - Visibility and monitoring of progress
  - Development team maturity and the need for bug fixes
  - Need to re-prioritize development or requirements
- Time boxes can run from a week to several months. Time box duration depends on overall project duration and internal planning times.
  - Maximum recommended interval is 3 months for a 6 or 12 month project (2 or 4 repetitions), but a 1 to 1.5 month interval (6 to 4 repetitions) is likely to be better for a 6 month project.
  - For a 1 month project, the time box interval should be based around 1 week (and then varied based upon experience). Use dynamic prioritization during development.
- Strict delivery dates are set and always kept:
  - A working product is always delivered at the defined delivery time.

- The amount of functionality varies depending upon the required functionality and the skill of the development team.
- The user learns firsthand the results of requests for new or enhanced functionality and changes, and their effect on the expected releases. Hence, slippage in functionality is ultimately managed by user.
- The user learns to manage their own expectations, the effect of unreasonable demands becomes apparent and the user learns to make hard decisions on what requirements to prioritize and hence develop.
- Regular small releases indicate amount of progress.

We found that understanding ISO/IEC 15504 helped us to implement high capability processes in a short time. We did this using a techniques I invented called Business Process Mapping (see chapter on Team Based Business Design Improvement).

In order to assess the capability we had to map our processes to the assessment model. There was no exact correlation between ISO/IEC 15504-5 base practices, and the actual practices implemented in the project. However, I highly recommend that the team creating the processes has business experts and process capability (ISO/IEC 15504) experts, as well as practitioners. In the cited project, I acted as the process capability expert and was the coach to the teams. It is important to carefully adapt process assessment to suit agile methodologies. It is possible to achieve this with ISO/IEC 15504 due to its flexibility in the process dimension, but it also requires deep understanding of the capability dimension.

Evolutionary development practices have several advantages to other agile methods described in this chapter. First it is possible to introduce practices one by one; something that Kent Beck insists is not viable in XP. Secondly, it can be adapted to the type of project, product and people. In my experience of introducing several agile processes in evolutionary development, we were able to tailor a solution that suited our particular needs. However, it is important to consider using a coach that understands both evolutionary development and process capability frameworks in order to achieve the best result. A coach will help reduce implementation time, learning curve and mistakes.

## eXtreme Programming

eXtreme Programming (XP) is an agile development methodology that focuses on embracing change by planning, analysing and designing software in very small iterative increments [47].

The methodology allows for highly volatile requirements, through the planning games and short development intervals. It is highly suited to smaller development teams using short verbal communication paths within the team and with the customer (in other words, immediacy of communication and feedback). It results in minimal written documentation, simpler and smaller design and programming increments.

Kent Beck and Ron Jeffries describe eXtreme Programming as a highly social activity (people oriented), rather than a documentation driven process. This important philosophical distinction shapes many aspects of eXtreme Programming. Kent Beck's book: eXtreme Programming Explained – Embrace Change [48] is considered the reference on XP.

In the following figure, I highlight the 3 factors that contribute to organizational and project success, using the People-Process-Product model.

Compared to other well-established process lifecycles such as the V-Model and the Rational Unified Process, eXtreme Programming dramatically shrinks the role of processes (greatly simplifying but not totally eliminating them) and places much greater emphasis on the role of people in a team, hence highlighting team social and cultural aspects.

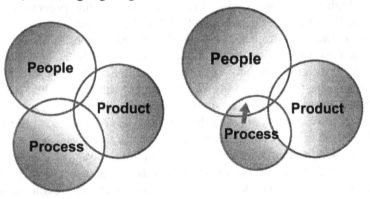

**Fig 31. People-process-product comparison: Process oriented and Agile.**

In order to determine whether process assessment can add value in an eXtreme Programming environment, it is important to understand the basics of eXtreme Programming.

Kent Beck describes in his book values and principles that he believes are the foundation for success within this social activity context. The values need to be appealing to people so they readily adopt and share them, and yet still meet the organization's commercial (business) needs. The main shared values are:

- Communication,
- Simplicity,
- Feedback,

- Courage, and
- Respect.

Communication is a necessary value in order to make many of the principles and practices work effectively and efficiently. A shared value of communication leads to common understanding with the team.

Simplicity means it is better to make simple solutions today (and further simple changes in the future as needed) rather than design something more complicated, which may never be used. This is based upon two premises. First, that the cost of change does not increase exponentially over time (see the book for further explanation). Second, that changing requirements may invalidate many design decisions made earlier.

The shared value of feedback is concerned with immediate, concrete feedback as well as longer-term feedback to the team. Immediate, concrete feedback to developers is provided by performing the already written tests (Kent Beck describes this approach in his book: Test Driven Development [49]).

Courage is about taking the simple path (simple changes), but also deciding when code is bad and should be completely rewritten. When shared communication and feedback are effective, then courage combines with simplicity to provide the team with the ability to effectively make changes. Finally, the combination of these four values leads to a shared value of respect within the team.

(Readers wishing to know more about the importance and benefits of shared values within a social and cultural context should look at the chapter on Improvement and Culture in the Practical Guide.) Kent describes sets of principles derived from these values. They include:

- Rapid feedback.
- Assume simplicity.
- Incremental change.
- Embracing change.
- Quality work.
- Teach learning
- Small initial investment.
- Play to win.
- Concrete experiments.
- Open, honest communication
- Work with people's instincts, not against them.
- Accepted responsibility.
- Local adaptation.
- Travel light.
- Honest measurement

In Extreme Programming Explained and in his second book: Planning Extreme Programming [50], Kent Beck explains in his typically clear and simple manner (the 2nd value and principle) how these values and principles provide the primary foundation upon which the rest of XP is based. When he describes aspects such as, courage, people's instincts, honest communication, travel light, and teach learning, he is describing both values and modes of behaviour he believes that the team must first accept and embrace in order to make eXtreme Programming succeed. Readers are encouraged to read the book to understand the importance of the values and principles, so that the following 12 practices are placed within the team social context of shared values and principles.

**Planning game.** Customers decide the scope and timing of releases based on estimates provided by programmers. Programmers implement only the functionality demanded by the stories in this iteration.

**Small releases.** The system is put into production in a few months, before solving the whole problem. New releases are made often—anywhere from daily to monthly.

**Metaphor.** The shape of the system is defined by a metaphor or set of metaphors shared between the customer and programmers. Note: The metaphor has been subject to debate in the XP community as to its usefulness. Ron Jeffries (the original XP coach) insists it provides value, while Kent Beck removed it in the second book he wrote about XP. I use metaphor when describing agile and process optimisation methods and find it often provides succinct and useful focus.

**Simple design.** At every moment, the design runs all the tests, communicates everything the programmers want to communicate, contains no duplicate code, and has the fewest possible classes and methods. This rule can be summarized as, "Say everything once and only once".

**Tests.** Programmers write unit tests minute by minute. These tests are collected and they must all run correctly. Customers write functional tests for the stories in an iteration. These tests should also all run, although practically speaking, sometimes a business decision must be made comparing the cost of shipping a known defect and the cost of delay.

**Refactoring.** The design of the system is evolved through transformations of the existing design that keep all the tests running.

**Pair programming.** All production code is written by two people at one screen/keyboard/mouse.

**Continuous integration.** New code is integrated with the current system after no more than a few hours. When integrating, the system is built from scratch and all tests must pass or the changes are discarded.

**Collective ownership.** Every programmer improves any code anywhere in the system at any time if they see the opportunity.

**On-site customer.** A customer sits with the team full-time.

**40-hour weeks.** No one can work a second consecutive week of overtime. Even isolated overtime used too frequently is a sign of deeper problems that must be addressed.

**Open workspace.** The team works in a large room with small cubicles around the periphery. Pair programmers work on computers set up in the centre.

Kent Beck emphasizes that the 12 practices should not be considered separately but as a complete set of practices. He emphasizes that the interactions between the practices are just as important as the practices themselves, and act as a self-reinforcing whole.

I add one important rule that Kent Beck emphasizes in his book.

**Just rules.** By being part of an eXtreme team, you sign up to follow the rules. But they're just the rules. The team can change the rules at any time as long as they agree on how they will assess the effects of the change.

### Studying eXtreme Programming values and principles in practice

One study of a company using eXtreme Programming [51] has focused on the deeper cultural values and principles mentioned in eXtreme Programming and how they operate. The study derived and highlighted 5 themes that provide the basis for how the company uses eXtreme Programming. The paper emphasizes that an effective eXtreme Programming team needs to display social and cultural behaviour that achieves the purpose of these themes. The themes are:

**Shared purpose, understanding and responsibility** – decisions are communal and collective; programmers changed pairs frequently so that everyone paired with another programmer at least once during a iteration of the development, and also could overhear other pair's discussion and join in as interested; the oral tradition meant story cards were transient and were used until understood and then discarded/torn up and the metaphor was important to maintain clear communication. Note: the discarding of written evidence on the cards makes the process assessment more difficult but not impossible (both due to lack of work products and (nearly total) reliance on interviews as the real source of evidence).

**Coding and Quality of code matters** – coding was considered the most important activity that should not be interrupted, hence a designated 'exposed pair' handled any customer enquiries; test first was always implemented; tension arose when refactoring was not allowed within the story card estimated work; and code was not released after 5 pm due to poor quality experiences in the past.

**Sustainability** – the team cared about the quality of life, there were no heated discussions; retrospectives (after completion meetings) used a fun referee (toy barking dog) to create moderate behaviour in the speaker; there were regular, communal breaks; and the team used a toy 'moo' box to announce code release.

**Harmonious Rhythm** – the team atmosphere was calm, competent and confident; discussions and meetings (e.g. planning game, stand-up meetings) started when enough people present and ended informally when people left; the daily rhythm fit inside the 3 week iteration rhythm.

**Fluidity** – the team members were fluid in their work allocation and retention of common ownership; physical space allowed fluid movement; there were recognized boundaries of different roles and responsibilities but members changed roles regularly.

The theme of shared purpose, understanding and responsibility highlights the team approach. In ISO/IEC 15504 at Capability Level 2, it states that "responsibilities and authorities for performing the process are defined, assigned and communicated", in eXtreme Programming there is an assigned customer and tester, the other responsibilities and authorities are assigned to the team as a whole, and at any time different persons can assume different responsibilities and authorities. This is not incompatible with ISO/IEC 15504 but highlights the need for an assessor to carefully interpret the process attributes in ISO/IEC 15504.

Themes such as Harmonious Rhythm and Fluidity emphasize the difference between a process orientation to a team social and cultural orientation. A process assessor needs to recognize and understand how these social and cultural orientations change the way a process is implemented. When Kent Beck states that the team members should only work a 40 hour week (sustainability), he emphasizes that if any overtime occurs for more than one week, then the project is in trouble and needs to go through new planning. This new planning in the planning game needs to look at scope, most often scope reduction and setting new priorities (shared responsibility).

All of the above values, principles and the way they are implemented (for example, as described themes) require careful understanding in order to 'translate' eXtreme Programming to a context where process assessment becomes viable and useful.

### eXtreme Programming, CMM and ISO/IEC 15504

The Software Engineering Institute has looked at how eXtreme Programming can be related to the CMM®. Mark Paulk [52] has provided an overview mapping in an attempt to address the debate about whether they are compatible and can co-exist, and he concludes that compatibilities allow CMM® to be applied. One issue that still troubles people is that the staged version of CMM® requires specific processes for each maturity level and this creates conflicts between the two at level 2 and above.

In the following table, I 'map' the implementation of the eXtreme Programming practices to several processes defined within the ISO/IEC 15504 compatible process reference and process assessment models.

While a comprehensive process mapping is beyond the scope of this book, the following table shows some of the main relationships between eXtreme Programming practices and ISO/IEC 15504 process descriptions (e.g. from the ISO/IEC 12207 PRM). This is a broad interpretation of relationships; it is not an exact equivalence due to the interdependent nature of the 12 practices and the relationship to values and principles.

**Table 22. eXtreme Programming Practices and ISO/IEC 15504 processes.**

| EXtreme Programming Practice | Related ISO/IEC 15504 Process |
| --- | --- |
| Planning stories, onsite customer, Continuous integration | Requirements Elicitation Requirements Management |
| Planning game, stories, small releases, project velocity | (Software) Project Management |
| Pair programming | Review (peer review) |
| Collective Ownership of code, small releases and continuous integration | Configuration Management |
| Metaphor, Simple Design, Refactoring, Pair Programming. | Software Design |
| Testing (unit and functional) | Software Testing |
| Continuous Integration. | Software Integration and Test |
| Coding Standard[31] | Software Construction |
| 40-hour Week. | No equivalent |

Even though I show the relationships, there are challenges in more precisely mapping eXtreme Programming to ISO/IEC 15504. This is because a practice is not the same level of granularity as a process. Issues include:

eXtreme Programming
- technical work oriented
- oriented towards smaller projects

ISO/IEC 15504
- broader management orientation
- oriented towards larger projects

---

[31] A coding standard is implied by collective ownership and pair programming, otherwise it is not possible for a programmer to improve code anytime he/she sees an opportunity. It does not imply that the coding standard is formally documented.

| | |
|---|---|
| with minimal documentation | with an emphasis on comprehensive documentation |
| • informal verbal communication means and information sharing | • formal means of communication and documentation |
| • few work products (code, tests) and fewer records of implementation | • many work products and records specified in the models |
| • larger project scaling open to debate [53] [54] | • small projects require extensive tailoring |
| • culture is personally and verbally oriented within a team | • culture is process oriented |
| • team driven selection of social interaction and practices | • management driven process oriented methodology (e.g. first a standard process (organizational), then a defined process for each team) |
| • discipline is exerted within the team by peer pressure | • discipline is (at least theoretically) driven by organization management[32] |

In Kent Beck's book, he has a diagram showing the relationship between the various practices that illustrates the inexact nature of the relationships in the above table. Pair Programming depends upon (and affects):
- Collective ownership.
- Coding standard.
- Continuous Integration.
- Metaphor.
- Refactoring.
- Simple Design.
- Testing.
- 40-hour week.

Kent Beck emphasizes that the 'richness' in eXtreme Programming comes from the way these aspects interact (i.e. a holistic view). What he is saying is that the team implementing eXtreme Programming must adopt all the values, principles and practices (in that order) to make it work.

If software construction is assessed as a process, we need to look at aspects that are relatively easy to assess such as the coding standard, but also at how all the aspects together enhance communication (one of the main values and principles) to make pair programming effective and efficient as a

---

[32] ISO/IEC 15504 specifies many organization and management processes, some of which support higher capability levels.

software construction process. Therefore, the assessor needs to decide which of the base practices are relevant (and from which processes in a PAM).

The lack of records (particularly permanent records) in eXtreme Programming makes process assessment more difficult. As an example, difficulties include finding records that meet the process attributes at Capability Level 2 (for example planning records).

Since permanent record capture is not required in eXtreme Programming, an organization that wishes to do so needs to consider how to do this without imposing additional restraints or effort upon the team. There have been studies to look into how to automatically capture sufficient records to track a project history to aid a process assessment [55], showing it is possible to do this, without impacting greatly upon the project team.

One possible assistance to address the lack of management coverage in eXtreme Programming is the adoption of SCRUM$^{TM}$ to handle more of the management aspects. This is called xP@Scrum [56]. This provides a method that integrates well with eXtreme Programming – some aspects of Scrum are also used in eXtreme Programming, for example, the Sprint Planning Meeting in Scrum shares similarities with the Planning Game.

One study [57] of the use of xP@Scrum highlights how the combination covers management aspects. In this report on xP@Scrum, the organization is creating its own combination of eXtreme Programming, Scrum, CMM and ISO 9000 compliant approach. The organization has added a broader management and quality process framework to eXtreme Programming. This amalgamation of eXtreme Programming with ISO standards or organization management procedures is becoming more common as organization management wishes to ensure that management reporting and controls meet their requirements.

In situations where eXtreme Programming practices are adopted within a broader process approach, process assessment using ISO/IEC 15504 can provide value. For example, determining how well eXtreme Programming meets the customer and project goals using metrics or qualitative means is one area that can be assessed using the process attributes in an assessment.

Process assessors need to modify their approach when assessing an XP project. It is not sufficient to just collect data in an XP project against an existing Process Assessment Model.

For example the exemplar assessment model in ISO/IEC 15504-5 has 40 Base Practices (BPs) in the software development [ENG] category (and another 7 for maintenance), and specifies a total of 76 input and 60 output work products (in reality many are repeated, so there are less actual work products). Since eXtreme Programming specifies 12 practices and many are very different to the base practices, the assessor needs to select the relevant eXtreme Programming practices and (minimal) work products and the relevant process attributes and base practices in a process assessment model.

The assessor needs to also understand how the team's culture, use of communication and informal information sharing complements/replaces some base practices and management practices. Currently there exists no detailed mapping of eXtreme Programming to any recognized process reference model or process assessment model. This means that it is more difficult to perform a conformant assessment.

An assessor therefore needs to understand the principles in eXtreme Programming, the 12 practices, and how the team applies then in their team culture in order to make a valid 'mapping' or translation between the implementation and a process assessment model, in order to perform an assessment.

To further complicate the assessor's task, at XP2003, Alan Francis (quoting Kent Beck) reported on the so-called XP-Maturity Model [58]. This consists of 3 levels:

- Level 0: follow all 12 practices all the time
- Level 1: modify the practices to suit the environment
- Level 2: it doesn't matter what you're doing as long as it works (see 'Just rules')

The 3 levels illustrate the basic cultural differences between eXtreme Programming and process-oriented methodologies, and the usual basis for process assessment. The suggested maturity levels are not aligned with ISO/IEC 15504 Capability Levels.

Level 2 in this XP Maturity Model is a prescription for extreme innovation and improvement, or extreme disaster – depending upon the level of discipline within the team (based upon collective ownership, respect, communication, courage, etc.).

The 'Just rules' rule is one of the more controversial aspects of eXtreme Programming. Opponents see it as an avenue for programmers to be hackers, proponents see it as an avenue to create strategic business advantage by optimising and further innovating the team approach and methods (which are ISO/IEC 15504 Capability Level 5 process attributes). Unfortunately, there is no one correct answer to this issue – a lot depends upon the discipline of the team – something that can worry management especially when first starting an eXtreme Programming project.

The range of implementations of eXtreme Programming is wide and some organizations are adopting only a few of the 12 practices within a process-oriented management approach. There have been other attempts to suggest alternate maturity models for eXtreme Programming, including one prepared by Poznan University in Poland [59]. This model looks at an order of implementation of the 12 practices.

Kent Beck expresses concern in his book about partial adoption, and states that this is no longer eXtreme Programming. The reason he provides is that the organisation first needs to adopt all the practices (and the values and principles) and successfully use them before it has sufficient understanding to change them. In other words: the 'No Rules' rule only applies once you have learnt how to apply eXtreme Programming properly and successfully. The reason is that the values and principles of eXtreme Programming must be the adopted basis for making decisions upon implementation of practices.

The cultural differences between process-oriented approaches and the social-cultural approach in eXtreme Programming means that process implementation may occur on a team-by-team basis, rather than an organization wide basis (a lot depends upon how much the experienced eXtreme Programming personnel including coaches move around between teams). Hence, process assessment has to recognize that team differences may be greater than in a more process-oriented approach.

Using process assessment to compare the way that eXtreme Programming is implemented in different project teams within one organization can therefore be a benefit to each team, as well as providing feedback to management.

Recommendations on the use of ISO/IEC 15504 process assessment for teams embracing eXtreme Programming and for assessors performing process assessments:

- Process assessment is more likely to be useful when eXtreme Programming is combined with some process-oriented methodology, rather than in an eXtreme Programming maturity level 2 team.
- Focus on a minimum set of software development processes (analysis and design, coding and testing), configuration management and customer requirements elicitation processes. When performing process mapping, use the most appropriate base practices to match the '12 practices', even if the base practices come from several different processes (in other words, don't restrict a process assessment to the base practices within a particular process but delete inapplicable practices and add applicable practices from other processes).
- Perform extensive (extreme) tailoring of the process attributes and indicators (base practices, generic practice indicators, generic work product indicators, generic resource indicators) to suit the team's project environment. In other words, it may be necessary to adapt the capability scale to suit the use of eXtreme Programming.
- Assessments should rely predominantly on interviews – using a team interview approach. (In any case, it is likely that the team will insist on this themselves).

- If an automated record-capturing product is implemented, use this as crosschecking evidence only when there is a dispute on how the method is implemented.
- Aim to use the assessment to provide value to the team and management. Comparative assessments between several teams in larger organizations can be useful.
- Try to capture the social and cultural aspects that indicate team cohesiveness and lead to team success, and/or note those aspects that are detrimental.
- Be open-minded and make the assessment enjoyable to all participants.
- Given the communication and information sharing orientation inherent in the social activity approach of eXtreme Programming, there should be consideration given to creation of a specific process assessment model that suits this and other agile development methodologies.

In the meantime, the use of explicit mapping prior to an assessment is more likely to lead to repeatable assessments. It will result in more consistent assessments than relying upon each assessor's judgment of what evidence to consider.

## SCRUM

Scrum is an agile project management method. It can be used with any agile development method including XP, Crystal, EVO and DSDM. Scrum was first documented by Takeuchi and Nonaka [60]. It is based upon Just In Time principles. Scrum's intended use is for management of software development projects Scrum can be used in running maintenance teams and program management.

The creators of SCRUM used the metaphor of a rugby football scrum where teams interlock into an ordered pack of opposing players in an attempt to win the football which is rolled into the middle of the pack. Like other agile methods, SCRUM has several typical agile characteristics. These include:

- The creation of self-organizing teams by encouraging verbal communication across all team members and disciplines in the project.
- Relatively little formal process documentation.
- There is a reduced division of work between individuals.
- There are small teams with a limited need for inter-team coordination.
- Short planning and estimation horizons.
- Higher reliance on having the knowledge immediately available within the team, and on very well documented software products.

- Reduced effort in recognising and mitigating risk (due to short planning horizon).
  - Accept that the problem cannot be fully understood or defined.
  - Focus on maximizing the team's ability to respond in an agile manner to emerging challenges.

SCRUM uses two types of meetings; Sprint meetings and daily status meetings (Scrum). The sprint meeting plans the work for a defined iteration (the 'sprint'), while the daily status meeting focuses on progress and problems.

- SCRUM has a living backlog of prioritized work to be done;
  - Completion of a largely fixed set of backlog items in a series of short iterations or sprints.
  - A brief planning session in which the backlog items for the sprint will be defined.
- Daily status discussion with the team is a must. Progress is explained, upcoming work is described and impediments are raised. Things to ask in the daily discussion are:
  - What did you do from yesterday?
  - What are you planning to do tomorrow?
  - Do you have any problems?
- A brief heartbeat retrospective, at which all team members reflect about the past sprint, occurs at the end of each sprint (lessons learnt).
- The customer must be a part of the development team.
- Frequent intermediate deliveries with a working functionality are a must.
- Transparency is a must in planning and different modules.
- If a feature has a problem, no delivery shall take place. No problems are buried under the carpet. No one is penalized for a problem.
- A frequent stakeholder meeting, to see the progress, is a must (show and discuss).
- Energized workplace and working hours is important.
- SCRUM suggests meeting after lunch, preferably having a stand-up meeting and people meet in front of a whiteboard. Because people tend to get tired after lunch, having a lively stand-up meeting at that time is the best thing to do.

**Fig. 32. Sticky information radiator in author's Agile SW project course.**

When a team uses hand written sticky notes to do planning, review and transmit information, they are using a low level of formality. The team works at a familiar, informal level of communication, with low power differences. The culture treats team members as relatively equal; everyone expresses their opinion and is treated with respect.

Practical care issues with SCRUM.

- SCRUM is a very 'loose' method with very thin process. It is therefore very easy to do but also can be done badly very easily.
- Hence the need for a coach who understands the method (called a Scrum Master, but she/he could be any coach experienced in agile project management).
- The product owner role is critical and can be a single point of failure
- SCRUM challenges the existing project culture. Trying to change a culture is always risky. The bigger the change, the bigger the risk. SCRUM is more challenging than adopting evolutionary project management approaches.
- SCRUM works quite well with XP, but using SCRUM and XP together challenge the existing culture even more. This is not just double as risky, but four times as risky (RISK$^2$).
- Starting the use of SCRUM therefore requires sponsor and management agreement to give the team time to learn. It requires a coach who can minimize mistakes and the time taken. The coach helps develop the correct practices and culture, which may require some shielding from existing enterprise culture until the project results produce benefits.

## Crystal

Crystal is a set of assembled agile software development methodologies [61]. It has been created using a methodology kit approach by Alistair Cockburn with the aid of many people, including Jim Highsmith.

In Alistair's book, Agile Software Development, he first focuses on the importance of communication and its impact on invention (read as software development). He discusses the art of listening at various levels as following, detaching and fluent. This is described as:

- Following a procedure.
- Finding the limits of procedures and adapting to the situation.
- Knowledge becoming almost subconscious in terms of what activities/techniques/procedures to apply in any situation.

Alistair similarly describes software development methodologies at three levels. The first is process centric with detailed techniques, standards and processes (suits process assessment). The second becomes less formulaic and more artistic, with several techniques available and explained for a variety of situations of use. The third level becomes a library of techniques that a programmer would choose based upon circumstances.

Alistair writes cogently about how to promote good communication (convection currents), and reduce bad communication (drafts) patterns and environments. He illustrates the advantages of collocated teams, pair programming and information radiators which all promote good communication. An information radiator could be a wall in a room showing all major project status information. This could include information such as development and test progress, work 'cards' and system status. Both location (a place people frequent gather or pass by) and the types of information displayed (graphical, simple to read and clear indicators) are important. Information should be 'sticky'; it should not be easily forgotten or lost. Self adhesive handwritten notes are good sticky information items. They are easily created, revised and moved around.

When a team uses hand written sticky notes to do planning, review and transmit information, they are using a low level of rigid formality. Alistair calls this 'ceremony'. The team works at a familiar, informal level of communication, with low power differences. The culture treats team members as relatively equal; everyone expresses their opinion and is treated with respect.

One characteristic of Crystal is that it varies depending upon team and project size. In small teams, all the persons may share several roles and each may perform any of the activities at different times. Hence, Alistair describes each methodology in 3 dimensions: roles, activities and lifecycle timing.

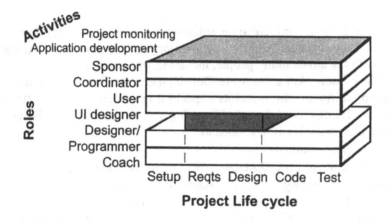

**Fig. 33. Scope of methodology: activities, roles and life cycle.**

As the team and project size increases, there may be separate defined roles and activities. The persons performing these roles may become distinct (one person – one role), although that is not a fixed rule.

The Crystal methodologies are a kit of methodology parts that a project team selects from and assembles into the specific project methodology. Alistair describes several available variants as 'starter sets'. A project team selects the most appropriate starter set or assembles a set based upon its experience. The selection of an appropriate starter methodology is based upon project team size and to a lesser extent upon project criticality. Team size is an important constraint on communication and coordination. As a team increases in size, it is more difficult for people to be co-located and to also communicate informally with everyone else. Coordinating more people requires a 'heavier' methodology. Crystal sets out various weight methodologies to handle different team sizes, rather than try to adapt one methodology to fit all team sizes. This approach is very sensible and adaptable. Alistair does not advise on use of the methodology for Life Critical (L) projects as he has yet to use it for this purpose. The Crystal methodologies are:

- Crystal Clear – for small teams with low rigor (criticality).
- Crystal Yellow – for teams up to 20 people.
- Crystal Orange – for teams from 20 to 40 people.
- Crystal Red – for teams from 40 to 80 people.

The larger the project, the more likely it is to handle discretionary and essential monies. Discretionary monies are those that a business can afford to lose should the project fail, while essential monies would cause business problems if the project fails.

Rigor/Criticality

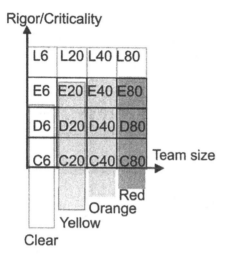

Fig. 34. Crystal Methodology chart.

The core Crystal elements for the above methodologies are the same. They are being people and communication centric, highly tolerant of cultural differences, and on-the-fly tuning of the methodology. There are several principles which shape the assembly and use of the methodology:

- The team can reduce intermediate work products when it uses richer communication and provides more running code releases.
- The team must adapt the methodology over time as projects evolve.
- The team bottlenecks (points where resources constrain throughput) determine where work overlap and sticky information is needed.
- The project uses incremental development of four months or preferably less. One to three months increments are better.
- The team must hold pre-increment and post-increment reflection workshops to decide what is working and should be kept, what is not working and should be altered or abandoned, and what should be added (on-the-fly tuning).
- The team should hold mid-increment reflection workshops to determine any critical barriers to achieving the increment release (on-the-fly tuning).

### Crystal Clear

Crystal Clear is the lightest methodology, for one team in one office with four roles: sponsor, senior designer/programmer, designer/programmer, and user. Crystal Clear suits D6 category (Discretionary monies) projects with a team of about six people. The senior designer/programmer is the critical person. Crystal Clear expects that:

- Software is delivered incrementally every 2-3 months.
- Progress is tracked by milestones of software delivery or major decisions.
- Some automated regression testing occurs.
- There is direct user involvement.
- There are 2 user viewings per release.
- Activities start as soon as there is 'stable enough to review' input.
- Pre and post reflection workshops occur.

Work products comprise:

- Release sequence.
- Schedule of user viewings and deliveries.
- Annotated use cases or feature descriptions.
- Design sketches and notes.
- Screen drafts.
- Common object model.
- Running code.
- Migration code.
- Test cases.
- User manual

Local team decisions cover whether to produce:

- Templates.
- Standards for coding and user interface.
- Standards for regression testing.

The team decides what versioning and configuration management system is used, and the use of a printing whiteboard.

Since the team is small and co-located, it uses verbal and simple visual communication to coordinate. Visual communication is hand written notes that may be created from the printing whiteboard. Hence, there is no requirement for specific project management documentation.

From a process assessment perspective, it would be possible to assess the engineering processes: design, construction (coding), and software testing, together with configuration management. Project management is partially covered, some base practices include schedule and specified deliverables. Some of the Capability Level 2 generic practices are covered, both for performance management and work product management, but it is likely that no Capability Level 3 generic practices are covered (unless the coding, user interface and testing standards cover procedural aspects).

### Crystal Orange

Crystal Orange is a more rigorous methodology designed for teams of 10 to 40 people. It covers medium sized production projects of 1 to 2 years duration where time-to-market is important. Increments can run from 2 weeks to 4 months. There is a need to communicate with present and future staff.

The project has 14 roles, some of which are:

- Business expert.
- Usage expert.
- Business analyst/designer.
- Architect.
- Design Mentor.
- Reuse point.
- Tester.

The roles are arranged in several teams, including system planning, architecture, technology, functions, project monitoring, infrastructure and external test. The work products include:

- Requirements document.
- Release sequence.
- Schedule.
- Status reports.
- User Interface design document.
- Common object model.
- Inter-team specifications.
- User manual
- Source code.
- Migration code.
- Test cases.

Local team decisions cover:

- Templates.
- Standards for coding.
- User interface standards.
- Standards for regression testing.

The team decides what versioning and configuration management system is used, and the use of a printing whiteboard. Each role decides what techniques to use. The team should be kept as small as possible and co-located. There is some more permanent work products required to allow information to be passed to future team members. The system planning team performs some project management. All teams and particularly the functions teams need to be cross-functional covering business analysis, user interface and design/programming/databases.

From a process assessment perspective, it would be possible to assess the engineering processes: requirements analysis, design, construction (coding), and testing, together with configuration management. Project management is covered in more detail in Crystal Orange. Some base practices include inter-team coordination, schedule and specified deliverables. More of the Capability Level 2 generic practices are covered, both for performance management and work product management, with some Capability Level 3 generic practices covered (standards for coding, user interface, regression testing).

The latest variant is called Crystal Orange Web, which covers internet projects. This variant looks closely at aspects such as maintaining a 'regular heartbeat' – a feedback/learning procedure for the team, a maximally defect free product approach and a maximum progress/minimum disruption approach to managing the team.

I have yet to perform a process assessment upon a Crystal methodology based project. Readers who are interested in having their projects assessed should contact me. I would also be interested in gaining more exposure to a variety of Crystal projects from users who are readers.

## Feature Driven Development

Feature Driven Development is an object oriented agile method. Features are any 'client valued function'. It consists of five major activities:
- Develop and overall model.
- Build a feature list.
- Plan by feature
- Design by feature.
- Build by feature.

Each of these activities has specified entry criteria, tasks, verification actions and exit criteria. The first activity: Develop and Overall Model has entry criteria based upon forming the core team for the work, consisting of the Domain experts, Chief Architect and programmers. The tasks consist of:
- Form modelling team.
- Conduct domain walkthrough.
- Study documents.
- Develop small group models.
- Develop team model.
- Refine overall approach.
- Wrote model notes.

Verification consists of internal and external assessment by modelling team and the business process/product owner. The exit criteria consist of the object model satisfying the Chief Architect. The object model consists of class diagrams, sequence diagrams and notes.

The second activity is to build a feature list. The entry criterion is that the modelling team has successfully created an overall object model. The tasks consist of forming the feature list team(s) and building a feature list. The verification consists of internal and external assessment of the feature list. The exit criteria consist of the feature list satisfying the project manager, the feature list consists of a list of the major feature sets (areas) and a list of features within each area.

The third activity is to plan by feature. The entry criterion is that the feature list team has successfully built a feature list. The tasks include:

- Form the planning team.
- Determine the development sequence.
- Assign feature sets to chief programmers.
- Assign classes to developers.

The verification consists of internal and external assessment of the feature sets and classes. The exit criterion consists of the planning team preparing a development plan that satisfies the project manager and development manager. The plan consists of feature list sets, a list of classes and the developers that own them.

The fourth activity is to design by feature. The entry criterion is that the planning team has successfully completed the plan by feature activity. The tasks consist of:

- Form feature teams.
- Conduct domain walkthrough.
- Study reference documents.
- Develop the sequence diagrams.
- Refine the object model.
- Write class and method prologue.
- Design inspection.

The verification consists of the design inspection by the feature team. The exit criterion consists of a successfully inspected design package. The design package comprises a covering memo that integrates and describes the design package, the referenced requirements, design alternatives, the updated object model, the class and method prologues (pseudo code) created during the process and a 'to-do' task list on affected classes for each team member.

The fifth activity is to build by feature. The entry criterion is that the Feature team has successfully completed the Design by Feature for each of the selected features. The tasks consist of:

- Implement classes and methods.
- Conduct a code inspection.
- Unit test.
- Promote to build.

The verification consists of the Code Inspection and Unit test by the Chief Programmer and the Feature team. The exit criterion consists of the Feature team completing the development of one or more features (client valued functions). This is done by promoting to the Build, the set of new and enhanced classes that support those features.

Ideally Feature Driven Development should be assessed using the object oriented process assessment method OO-SPICE.

## Practical Care Issues in Agile Methods

There are issues that require practical care in any methodology. These apply to agile methods.

Agile methods accentuate personal discipline as well as team discipline. In the authors experience this can lead to very positive performance, but also to gaming. Gaming is basically cheating the system. For example, it may include writing unit tests that do not actually test any functionality or performance. In some agile methods it is easier to subvert the correct approach because there is no formal standard process and this is more likely to occur when the team culture encourages expediency instead of discipline.

Therefore the project leaders need to be careful to ensure these issues are properly addressed, and an assessor should determine if these issues occur within an agile team.

- Interactive, face to face communication is the cheapest and fastest way to exchange information.
  - Best one to one, few to few.
  - Problem with 'memory'. Things are forgotten, sticky memory aids are needed.
- Good communication and analysis turns information into knowledge. Increasing knowledge reduces need for intermediate documentation.
- Excess methodology is costly.
- Larger teams need heavier methodologies.
- Greater rigor and formality is needed as projects become more critical.
- There is a need to balance the continuum between the people and process to suit the project, the people and the products being produced:
  - Discipline ←→ Process
  - Skills ←→ Formality
  - Understanding ←→ Documentation
- Some people try to hide their ignorance of what are good software working practices.
  - Leads to poor working practices and sometimes even hacking!
  - Quickly found out in most agile methods where teamwork is important.

- Many software developers are 'anti quality management processes' – often seeing quality standards as a worthless overhead to what they have to do. They lack 'system' understanding. They mistakenly believe that they can do everything perfectly and fail to understand how even small mistakes at a personal level may have significant impact at a systems level.
- Many software developers see the need for management visibility as an unwanted burden on their precious time. They sometime only provide rudimentary or incomplete status reporting. Good agile methods provide accurate, complete and yet simple status reporting and visibility.
- Many developers may be ignorant of overall business processes of which the software development is just one part.
- Subversion of the official processes is quite common when expediency and time pressure are high. In some teams, this becomes a habitual practice.
- The actual processes as implemented may significantly deviate (for good or bad) from the 'official' processes. This requires understanding of the reasons for deviation.
- Assessors may be too pedantic and do not see that a modified process is adequate or even better that the 'official' or standard process.
- Highly skilled practitioners can operate well with less formal processes and should have latitude to adapt processes to suit the project and products being produced.

The Team Based Business Design Improvement approach to agile methods addresses these practical care issues. It uses a facilitated and coached method working with the team (both customer and supplier) to create an enterprise tailored solution. It can integrate within existing cultures to lessen risk of rejection and adoption problems. Some advantages include:

- Reduces management nervousness associated with fear of failure.
- Can be used to improve the entire organization, not just the software development method. This is very useful when the software team is better organized than the enterprise management.
- In most organizations the greatest benefit comes when both management and software teams improve together.
- Can be used to eXtremely change project management when desired (allowing time for culture change to take effect).
- Learning and improving is inherent to the approach.
- It is flexible and adaptable to the particular application and the persons involved.
- Uses a coach to get team started:
  - Normally one or two major iterations are sufficient for a stable process.

- Then team can make further improvements without need for a coach.
- Different to SCRUM, where the Scrum Master remains always required.

Team Based Business design Improvement is agile in its ability to work on small or large improvements and changes, and incorporates sound change management principles.

# Standards View - Performing Assessments

## Performing Assessments

In this chapter, I describe how to perform process assessments. The success factors are raised. The generic assessment procedure based upon the standard and the SPiCE for SPACE variant is described in detail. Finally the various types of assessment are described, including self-assessment, quick assessments, external and comprehensive assessments. This chapter will be of interest to assessment sponsors and assessors.

ISO/IEC 15504-2 specifies requirements for performing conformant process assessments. Assessment must be performed according to a documented, conformant assessment process (see Reference book). ISO/IEC 15504 defines the requirements for a conformant assessment as follows:

- Use a documented assessment process, which must be capable of meeting the assessment purpose.
- Define roles and responsibilities of the sponsor, the competent assessor and assessors.
- Define the assessment inputs for each assessment.
- Conduct the assessment according to the documented assessment process.
- Record the assessment output according to the standard.

The major selection criteria for a documented assessment process are:

- Ensure that the assessment purpose and all desired assessment outcomes are achieved (covers process improvement, capability determination and use of a conformant Process Reference Model);
- Its suitability for the context of the assessment (factors in the organizational unit that affect the assessment process);
- Ensure it covers the planned scope of the assessment and the process context of the selected processes (covers a conformant Process Assessment Model); and
- The assessment approach conforms to the requirements of ISO/IEC 15504.

Larger, more complex organizations may also be constrained to select documented assessment processes that have the ability to cover the range of business activities to ensure consistency of approach, reuse of competencies, etc. The selection may also be constrained by important, secondary considerations such as such as cost, duration, and availability of specialist resources, especially the trained and competent assessors needed to conduct the assessment.

The assessment purpose, scope and overall approach will impact on the way in which the required activities are performed. Therefore, the assessment process has to be suitable for tailoring for individual assessments. Tailoring may include the addition or deletion of specified tasks, as long as the minimum required set of activities is performed. Tailoring guidelines may address:

- the level of detail required in the assessment plan(s);
- the source and means of collection of data;
- the mechanisms for storage and retrieval of data;
- the additional tasks to be performed as part of the assessment;
- the means for achieving agreement on process ratings; and
- the reporting of assessment results

There are several conformant assessment methods available including:

- ISO/IEC 15504 part 3: Guide on performing an assessment.
- SCAMPIˢᴹ for CMMIˢᴹ.
- SPiCE for SPACE Method [62].

The methods comprise similar sets of generic activities. The generic assessment procedure described in this chapter is based upon SPiCE for SPACE, a conformant method developed for the Aerospace industry.

## Success Factors for Process Assessment

The following factors are essential to a successful process assessment.

### Commitment

Commitment to the complete assessment process and use of the results is of vital importance. Sponsors have the key role to promote commitment. Depending upon business needs, there are potentially several sponsor roles. The first is a process improvement sponsor, the second is a process capability determination sponsor, and the third is an assessment sponsor. These roles may be allocated to one person, or an organizational entity (for example, senior management), or across one or more organizations.

For example, in the Process Improvement section of chapter 6, the responsibility for the process improvement sponsor role is accepted by the process improvement programme steering committee. The committee may then allocate the assessment sponsor role to allow one or more persons to sponsor individual assessments or sets of assessments and these assessment sponsors may also (but not necessarily) be in the steering committee.

Regardless of the allocation of the sponsor roles, it is vitally important that the sponsor(s) should commit themselves to the established goals and objectives that provide the reason to perform process assessment, and to the use of the assessment results. This commitment requires that the necessary resources, time and personnel are available to undertake the assessment and the agreed implementation of the results. Early on, an estimated budget of resources, time and people must be explicitly agreed and then refined in the planning.

The allocated assessment sponsor must be committed to the assessment purpose and provide the authority and resources to undertake the assessment within an organization. The commitment of the assessment team is also very important to ensuring that the assessment objectives are met.

### Motivation

The attitude of the organizational unit's management, and the documented assessment process by which the information is collected, has a significant influence on the outcome of an assessment. The management of the organizational unit, therefore, needs to motivate participants to be open and constructive. Process assessments focus on the process, not on the performance of organizational unit members implementing the process. The intent is to make the processes more efficient to support the defined business goals, not to allocate blame to individuals.

Providing feedback and maintaining an atmosphere that encourages open discussion about preliminary findings during the assessment helps ensure that the assessment output is meaningful to the organizational unit. The organization needs to recognize that the participants are a principal source of knowledge and experience about the process and that they are in a good position to identify potential weaknesses.

### Confidentiality

Respect for the confidentiality of the sources of information and documentation gathered during the assessment is essential in order to secure that information. If discussion techniques are utilized, consideration should be given to ensuring that participants do not feel threatened or have any concerns regarding confidentiality. Some of the information provided might be proprietary to the organization. It is therefore important that adequate controls are in place to handle such information.

### Benefits

The organizational unit members should believe that the assessment will result in some benefits that will accrue to them directly or indirectly.

### Credibility

The sponsor and the management and staff of the organizational unit must all believe that the assessment will deliver a result, which is objective and is representative of the assessment scope. It is important that all parties can be confident that the assessors have adequate experience of assessment, are impartial and have an adequate understanding of the organizational unit and its business to conduct the assessment.

## The Generic Assessment Procedure

A conformant assessment must follow a documented method. The generic assessment procedure in this section is one conformant assessment method[33].

An assessment can be divided into the following seven activities: Initiation, Planning, Briefing, Data Acquisition, Data Validation, Process Rating, and Reporting.

In addition, the assessment roles are defined and are assigned to tasks. Five mandatory roles needed are the assessment sponsor, assessment team leader, other assessors, assessment participants (interviewees) and the local assessment coordinator. Two optional roles include technical specialists and observers.

### Initiating the Assessment

The assessment process begins when the sponsor decides that process assessment should occur (see section on commitment above). In some cases, an assessment sponsor must first be found who willingly assumes the responsibility, has sufficient power and authority, and is prepared to commit

---

[33] The generic assessment procedure described here is based upon the assessment method in SPiCE for SPACE. This description includes some refinement of the steps, based upon best practice and the authors' experience in performing process assessments.

the resources needed. The sponsor also needs to ensure that human and cultural factors are addressed in order to facilitate successful process assessment.

Note: Where the sponsor is external to the organization being assessed, it is important to also obtain an equivalent 'internal sponsor' within the organization being assessed to ensure that the organization is committed to participation and cooperation.

The sponsor must define a clear assessment purpose (for example, process improvement and/or capability determination) and a suitable budget (resources, time and people) formulated.

If the sponsor is unable to obtain the willing commitment of the organization to be assessed, the process assessment should be delayed until the commitment to the entire process is established.

Once the commitment is established, the next step is defining the scope of the assessment (which processes are being assessed, and up to which Capability Level), what constraints (time, budget) apply to the assessment, and any additional information that needs to be gathered.

The assessment team leader and the assessment team are chosen and the roles of team members are defined. A competent assessor is selected to oversee the assessment. The assessment team defines the assessment inputs, which must then be approved by the sponsor.

## Assessment Planning Steps.

1. **Sponsor commitment to proceed**. Recognize and document the identity of the sponsor (may already exist), the sponsor's relationship to the organizational unit(s) being assessed, and the sponsor's and organization's commitment to proceed and an estimated budget. [34]

2. **Select the Assessment Team Leader.** Select the person who will lead the assessment team and ensure that the persons nominated possess the necessary competency and skills.

3. **Define the assessment purpose**. The sponsor defines the assessment purpose, aligned with business goals (may be previously defined). Ensure that business needs are available as input to the assessment.

---

[34] Note: There may be multiple organizational units involved in a constructed capability as described in the capability determination section in chapter 6. If this is the situation, there may be multiple internal sponsors, Local Assessment Coordinators, and differing participants. In this section we assume assessment of the organizational unit(s) within one organization (e.g. one supplier) for simplicity.

4. **Sign confidentiality agreement**. Identify and sign the conditions of confidentiality covering assessment input and output products (as required).

5. **Select the Local Assessment Coordinator**. The Local Assessment Coordinator manages the assessment logistics and interfaces between the organizational unit(s) and the Assessment Team.

6. **Submit the Pre-Assessment Questionnaires to the Local Assessment Coordinator**. The Pre-Assessment Questionnaires help structure the on-site interviews by gathering information about the organization and projects of the assessed organizational unit(s). There should be one questionnaire per project and per unit being assessed.

7. **Build the assessment team and assign team roles.** Normally, the team should consist of at least one assessor in addition to the team leader. Assessment team members should have a balanced set of skills necessary to perform the assessment. For a conformant assessment, there must be at least one Competent Assessor. The other assessors should preferably be Provisional Assessors but for internal process improvement assessment, it is also useful to include persons from the assessed organizational unit (to improve commitment, understanding and manage any cultural issues) and/or those who will implement the assessment results. The team shall have access to the assessment input, to any other relevant information and guidance on assessment techniques or tools.

8. **Check** the returned Pre-Assessment Questionnaires for completeness.

9. **Define the assessment context.** Identify factors in the organization that affect the assessment process and the validity of comparisons of assessment results. These factors include, at a minimum:

   - the number of organizational units to be assessed,
   - the size of each organizational unit,
   - the demographics of each organizational unit,
   - the application domain of the products or services of each organizational unit,
   - the size, criticality and complexity of the products or services,
   - the quality characteristics of the products.

10. **Define the assessment scope** including the processes (firstly the key processes, then the additional supporting processes) to be assessed within the organizational unit, the highest Capability Level to be assessed for each process within the assessment scope and the

organizational unit that deploys these processes. For processes describing cross-organizational activities, the source of data to be used for rating must be defined and documented. Note: A subset of the processes performed by the organizational unit may be selected for assessment, especially when the assessment cost constrains the definition of the scope.

11. **Specify constraints** placed on the freedom of choice of the assessment team regarding the conduct of the assessment and use of assessment outputs. The assessment constraints may include:

    - availability of key resources,
    - the maximum amount of time to be used for the assessment,
    - specific processes or organizational units to be excluded from the assessment,
    - the minimum, maximum or specific sample size or coverage that is desired for the assessment,
    - the ownership of the assessment outputs and any restrictions on their use,
    - controls on information resulting from a confidentiality agreement,
    - definition of data consolidation criteria,
    - definition of validation criteria and methods (e.g. data corroboration).

12. **Map the organizational unit to the assessment model.** Establish a correspondence between the organizational unit's processes specified in the assessment scope and the processes in the process assessment model (process mapping). This may require assistance from the Local Assessment Coordinator. Identify any conflicting nomenclature between the organizational unit and the assessment model.

13. **Select the assessment participants** from within the organizational unit. The participants should adequately represent the processes in the assessment scope.

14. **Define responsibilities.** Define the responsibilities of all individuals participating in the assessment. Assign tasks to individuals.

15. **Identify ownership of the Assessment Record** and the person responsible for signing the assessor logs. The sponsor may designate another actor to accept the Assessment Record and/or to sign the logs. If so, this shall be documented.

16. **Identify any additional information** that the sponsor requests to be gathered during the assessment. Examples include measurement data or staff feedback on certain organizational issues.

17. **Document the assessment inputs.** Throughout the initiation phase, assessment inputs should be documented as they are developed and assembled into the Assessment Initiation File.

18. **Review all inputs** with the assessment sponsor and obtain sponsor approval.


## Planning the Assessment

The assessment team creates a plan describing all activities performed in conducting the assessment. Using the project scope, resources necessary to perform the assessment are identified and secured. The organizational unit processes are mapped to the assessment model. The method of collating, reviewing, validating and documenting all information required for the assessment is determined. The plan also provides for the logistical needs of the assessors by specifying the responsibilities of the organizational unit. If appropriate, a tool to collect and store the information is specified. Finally, coordination with participants in the organizational unit is planned.

1. **Determine the necessary resources and schedule for the assessment.** From the scope, identify the time and resources needed to perform the assessment. Resources may include the use of equipment at the organizational unit such as overhead projectors, etc.

2. **Identify the key process mandatory base practices**. In some contracts, or in processes required to comply with standards there may be mandatory base practices. The performance of mandatory base practices is therefore necessary to achieve Capability Level 1 for these processes.

3. **Define how the assessment data will be collected, recorded, stored, analysed and presented.** Select an assessment instrument to support handling of data. To ensure optimum performance (effectiveness and efficiency), instruments and tools should be selected or designed to match the assessment process. Ensure that all confidentiality requirements will be met.

4. **Define the planned outputs of the assessment.** A report of the assessment results shall be part of the outputs. An assessment record is also to be specified.

5.  **Verify conformance to requirements.** Detail how the assessment will meet all of the requirements in the standard, and, in particular, how an assessment record will be established so that conformance can be verified later.

6.  **Manage risks.** Potential risk factors and mitigation strategies are communicated to the sponsor. Throughout the assessment, monitor all identified risks. Potential risks may be changes in the commitment of the sponsor, changes to the assessment team, organizational changes, new standard processes, changes to the assessment purpose/scope, resistance/unwillingness of the organizational unit members, lack of resources for assessment, and confidentiality.

7.  **Coordinate assessment logistics with the Local Assessment Coordinator.** Ensure the compatibility and the availability of technical equipment at the organizational unit. Confirm that identified workspace and scheduling requirements will be met.

8.  **Review and obtain acceptance of the plan.** The sponsor identifies who will approve the assessment plan. The plan, including the assessment schedule and logistics for site visits is reviewed and approved by that authority.

9.  **Confirm the sponsor's commitment to proceed with the assessment.**

## Briefing

The Assessment Team Leader reviews the plan with the assessment team and ensures that the assessment team understands the assessment input, process and output. The team presents an overview of the assessment method to the organizational unit.

1.  **Brief the assessment team.** Ensure that the team understands the requirements for a conformant assessment, the assessment inputs and outputs, and is proficient in using the selected assessment instrument. Ensure that the team has sufficient knowledge about the assessment input.

2.  **Brief the organizational unit.** Explain the assessment purpose, scope, constraints, and model. Stress the confidentiality policy and the benefit of assessment outputs. Present the assessment schedule. Ensure that the staff understands what is being undertaken and their role in the process. Answer any questions or concerns that they may have. Potential

participants and anyone who will see the presentation of the results should be present at the briefing session.

## Data Acquisition

The assessment team collects evidence of process performance in a systematic and ordered manner. Data is gathered primarily through interviews. As far as necessary, organizational documents are examined to corroborate participants' testimony.

Each process identified in the assessment scope is assessed based on objective evidence. The objective evidence[35] gathered for each attribute of each process assessed must be sufficient to meet the assessment purpose and scope. Objective evidence that supports the assessors' judgment of Process Attribute ratings is recorded and maintained in the Assessment Record. This Record provides evidence to substantiate the ratings and to verify compliance with the requirements. This assessment data may be gathered with the aid of a tool.

The strategy and techniques for the selection, collection, analysis of data, and justification of the ratings are explicitly identified and demonstrable to both the assessment participants and the sponsor.

1. **Collect evidence of process performance for each process within the scope.** Evidence includes observation of work products and their characteristics, testimony from the process performers, and observation of the infrastructure established for the performance of the process.

   - The team needs to ensure that the evidence in general indicates that the process mapping performed earlier was substantially correct and that there is not a misunderstanding between the assessment team and the assessment participants of the organizational unit.
   - The purpose of work product observation is not to detect errors; however, if work products are flawed, this may be an indication of low process capability.

3. **Collect evidence of process capability** for each process within the scope.

4. **Record and maintain the references to the evidence** that supports the assessors' judgment of Process Attribute ratings.

---

[35] Objective evidence is founded on observation, measurement or test and can be verified.

5. **Verify the completeness of the data.** Ensure that for each process assessed, sufficient evidence exists to meet the assessment purpose and scope.

## Data Validation

The assessment team validates the evidence before using it to assign process ratings. Actions are taken to ensure that the data is accurate and sufficiently covers the assessment scope, including seeking information from first hand, independent sources; using past assessment results; and holding feedback sessions to validate the information collected.

1. **Assemble and consolidate the data.** For each process, relate the evidence to defined process indicators. Relate the indicators to the appropriate Process Attributes.

2. **Validate the data.** Ensure that the data collected is correct and that the validated data provides complete coverage of the assessment scope.

## Process Rating

For each process assessed, a rating is assigned for each Process Attribute up to and including the highest Capability Level defined in the assessment scope. The rating scale, described in chapter 2, ensures the consistency and repeatability of the ratings.

1. **Establish the decision-making process used** to reach agreement on the ratings (e.g. consensus of the assessment team, majority vote, competent assessor casting vote, or combined assessment team-organizational unit participant rating). Document this process in the Assessment Report. If necessary, document any dissenting rating.

2. **For each process assessed, assign a rating to each Process Attribute.** Use the defined set of assessment indicators in the assessment model assessment to support the assessors' judgment.

   - The process context, recorded in the assessment input, influences how an assessor should judge and rate the Process Attributes for an implemented process.

   - When more than one instance of a process is assessed, the assessor will be required to use the recorded assessment information collected on all of the instances to make a judgement on the rating of each of the Process Attributes assessed for that process.

3. **Record the set of Process Attribute ratings as the process profile** and calculate the Capability Level rating for each process using the Capability Level Attribute Model.

## Reporting the Results

The assessment team documents the assessment results with any required analysis, and reports them to the participants and the sponsor. The report may be either preliminary or final, for example, it should be considered preliminary when the assessment participants have had no opportunity to provide feedback on the results and corroborate the evidence. Use of preliminary reporting can aid longer-term assessment result acceptance in case of disputes over the rating by allowing further assessment to obtain more evidence.

The report also covers any key issues raised during the assessment such as observed areas of strength and weakness, findings of high risk, or the unsuitability of an assessed process for its intended purpose. Assessment records are produced for benchmarking database and for assessor certification.

1. **Prepare the assessment report.** Summarize the findings of the assessment, highlighting the process profiles, key results, observed strengths and weaknesses, identified risk factors, and potential improvement actions. Compare the results of the current assessment to those of previous assessments where applicable, or to any industry benchmarks available. Relate the findings to the original purpose of the assessment.

2. **Present the assessment results to the participants.** Focus the presentation on defining the capability of the processes assessed. For processes with Capability Level 0, ensure that participants view and understand the underlying Process Attribute ratings. In general, encourage the organizational unit to accept the results, highlighting both strengths and weaknesses and seeking input to a proposed action plan.

3. **Present the assessment results to the sponsor.**

4. **Submit the assessment report to the sponsor.**

5. **Verify and document that the assessment** was performed according to the agreed process assessment model and requirements.

6. **Incorporate key findings into the assessment record.** Verify that the assessment record is complete and satisfies the ISO 15504 requirements.

7. **Submit Assessment Record**. Provide the Assessment Record to the sponsor for retention and storage.

8. **Prepare and sign assessor records.** For each assessor, records to prove the participation in the assessment are produced. The sponsor or the assessment record authority signs the records.

## Assessment Work Products

### Assessment Input

#### Business Needs

The needs either are directly obtained as a specific input, or are indirectly applied from a process improvement programme or capability determination requirement.

#### Industry Benchmarks

Industry benchmarks may be derived from assessment records collected over time. Only records of ISO 15504 conformant assessments should be used.

#### Reports from Previous Assessments

Previous Assessment results may be used to evaluate the effect of process improvement programs in the organization.

#### Organizational Documents and Records

To qualify as evidence of a process work product, a document or record must:
- address key issues for the process under assessment
- show evidence that reasonable control has been achieved.
Examples include:
- contracts with customers and suppliers
- plans
- specifications
- procedures
- meeting minutes
- review reports

**Assessment Instrument**

Tool for information gathering, processing, and presentation, which may be computer-based or paper-based. The tool helps the assessor perform the assessment in a reliable and consistent manner.

## Assessment Output

**Statement of Confidentiality (optional)**

Defines the agreement on confidentiality between the assessment team, the sponsor and the organizational unit. Covers the confidentiality of the sources of information and documentation gathered during assessment and defines controls for any proprietary information.

**Pre-Assessment Questionnaire (PAQ)**

Collects information about the organizational unit's software development approach and local environment needed for planning the assessment. Provides information to specify the assessment context. Topics include:

- motivation for assessment
- company profile (business sector, key products, size, revenues of business unit, organizational structure)
- demographics of organizational unit being assessed
- the organizational unit staff
- size, criticality and complexity of the products or services
- quality characteristics of the product
- software development in the organizational unit (software life-cycle, development environment)
- quantitative measurements (metrics)

**Assessment Initiation File**

Records the assessment inputs:

- the sponsor's commitment
- the ownership and distribution of the assessment report and record
- Statement of Confidentiality and how it is fulfilled
- the assessment purpose, scope, context, and constraints
- the identities and responsibilities of the assessment team members and the participants
- the completed Pre-Assessment Questionnaire

**Assessment Plan**

The set of instructions and procedure for conducting the assessment is based on the Assessment Initiation File and the completed PAQ. Specifies or references, at a minimum:
- activities and tasks to be performed in conducting the assessment
- resources and schedule assigned to these activities
- assessment risks and risk management strategy
- mapping of the organizational unit to the Assessment Model
- mandatory base practices from the Assessment Model (if applicable)
- use of tools and techniques for data collection
- criteria for verification of the performance of the requirements
- planned assessment outputs

**Evidence of Process Performance and Capability**

Objectively demonstrated characteristics of work products and practices associated with the assessed processes, which supports the assessors' judgment of Process Attribute ratings.

Includes:
- References to Organizational Documents.
- Questionnaires.
- Input of Participants.

**Assessment Report**

Summarizes the findings of the assessment. It contains:
- configuration control.
- document history.
- revision history.
- change forecast.
- executive summary.
- roles and responsibilities.
- assessment inputs (or references to assessment input).
- key assessment activities.
- assessment outputs (including assessment record).
The assessment report highlights:
- process profiles (the set of Process Attribute ratings and Process Capability Level ratings).
- key findings
- observed strengths and weaknesses
- identified risk factors
- improvement opportunities

The report provides comparisons to a target capability profile or to other assessment results, if these exist.

### Assessment Record

Compiles information pertinent to the assessment. Supports understanding the output of the assessment. Retained by the sponsor. Contains, at a minimum:

- the date of the assessment;
- the assessment input (or references to assessment input);
- the identification of the objective evidence gathered;
- the assessment model and method used;
- the set of process profiles resulting from the assessment (i.e., one profile for each process assessed);
- any additional information collected during the assessment to support process improvement or process capability determination; and
- any sponsor agreed changes to the assessment inputs.

### Assessor Records

Records kept by Provisional or Competent space assessor to demonstrate competence. It includes:

- Assessment Log used to record an assessor's participation in conformant assessments, conducted according to the provisions of ISO 15504. Verified by the sponsor of the assessment, a Competent Assessor or the Assessment Team Leader.
- Training Record used to maintain a record of the assessor's training in ISO 15504, S4S, or related topics.
- Professional Activities Log to demonstrate continuing competencies of skills, knowledge and training.

## Self Assessments

In general, self-assessments (internal) by an organization are performed as part of a process improvement programme. They can be used to either start the programme or in support of an existing programme. In exceptional cases, they may be performed to provide a capability determination in anticipation of an external requirement for capability determination. In either situation, the general assessment procedure should apply, but may be relaxed in some respects and expanded as described in this section.

The assessments should provide process 'opportunities for improvement' as the main output as they have a greater benefit internally to the organization than just a capability rating. The opportunities for improvement also provide a positive form of feedback and motivation to the sponsors and participants (especially since the assessment takes time away from their normal work activities). It should reduce focus on the Capability Level 'number', while highlighting good practices and potential improvements.

Initiation is often simplified when a process improvement programme is already in place. In addition, the **initiation**, **planning** and **briefing** steps may be iteratively formulated in shorter time (especially in small and medium size organizations). The sponsor may already exist, with a previously estimated budget for assessment and follow-on improvement activities. For internal persons no confidentiality agreement will normally be needed.

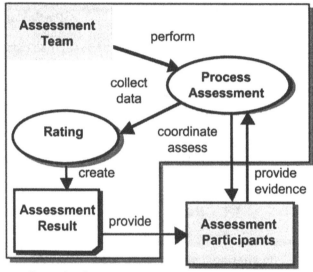

Fig. 35. Standard Process Assessment approach.

In the standard approach, the assessment team performs the assessment, rating and results reporting. For most organisations starting process assessment, this approach is followed.

In a previous employer, where I led process assessments for improvement purposes, we modified our approach from the standard assessment approach (see diagram above: Standard Process Assessment approach) as we performed more assessments. We migrated to a participatory process assessment approach where we involved assessment participants in the planning and preparation, as a training exercise for the participants and assessors. This also helped participants understand ISO/IEC 15504, what evidence we were looking for in processes and established some rapport between the assessors and the participants prior to the assessment (positive cultural enablers). It created a positive feeling of anticipation, encouraged understanding of the value of assessments before the assessment took place, and acceptance of the results.

Initially we held larger briefings with several assessment participants from the participating organisational units. We migrated towards a specific assessor/assessment team working with the specific unit(s) in planning and preparation. In this way, the assessment participants became a part of the assessment team in spirit and shared understanding.

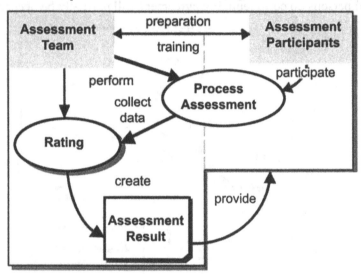

Increasing maturity - participatory assessment

**Fig. 36. Participatory Assessment approach.**

We still employed external assessors as part of the assessment team, but reduced the social interaction distance by encouraging participation of the assessed organisation through the preparation, planning and performance of assessments.

The assessment participants participate in interpreting the assessment indicators, not just in providing evidence requested by the assessors, but also in any need to map or interpret their implemented processes against the base and management practices.

We then began migrating to a complete integrated team approach, using joint assessment performance, team rating and results preparation.

This approach almost eliminated social distance, as assessments became not just organisational self-assessments, but also an assessed organisation unit self-assessment, facilitated by the lead assessors/assessors. Assessment results were jointly derived and agreed, guided by the lead assessor. In general, disputes of the assessment results, especially improvement opportunities (and any rating) were less frequent (in fact almost absent) compared to the standard assessment approach. In the extremely rare cases where the team could not agree, then the lead assessor made the final judgement and this was respected by the team members.

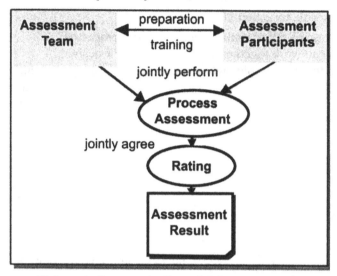

High maturity organization - joint assessment

**Fig. 37. Joint Process Assessment approach.**

We eventually incorporated this into the Team Based Business Design Improvement approach as described in the Improvement chapter. This provided an even greater qualitative and quantifiable advantage in improvement culture and performance. Advantages and constraints:

✓ Move away from assessor and (versus?) assessed people.

✓ Move towards team approach with shared values, respect and responsibilities. Distinct roles are retained (e.g. lead assessor ensures a valid assessment result).

✓ People in the assessed organisation learn the value and application of the practices of ISO/IEC 15504 in detail. And they apply them in improvement!

✗ Requires more training for assessed organisation participants.

✗ Takes time to learn best method for new organisations just starting assessments.

✗ Possibly harder to ensure rating honesty (not found in practice).

✗ Does not suit competitive assessment focus – where parts of an organisation are competing for the best rating or least number of improvement actions to perform. This is a sign of a dysfunctional organisational culture that requires improvement anyway! Not found in practice.

➢ Participatory assessment and joint assessment require a higher level of maturity of the organisation towards assessment.

➢ Not useable for external assessments.

✓ Suits organisations with higher capability processes.

✓ Team can work together on improvements if desired.

✓ Leads to a more rapid and sustained focus on improvement.

✓ Works even better with a 'Design first - then assess' approach (see improvement chapter and Team Based Business Design Improvement).

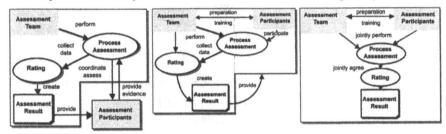

**Fig. 38. Migrating from standard to participatory to joint assessment.**

I believe that more mature organisations should follow a similar path of migration in their approach to assessments.

## Self Assessment Initiation

The assessment purpose may be predefined. Check the purpose meets any changing business needs when part of longer-term programmes (and also after organizational strategy workshops). Identify any additional information that the sponsor requests to be gathered during the assessment. Identify the sponsor and budget if not already known.

Build the assessment team. The Assessment Team Leader will normally be an internal person. This is an opportunity to train a provisional assessor to be a competent assessor (they must lead at least one assessment successfully) so share the role and duties for each assessment. If the results must be externally verifiable, ensure a competent assessor is involved [this may mean using an external assessor for the first assessment(s)]. The team could also comprise participants of the assessed organizational unit when improvement is the aim. When the participants are involved in the team, the degree of commitment and motivation is much higher for both the assessment and subsequent improvement actions.

The Local Assessment Coordinator is often the assessed organizational unit manager. Select the additional assessment participants with the manager. Define each person's responsibilities in the team and the unit(s).

No Pre-Assessment Questionnaires is needed unless the organizational unit is remote and not much is known about their operation (possibly needed in large, dispersed organizations). The aims of the questionnaire can better be handled in an interactive briefing with all the participants.

Define the assessment context when multiple units will be assessed, and define each unit's assessment scope including the processes and to what Capability Level they will be assessed. Note: This may also be done with the potential participants as part of the briefing step.

Specify any special constraints placed on the freedom of choice of the assessment team regarding the conduct of the assessment and use of assessment outputs.

Map the organizational unit's process to the process assessment model. In some cases, there will be no direct mapping correspondence to a particular process. The mapping may then use base practices from different processes that are closest the purpose of the organizational unit process (for example, a company tendering process may be mapped partially to the Requirements Elicitation process and the Supply process).

The sponsor should normally freely share the Assessment Record but determine the requirement if not.

Document the assessment inputs and review all inputs with the assessment sponsor for approval to proceed.


## Planning

Planning will normally partially occur in parallel with initiation activities and should involve the assessment team (and if possible the assessment participants).

Determine the necessary resources, schedule and logistics for the assessment.

Define how the assessment data will be collected, recorded, stored, analysed and presented, including use of an assessment instrument. Planned outputs may include a preliminary report to the organizational unit before a final report. Verify conformance of the requirements to the standard if a conformant assessment.

Identify and manage risks together with the sponsor and the local assessment coordinators. Formalize the planning in an assessment plan, review and obtain acceptance of the plan from the sponsor.

## Briefing

Briefing can help ensure cooperative planning of the assessment. When the organizational unit is briefed as part of the planning activities, they have a strong motivation to understand what the assessment purpose means and may help select the most appropriate processes to assess. By ensuring their input early in the planning process, their commitment to the assessment and use of the results is greatly enhanced. Potential participants and anyone who will see the presentation of the final results should be present at the briefing session.

Time permitting, the briefing should be run one to two weeks before the assessment. In the briefing, explain the assessment purpose, scope, constraints, and model. It is then useful to divide the briefing into multiple parallel mini-meetings where each assessor in the team describes the specific processes to the person(s) who will participate in that process assessment. This will help the participants understand what evidence is needed and how the evidence and ratings apply to their processes. The assessor will gain a better understanding of the actual processes and if needed can revise the process mapping. After each individual session is ready, collate and present the tentative assessment schedule and obtain agreement.

The positive change in attitude of participants involved in cooperative assessment planning versus those who are presented with a prepared assessment plan is worth the extra effort involved in an interactive briefing and planning session. By allowing time between the briefing and the assessment for the participants to reflect on what is required, they can gather the evidence and clarify with the internal assessors any issues they have.

## Data acquisition and validation

During the assessment data acquisition, collect evidence of process performance for each process within the scope. This is easier if cooperative assessment planning occurred as the participants are better prepared and understand what is needed. At the same time, collect evidence of process capability for each process within the scope, record the references to the evidence and verify the completeness of the data. Look especially at how the collected evidence can suggest opportunities for improvement, when possible it is better to describe incomplete process assessment attributes in positive 'opportunities for improvement' terms than in negative 'failure to achieve' terms. Participants may also offer additional useful information that should be noted as such.

Ensure with the participants that the data collected is correct and that the validated data provides complete coverage of the assessment scope.

## Process rating

If the rating of process capability is part of the output, the assessment team validates the evidence before using it to assign process ratings. For each process, relate the evidence to defined assessment indicators. Relate the indicators to the appropriate Process Attributes. For each process assessed, the assessment team assigns a rating for each Process Attribute up to and including the highest Capability Level defined in the assessment scope. Depending upon time constraints, it is useful to collect rating evidence of Process Attributes at higher Capability Levels as a sign of positive performance (even if the lower Capability Levels is not fully achieved). In self-assessments, it is normally useful to collect as much positive evidence as possible with the aim to promote achievement of higher capability.

In self-assessments, the assessors may also be asked to provide advice to the participants on how to take actions to improve the assessed processes. This should be encouraged, unless the organization specifies otherwise. Providing help during the assessment will improve motivation and commitment to improve, and may allow the organizational unit to start improvements sooner.

Where possible, use a consensus approach to rating decisions. Including the assessment participants and performing the process ratings immediately following the data validation will further educate the participants and raise their commitment to both the result and subsequent use of the results. If clear evidence supports a rating (either positive or negative) then the team will normally accept this (even if their pre-conceived rating was different).

By carefully noting the evidence with each Process Attribute rating, the team and participants know what needs to be done to improve.

As required, record the set of Process Attribute ratings as the process profile and calculate the Capability Level rating for each process using the Capability Level Attribute Model.

## Reporting

Present the preliminary assessment results to the participants after each organizational unit assessment or as a combined presentation together with the sponsor as decided in the planning. Allow for feedback and a potential need to re-examine evidence in support of higher ratings. Focus on the opportunities for improvement and/or the ratings depending upon the assessment purpose.

Prepare the assessment report. Summarize the findings of the assessment, highlighting the process profiles, key results, observed strengths and weaknesses, identified risk factors, and potential opportunities for improvement actions. Compare the results of the current assessment to those of previous assessments where applicable, or to any industry benchmarks available. Relate the findings to the original purpose of the assessment.

Verify and document that the assessment was performed according to the agreed process assessment model and requirements. Verify that the assessment record is complete and satisfies the ISO 15504 requirements. Prepare and sign assessor records as needed.

Incorporate key findings into the assessment record. Submit the assessment report and record to the sponsor. If a process improvement programme exists, the results should be used as an input to the next step in the improvement programme (see chapter 6), where a results and risk analysis uses the assessment results. Note when the organizational unit has decided to start improvement actions as a result of discussion during the assessment.

## External Assessments

External Assessments are normally performed for Capability Determination purposes[36] or by the organization itself to independently verify that an organization's own assessment programme is functioning correctly. The sponsor of a Capability Determination assessment is normally external to the organizational unit being assessed, such as an acquirer who wishes to have an independently derived assessment output. For independent verification, the assessment sponsor will belong to the same organization but not necessarily the organizational unit being assessed.

An external assessment generally uses an independent assessment team.

The assessment team follows the Generic Assessment Procedure described in this chapter (this procedure is designed for external assessments). The assessment team must formally follow the standard assessment procedure so that all steps and the evidence collected are properly recorded and able to be verified later if requested.

During the initiation, planning and briefing, the assessment team should clearly ensure the assessed organization understand the data collection and validation requirements and how the process rating will be performed, including the decision-making process that is performed by the external assessment team (e.g. consensus of the external assessment team or majority vote or competent assessor casting vote).

---

[36] See the section on Process Capability Determination in chapter 6.

## Data collection and validation

One critical aspect of external assessments for capability determination is to ensure that the data collected is validated during the assessment. This affects the data collection activities as at least two sources of information need to be found.

For a single organizational unit instance (for example, one project) the assessors should check that the evidence from both the interview testimony and work products matches, and that sufficient evidence exists as assessment indicators of the process indicators/Process Attributes/Capability Levels to meet the assessment purpose and scope.

The assessment team should assess at least two organizational instances (two projects) that management has clearly identified as typical and relevant to the assessment scope (preferably they are part of the capability being used/offered). If the assessors find variation in implementation/capability found by the assessors between different instances of implementation of the same process, they might need to assess more instances in order to derive a valid organizational rating. The assessment team may also seek information from independent sources, check past assessment results and hold feedback sessions to validate the information collected.

## Process Rating

For each process assessed, the assessment team assigns a rating for each Process Attribute up to and including the highest Capability Level defined in the assessment scope. If necessary, document any dissenting rating.

When more than one instance of a process is assessed, the assessment team will be required to use the recorded assessment information collected on all of the instances to make a judgment on the rating of each of the Process Attributes assessed for that process.

Record the set of Process Attribute ratings as the process profile and calculate the Capability Level rating for each process using the Capability Level Attribute Model.

## Reporting the Results

The assessment team documents the assessment results with any required analysis, and reports them to the participants and the sponsor. This may be at the end of the assessment period, or there may be interim reporting if the assessment is over an extended period or the assessment team requires feedback.

The assessment team focuses the presentation on defining the capability of the processes assessed. For processes with Capability Level 0, ensure that participants view and understand the underlying Process Attribute ratings. The report covers any key issues raised during the assessment such as observed areas of strength and weakness, findings of high risk, or the unsuitability of an assessed process for its intended purpose.

Submit the assessment report to the sponsor.

Verify and document that the assessment was performed according to the agreed process assessment model and requirements. Incorporate key findings into the assessment record. Verify that the assessment record is complete and satisfies the ISO 15504 requirements.

## Quick Assessments

In general, a quick assessment is considered to involve no more than 2 days at the organization, possibly one day when a small enterprise is being assessed. There are two fundamental choices in quick assessments:

- Perform a conformant assessment with a very limited number of processes and assess only to Capability Level 1 or 2; or
- Perform a nonconformity assessment covering more processes at varying Capability Levels based upon interviews only.

There are several methods available for quick assessments. The method described here is called Quick Scan [63]. Methods include RAPID [64] and a light version of SYNSPiCE [65]. Quick Scan is suited to small enterprises, and to small-medium enterprises with similar project implementations. It assumes no constructed capability spanning several enterprises. Quick Scan's aim is to:

- Provide a high level overview of which processes exist.
- Quickly determine whether a process is being performed.
- Estimate the level of implementation (process capability).
- Provide limited improvement opportunities based on the missing practice indicators (base practices, work products and management practices/generic practice indicators).

The assessment is run as an interview. There is no review of documentation to ensure that work products exist or meet the detailed requirements of ISO/IEC 15504. The assessment will reflect the information and its accuracy as provided by the interviewees. The interviewee selection must be carefully managed by the organization management (sponsor and/or local assessment coordinator) to ensure participants not only have sufficient working process knowledge but also perform the activities (so they are quickly able to describe the process in operation, and hence the Capability

Level up to level 2). The aim is to maximize the value to the client while minimizing the time taken in the client interview. In order to do this, a team of two Quick Scan assessors prepares and run the assessment as follows:

- Send out the pre-interview questionnaire to select the processes to assess. The questionnaire is general and focussed on how many people are involved in each process category as well as their organizational process knowledge, it includes questions such as:
  - How many people are involved in software development and maintenance?
  - How many have you selected for a 1 day interview?
  - For your selected people, what part of the organization do they represent (**Entire**, **Wide** coverage, **Department**, one **Project**, **Part** of project/section)?
  - How well will they be able to describe what is happening in regard to software related work (**Excellent**, **Good**, **Okay**)?
  - When can the interview be held?
- Prepare the interview questionnaire sheet for the selected processes. Normally around 5 - 6 processes can be assessed, depending upon the degree of complexity and variation within the interviewed group.
- Check with the assessment sponsor to ensure that sufficient persons (roles) covering all the processes to be assessed will be available for the interview. It is critical that the actual person(s) doing the work are available to describe how they do the activities during the interview. If they are not available there are 2 choices:
  - Postpone the interview to a date when all are available; or
  - Delete the processes that these people would cover.
- The leading competent assessor asks the group of persons to go through how they work in the interview. The leading assessor prompts for additional information or clarification based on the questionnaire but does not use the questionnaire as the main interview method. The aim is to have the people describe their activities in their own terms and for the assessors to match them to the questionnaire.
- The second assessor notes where activities are performed that match the requirements for the various processes on the questionnaire.
  - Experienced assessors are needed in order to be able interpret the client statements into the practice indicators, and the Process Attributes and rating scale of ISO/IEC 15504.
- Where there is a difference of opinion on how an activity is performed, this is:
  - clarified if possible,
  - noted if considered more than minor, and

- if necessary, a simple 'vote' of the interviewees used to decide whether it meets the questionnaire criteria.
- The accuracy of the result is highly dependent on the accuracy of the information provided. The competent assessors need enough experience to help interpret the information provided and should also be able to detect in some cases where inconsistent information is provided (and note this on the questionnaire).
- A copy of the questionnaire is left with the sponsor at the end of the interview where agreed.
- The assessors convene within 1-2 days to create a report highlighting positive aspects and Opportunities for Improvement.

Quick Scan assessments are not intended to be comprehensive and therefore are not conformant assessments, but are intended to provide the clients with rapid feedback of a limited set of processes from competent assessors familiar with the domain assessed. The 'favourite' set of processes to assess for a software development organization is:

- Requirement Elicitation
- Software Design
- Software Construction
- Software Testing
- Project Management
- Problem Resolution
- Configuration Management

## Intensive Assessments

Organizations may wish or need to perform intensive assessments for the following reasons:

- Achievement of a specific process maturity as part of a Certification programme (e.g. for aerospace).
- As a baseline to perform a comprehensive improvement programme.
- In response to a detailed capability determination request or to demonstrate a specific capability/maturity level.

An intensive assessment is one that assesses:

- A comprehensive set of processes covering all the fundamental activities of the primary lifecycle processes in the organization. This would include:
  - All the customer-supplier, operations and engineering key processes that are relevant.
  - All the performed support and management processes.

- The organization processes that directly impact on the operations of the organization.
- This does not assume all processes in the process assessment model are assessed. (However in order to be assessed as Capability Level 5, there are few processes that are required to be assessed.)
- Multiple instances of the processes across multiple organizational units (for example at least one (preferably at least two) project in each organization division/department).
- All Capability Levels, even if the Target capability profile is level 3 or 4.

The effort involved in performing intensive assessments is substantial. Therefore, the complete approach described in the section on the Generic Assessment Procedure should be followed. It is important to ensure that the Assessment Sponsor understands the required effort and budget (for a comprehensive programme including assessment and improvement).

At the start, the lead assessor or team defines with the Assessment Sponsor the expected results and potential benefits before starting intensive assessments. Also, it is important to ensure that Local Assessment Coordinators are appointed and active in first scheduling the assessment interviews. This person must ensure that suitable persons with both process and organization knowledge will be available for the assessment briefing, the interviews and follow up.

It is common to use several teams of assessors when time is limited. This requires several competent assessors who are able to coordinate and analyse the results of the multiple teams to ensure a consistent assessment occurs. Alternatively, when the organization has more time, it can use one assessment team, thereby ensuring less coordination and analysis. Either approach is valid. The selection of one or more teams should be based upon the specific reasons driving the assessment purpose.

The following table provides indicative guidance on which ISO/IEC 12207 processes should be assessed for two example organizations.

Organization 1 (Org One) is a System Prime Contractor of a large aerospace project (with subcontractors) responsible for supporting the system.

Organization 2 (ORG Two) is a software developer with no systems responsibility.

**Table 23. Intensive assessment – indicative process selection table.**

| Process Category | Processes | Org One | Org Two |
|---|---|---|---|
| Customer - Supplier | Acquisition | Assess | - |
| | Supply | Assess | Optional |
| Operations | Operation Use | Assess | - |
| | Customer Support | Assess | - |
| Engineering | Requirements Elicitation | Assess | - |
| | System requirements | Assess | - |
| | Analysis | Assess | - |
| | System Architecture Design | Assess | Assess |
| | Software Requirements | Assess | Assess |
| | Analysis | Assess | Assess |
| | Software Design | Assess | Assess |
| | Software Construction | Assess | Assess |
| | Software Integration | Assess | - |
| | Software Testing | Assess | - |
| | System Integration | Assess | Optional |
| | System Testing | | |
| | Software Installation | | |
| Support | Documentation | Assess | Level 3 to 5 |
| | Configuration Management | Assess | Assess |
| | Quality Assurance | Assess | Assess |
| | Verification | Level 3 to 5 | Optional |
| | Validation | Level 3 to 5 | Optional |
| | Joint Review | Assess | Optional |
| | Audit | Level 3 to 5 | Level 3 to 5 |
| | Product Evaluation | Assess | - |
| | Usability | Assess | Optional |
| | Problem Resolution | Assess | Assess |
| Management | Organizational Alignment | Level 3 to 5 | Optional $\geq$ level 3 |
| | Organization Management | Level 3 to 5 | Optional $\geq$ level 3 |
| | Measurement | If level $\geq 4$ | If level $\geq 4$ |
| | Project management | Assess | Assess |
| | Quality Management | Assess | If level $\geq 4$ |
| | Risk Management | Assess | If level $> 4$ |
| Organization | Infrastructure | Level 3 to 5 | Level 3 to 5 |
| | Improvement process | If level $\geq 4$ | If level $\geq 4$ |
| | Human Resource | Level 3 to 5 | - |
| | Management | Assess | - |
| | Asset Management | Optional | Optional |
| | Reuse Programme | Assess | - |
| | Management | | |
| | Domain Engineering | | |

# The assessor as guide and coach

## The assessor as guide

A trained SPICE assessor acquires detailed knowledge about using ISO/IEC 15504 [1]. This knowledge includes a large amount of information about:

- Assessing the work of people within the enterprise.
- Ways to measure enterprise effectiveness.
- Processes and process lifecycles particularly related to assessing system and software development.
- What comprises basic, good and best work practices for each process.

The scope and depth of knowledge is one reason why there is a set of requirements on people wishing to become assessors, such as formal educational qualifications and industry experience. These requirements are aimed at ensuring people can learn all the required knowledge and also competently apply it. This knowledge is valuable to the individual and to an enterprise. The depth of knowledge depends upon the level of competence of the assessor.

A qualified assessor must have good working knowledge of the various processes, a very detailed knowledge of the management of any process (the generic practices in the capability levels) and an excellent level of knowledge in how to plan and perform assessments. He or she will also have a good knowledge of how to guide people into becoming competent assessors and be able to judge whether they meet the requirements to be competent assessors.

A competent assessor must also have good working knowledge of processes and their management and a good level of knowledge in how to plan and perform assessments. As a lead assessor, he or she will also know how to form and manage assessments teams.

A provisional assessor must have a good working knowledge of processes and their management, but will have only basic knowledge in how to perform assessments gained in training during the 5 day assessor course.

The knowledge of an assessor is used not only to perform assessments, but also to guide others in the meaning and use of the standard. The first type of guidance is related to helping assessors, especially provisional assessors to become competent assessors. A qualified or competent lead assessor must act as a guide to the assessment team, especially to provisional assessors. This guidance covers the entire assessment approach, including:

- Planning the assessment, including guidance on which processes to select and the selected capability level.
- Checking that (provisional) assessors correctly follow the assessment method, conduct interviews, collect evidence and record their findings. Provisional assessors generally take longer to collect evidence and derive an assessment finding. A skilful qualified assessor will moderate the time and depth required by a provisional assessor in the assessment so that interviews take the minimum effort to perform but still acquire sufficient evidence to support an assessment finding.
- Guiding provisional assessors in interpreting the base practices and the generic practices correctly. This is particularly important to do well, because provisional assessors will tend to follow the interpretation in future assessments. Good guidance will be provided in an open, non-argumentative way. The guidance will not only describe the meaning of the practices and use of work products but also how to interpret them in a given assessment situation. The aim is to provide guidance that builds assessor judgment. It will inform not only the assessor but also assessment participants.
- Guiding provisional assessors in presenting the assessment findings, both at the preliminary result presentation and in the final assessment report. I have attended assessments where provisional assessors have broken one of assessment 'rules' by getting into arguments with the assessment participants when presenting the preliminary results. The presentation of results at the end of the assessment is called preliminary specifically for this reason, that it gives the assessment participants the opportunity to indicate if they believe that not all relevant evidence has been collected. Instead of taking the criticisms as a need to revisit the assessed processes, in this case the provisional assessor escalated his argument that his interpretation was correct. The qualified assessor had to stop the argument and offer to perform further assessment to resolve the matter (which the provisional assessor should have offered). In this particular case, the provisional assessor was judged not to have met the requirements to become a competent assessor purely due to the failure to perform the preliminary reporting correctly.

- Guiding assessment participants in interpreting the assessment questions and the interpretation of practices and work products during interviews and other evidence collection activities.

The last point is one of the most important. All assessors need to act as guides for assessment participants, because ISO/IEC 15504 knowledge is not very common and not always self evident. In particular, the detailed interpretation of the generic practices related to management of processes is not always obvious. When an assessor acts as a good guide, the assessment participants will better understand how the way they work compares to the basic, good and best practice.

Assessment as a separate activity is purely a cost without benefit. It is the reason why Mark Paulk calls focusing on the numerical assessment result (i.e. a maturity or capability level) is dysfunctional behaviour.

The assessor acts as a guide when she/he runs a preparatory workshop with the personnel to be involved in assessments. The aim is to prepare them better for the assessment and form small teams of one assessor and several assessment participants. In effect, the assessment participants receive the initial half day training that all provisional assessors receive in the five or two day course, in this case focussed on their particular processes.

In the two weeks leading up to the assessment, the participants are given the opportunity to use the assessor to help them prepare for the assessment. In general, the participants and their assigned assessor take a couple of hours in these two weeks to prepare. The initial guidance and help during the assessment preparation has several benefits:

- Assessment participants understand how the unit's processes will be assessed.
- Assessment participants know what information to prepare or have available for the assessment, removing the assessment interview stress and time. Working with the assessor helps them prepare and gives them the chance to become better informed.
- Assessment participants realise that they are not being personally examined.
- Assessment participants have an influence on the scope of assessment and become more willing collaborators in the assessment (cooperation and collaboration).
- Assessment participants can contribute to the goals in terms of what improvements should be sought (empowerment).
- The overall knowledge and utility of ISO/IEC15504 as a means to investigate and propose improvement is enhanced (education).
- Participants realise that they can use the assessment process as a means to focus improvements.

The result of the extra assessor guidance to participants in the assessment preparation phase has a direct benefit in reducing the time and effort in the assessment. Because the assessor's first contact with participants is as a guide and helper rather than an examiner, there is less stress and a more relaxed and open environment during the assessment.

When the assessment is seen as collaborative, this situation can be moderated through the guidance of the assessor. The aim is that at the end of the interview, there is an agreed assessment result. When the assessor acts as a guide, this is achievable because both the assessor and participants collaborate. As a further result, after the assessment, the participants are happier seeking out the help of the assessor in planning and performing improvements.

Assessment has a high value when it indicates things that can be improved. For internal assessment, the benefit comes when the results of an assessment are used to improve the enterprise. This improvement will result in various types of benefit including better quality of products (and hence higher customer satisfaction), more effective and efficient processes, and better people. These can all lead to better business results (lower costs due to reduced quality problem rework). The role of assessor as guide and leader consequently must be primarily focused on achieving benefit to the enterprise through improvement.

## Improvement guide and coach

How can an enterprise maximise the benefit of improvement? This example comes from work performed in high quality enterprises that achieved high capability levels in many of its software project processes. The reason that this enterprise achieved these levels was not due to process assessment per se, but because of the way the ISO/IEC 15504 standard was used in the enterprise.

The change in the perceived role of a SPICE assessor from an examiner to a guide can be taken much further and to greater benefit. SPICE assessors and assessment providers have a blind spot in terms of measurement of their own work. An assessment report focused on improvement will have a number of recommendations or opportunities for improvement. Few if any assessors measure how many of these improvements are successfully performed.

My experience is that the number of improvements successfully performed is less than 25% for the standard assessment method, in some cases as low as 5%. The figures are often this low because the effort in improvement is greater than in assessment and occurs over much longer time. The longer time period needed for improvement is particularly significant because improvement is often disrupted by 'everyday business crises' and reorganisations.

When a SPICE assessor acts as a guide, the improvement success rate can rise closer to 40% (two out of five opportunities for improvement are actually implemented). I keep contact with my assessed organisations to ensure this is monitored. While this is itself an improvement, it is still far below an optimal investment. It means 60% of started improvement efforts fail. This is a sub-optimal cost/benefit ratio. It raises the question "why perform an assessment if you don't use the results?"

This is where a different paradigm is needed for the use of assessment to become valuable to the business. If the role of a SPICE assessor is to create a business benefit, then a means is needed to use the knowledge of the assessor to help in improvement. The following method has a proven success rate over 95%. Virtually all improvements started are successfully implemented. The method uses Team Based Business Design Improvement (TBBDI). The fundamental aim of TBBDI is to successfully implement improvements.

- It uses a 'design first – then assess' approach.
- It uses a team comprising the assessor as a guide and the business unit personnel.

The approach uses the role of process champion to improve a particular business process. She/he normally employs a facilitator so that the internal business politics are handled carefully. The SPICE assessor acts as a dedicated guide to the team by:

- Training team members in the ISO/IEC15504 standard – specifically in the meaning of the base, good and best practices and the relevant work products relevant to the business process being improved.
- Helping the team select the appropriate capability level for the process, both generically and for particular instances (i.e. tailoring).
- Coaching team members on the meaning and application of the practices and work products.
- Guiding the team on the way the improved process will be assessed after implementation.

The team selects and applies the information in the design of the selected business process. The approach is highly suited to motivating teams to adopt, design and implement processes at Capability Level 4 or 5 but can be used with experienced guidance at lower levels. It favours teams with a level of experience of process design at these Capability Levels.

One of the intended effects of the guidance by the SPICE assessor is that the team members become very familiar with the standard and understand the value of the management or generic practices defined in the process capability dimension.

The cooperative and participatory approach embodied in Team Based Business Design Improvement approach is psychologically better suited to motivate teams and people. The team embraces the paradigm of 'Innovation and Improvement from WITHIN'.

The approach fosters a culture of "Striving for Excellence".

# Application View – Assessment results

## Viewing assessment results

In this chapter, we show an example assessment result and explain some of the important characteristics to help sponsors interpret the results.

The results are fictional and are used for illustrative purposes only. The plots are obtained using the SPICE 1-2-1 Tool (see the annex on Assessment tools) This chapter will be of interest to assessors, assessment sponsors, customers, improvement sponsors, process capability determination sponsors, process experts and quality professionals.

---

### Capability Determination example

First, we must set a target capability profile, either as the customer or the process capability determination sponsor.

**Table 24. Capability determination example.**

| Key Process | Process Attributes | Process attribute ratings required | Capability Level |
|---|---|---|---|
| ACQ.2 Supplier Selection | PA1.1, PA2.1, PA2.2, PA 3.1, PA 3.2 (i.e. all up to and including the *Established* Capability Level) | Fully Achieved | Level 2 |
| ENG.5 Software Design | PA1.1, PA2.1, PA2.2, PA3.1, PA3.2 (i.e. all up to and including the *Established* Capability Level) | Fully Achieved | Level 3 |
| ENG.8 Software Testing | PA1.1, PA2.1, PA2.2, PA3.1, PA3.2 (i.e. all up to and including the *Established* Capability Level) | Fully Achieved | Level 3 |
| SUP.8 Problem resolution | PA1.1, PA2.1, PA2.2 | Fully Achieved | |
| | PA3.1, PA3.2 | Largely Achieved | Level 3 |
| MAN.3 Project management | PA1.1, PA2.1, PA2.2 | Fully Achieved | |
| | PA3.1, PA3.2 | Partially Achieved | Level 2 |

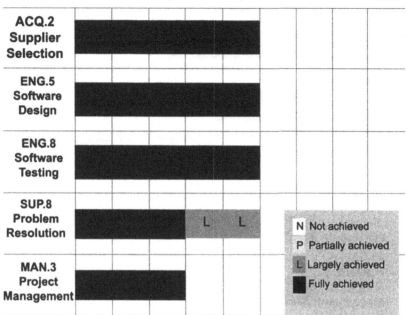

**Fig. 39. Target Capability Profile.**

In the target profile, we set Capability Levels as shown. When Process Attributes are set to largely (in SUP.8) it is taken as a Capability Level 3 target. When Process Attributes are set to partially (in MAN.3), the target is Capability Level 2. Next, we obtain the actual process performance by process assessment. This is called the Assessed or Measured Process Capability Profile.

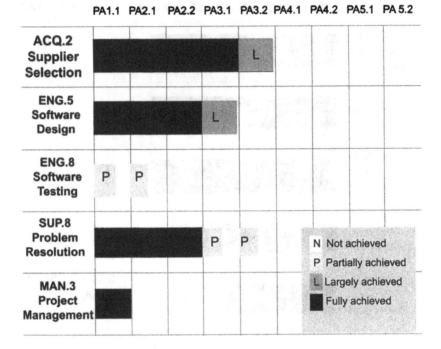

ig. 40. Assessed Capability Profile.

The next step is to compare the target and the measured process profiles nd determine any gaps.

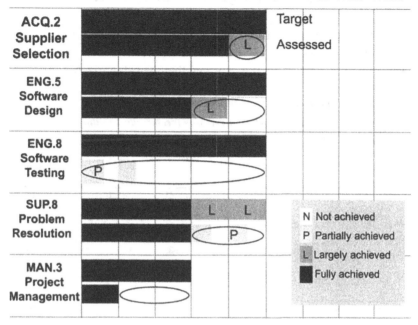

**Fig. 41. Target to Assessed Process Capability Gaps.**

The gaps are circled and can be categorized at various capability gap levels, Process Attribute gap level and practice indicator gap level using the following the Process Attribute to Capability level gap relationship.

**Table 25. Process Attribute to Capability level gap.**

| Number of Process Attribute gaps within Capability Level | Capability level gap |
|---|---|
| No major or minor gaps | None |
| Minor gaps only | Slight (unlikely) |
| A single major gap at Levels 2 - 5 | Significant (moderately likely) |
| A single major gap at Level 1 or more than one major gap at Levels 2 - 5 | Substantial (highly likely) |

The gaps are:
- ACQ.2 has slight Capability Level gap, due to a minor Process Attribute gap in PA 3.2.
- ENG 5 has capability gap at Capability Level 3, minor Process Attribute gap in PA 3.1 and a major Process Attribute gap in PA 3.2.
- ENG .8 has capability gaps at Capability Levels 1, 2 and 3.

- SUP.8 has a capability gap at Capability Level 3 only, caused by major Process Attribute gaps in PA3.1 and PA 3.2.
- MAN.3 has a capability gap at level 2, and minor Process Attribute gaps at level 3.

The risks associated with the gaps can then be categorized. [66]

**Table 26. Capability gap process-oriented risk**

| *Capability Level Gap (severity, impact)* | *Extent of Capability Level Gap (probability, likelihood)* | | | |
|---|---|---|---|---|
| | None | Slight (unlikely) | Significant (moderately likely) | Substantial (highly likely) |
| Performed | No Identifiable Risk | Medium Risk | **High Risk** | **High Risk** |
| Managed | No Identifiable Risk | Medium Risk | Medium Risk | **High Risk** |
| Established | No Identifiable Risk | Low risk | Medium risk | Medium Risk |
| Predictable | No Identifiable Risk | Low Risk | Low Risk | Medium Risk |
| Optimising | No Identifiable Risk | Low Risk | Low Risk | Low Risk |

The process-oriented risks are:

- ACQ.2 has slight, low risk due minor Process Attribute gap in PA 3.2 (Established).
- ENG.5 has significant, medium risk due to capability gap at Capability Level 3.
- ENG.8 has substantial high risk due to capability gaps at Capability Levels 1, 2 and 3.
- SUP.8 has a significant, medium risk due to a capability gap at Capability Level 3.
- MAN.3 has a significant medium risk due to the capability gap at level 2.

# Application view - Industry Experience

## Industry Experience

In this chapter I look at the overall, published results of industry experience, first in the SPICE Trials, and then at experiences in some industry sectors. ISO/IEC 15504 has a wide application in industry within Europe and is expanding in other parts of the world. This industry overview spans the sectors discussed as well as other sectors including the finance and insurance industry, large software developers and aerospace companies.

This chapter will be of interest to managers, improvement sponsors, process capability determination sponsors and quality professionals.

## Overview of industry experience – the SPICE Trials

As part of the creation and evolution of the ISO/IEC 15504, the SPICE project initiated a programme to capture the experience of process assessment and use it to improve the draft versions of the standard. The results of this experience are captured in a series of reports (Phase 1 [67], Phase 2 [68]). The most interesting information comes from the phase 2 trials as this most closely resembles the version of the standard described in this book (ISO/IEC TR 15504:1998). The following overview has been extracted from these reports.

The trials were conducted across five regions: Canada, Europe, North Asia-Pacific, South Asia-Pacific and USA. Only 3 regions provided significant numbers of results: Europe, North Asia-Pacific and South Asia-Pacific. USA and Canada only provided 1 result each.

About half of the results were for small organizational units (less than 50 IT staff). Another significant IT staffing size was around 100 to 150 IT staff.

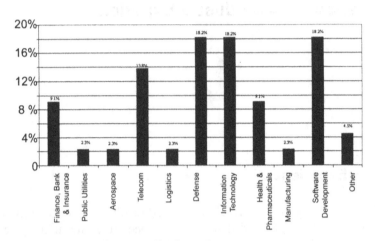

**Fig. 42. Assessments by Primary Business Sector.**

The assessment coverage indicates which businesses were adopting ISO/IEC 15504 process assessment in the period of the trials, the leading industries being Information Technology, Software Development and Defence, followed by Telecommunications and then Finance and Health/Pharmaceuticals. It should be noted that since completion of the trials, the space industry in Europe has increased ISO/IEC 15504 process assessment and the Defence industry (at least in Australia) has moved more towards CMMI[SM].

As an indication of process assessment coverage, 691 process instances were assessed across 169 projects. More than half the assessments assessed only one project.

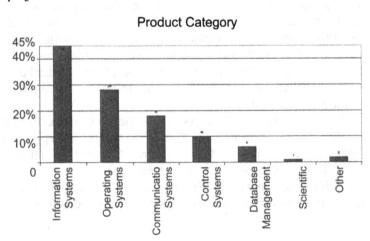

**Fig. 43. Product category for assessed projects.**

The reasons for software process assessment were also surveyed with assessment sponsors.

**Table 27. Reasons to perform process assessment**

| Reasons for process assessment | Rationale |
|---|---|
| 1. Establish baseline and/or track the organization's process improvement. | Measurement orientation |
| 2. Improve efficiency. | Improvement |
| 3. Establish best practices to guide organizational process improvement. | Improvement |
| 4. Establish project baselines and/or track projects/process improvement. | Improvement |
| 5. Improve customer service. | Improvement |
| 6. Customer demand to improve process capability | Improvement |
| 7. Generate management support and buy-in for software process improvement. | Buy-in |
| 8. Generate technical staff support and buy-in for software process improvement. | Buy-in |
| 9. Improve reliability of products. | Buy-in |

Three additional potential reasons (improve reliability of services, gain market advantage, and competitive market pressure) were not found to be important reasons for process assessment.

It should be noted that the organizations assessed often fit into the early adopter category and are generally considered more active in process establishment, assessment and improvement.

In the total of 691 assessment instances, 301 were not rated at level 5, 299 were not rated at level 4, and 56 were not rated at level 3. This should be taken into account when looking at the overall Capability Level ratings (although it could be surmised that most process instances were not rated to these Capability Levels because the assessors could guess that processes would not achieve these Capability Levels).

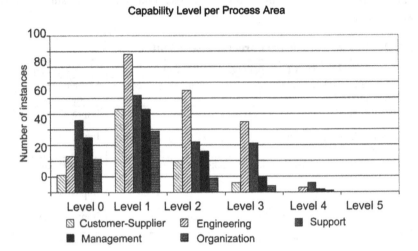

**Fig. 44. Phase 2 trials – process capability per process area.**

It is clear from the results that nearly all of the assessed organizational units are between levels 1 and 3. The report states that software process capability, as measured by ISO/IEC TR 15504:1998 can be considered a two dimensional construct: Process Implementation (levels 1 to 3) and Quantitative Process Management (levels 4 and 5). In other words, most organizations that were assessed during the trial period were focused on process implementation, and very few organizations were focused on the *'next level of performance'*. In addition, the trials reported the following:

- At Capability Level 2, the performance management attribute was more often rated higher than work product management.
- At Capability Level 3, the process resource attribute was more often rated higher than the process description attribute.
- At Capability Level 4, the process measurement attribute was more often rated higher than the process control attribute.

The confidence of achievement of Capability Levels was analysed for various processes and varies considerably across the 15 processes that had statistically significant sample sizes.

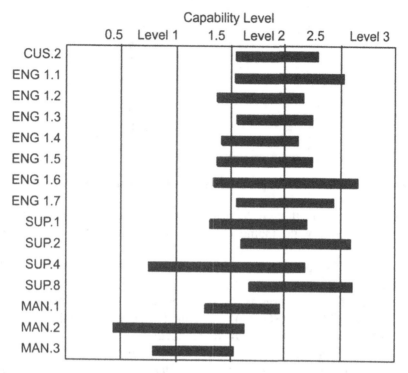

**Fig. 45. 95% Confidence interval for ISO 9001 accredited organizations.**

One clear result was that ISO 9001 accredited organizations achieve a higher level of capability than non-ISO 9001 organizations for specific processes[37], which were: CUS.3 – Requirements Elicitation, ENG.1.4 – Software Construction, ENG.1.5 – Software Integration, SUP.1 - Documentation, SUP.2 – Configuration Management, SUP.3 – Quality Assurance, SUP.8 – Problem Resolution, MAN.2 – Project Management, ORG.2 – Process Improvement and ORG.4 - Infrastructure.

---

[37] I have changed the ENG and MAN identification numbering to reflect the ISO/IEC TR 15504 process identifiers (rather than the Preliminary Draft TR identifiers).

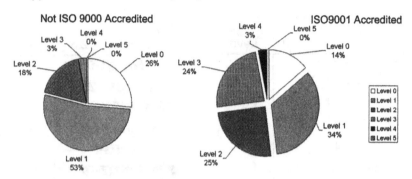

**Fig. 46. Capability levels of processes non ISO 9000 versus ISO 9001.**

The report also attempts to analyse the amount of assessor effort and suggests the following (some of which would appear to be obvious to assessors):

- Assessor effort per process increases as the number of Process Attribute assessed increase.
- Assessor effort decreases as assessors conduct more assessments.
- Assessor effort for ISO 9001 accredited organizations takes less effort than for non ISO 9001 accredited organizations.
- Assessor effort decreases for larger IT units compared to smaller IT units, although fewer process attributes were often assessed in larger IT units.
- Assessor effort increases as the difficulty to achieve consensus increased.
- Assessors find it hardest to differentiate between partially and largely when rating processes.

Some other general conclusions of the report are:

1. The median number of projects assessed per Organizational Unit was 1, but goes as high as 26.
2. The median number of process instances per assessment was 6.5.
3. In general, the attributes corresponding to the higher Capability Levels less often receive the higher ratings than those corresponding to the lower Capability Levels. In a significant number of cases process instances failed to achieve a particular Capability Level because of inadequacies at the previous level, rather than at the level in question.
4. The most costly activity during an assessment is the collection of evidence (47% of assessment effort), and the least costly is the final presentation (3% of effort). Preparation consumed 12% of the total assessment effort [averages given].
5. The median cost of an assessment is US $833 per process instance assessed.
6. The median experience of competent assessors in software engineering is 12 years, and the median experience with assessments is 3 years.

7. Approximately 83% of the competent assessors had received prior training on assessments and 93% received training on 15504 specifically.

In addition, there are a wide variety of experience reports published in magazines and SPICE conferences [69].

## Space industry: risk oriented process assessment

The space industry experience with ISO/IEC 15504 is focused on the efforts of the European Space Agency (ESA) through the quality department of the European Space Research and Technology Centre (ESTEC) who are actively sponsoring and using the standard.

The space industry has particular requirements due to human safety and mission criticality concerns (it is hard to recall a space probe to a repair depot!). Mistakes made with software are harder to correct when a space mission has been launched, although earth orbit missions (such as communications satellites and ground observation satellite) are now able to accept some reprogramming while in orbit. In addition, the computing processing capability is restricted both in terms of processing power (MIPS), and in the types of processor that are qualified for space use. The latter is important as space radiation effects can cause processing failures in unqualified integrated circuit electronics. Thirdly, space projects take a long time from instigation to completion, and have to be supported even longer (10-15 years is not unusual).

Therefore, the space industry has taken an appropriately conservative approach to software development with highly specified system and software engineering processes and documentation. The approach has a strong Risk Management focus in addition to the expected management and engineering process focus. The approach is documented in a series of standards called the European Cooperation for Space Standardisation (ECSS) standards that are the result of cooperation between the European Space Agency and its industrial partners.

Risk management in the space industry includes processes to ensure the required degree of safety and dependability of the software product (where required by the system/software criticality classification). In addition, there are processes to ensure that independent software verification and validation will be performed throughout development by a team of specialists from all disciplines including software product assurance (again where required by the system/software criticality classification). Industry organizations maintain an active risk management approach as mitigating risks is more efficient and effective than having to handle risks that eventuate into problems. Organizations make use of risk folders to monitor risks and take analysis and mitigation actions as needed.

The European Space Research and Technology Centre recognized the domain specific needs of the space industry when adopting ISO/IEC 15504 and sponsored development of SPiCE for SPACE [70] which incorporates ECSS specific needs including additional processes, base practices and work products.

During my time in SYNSPACE, we were heavily involved in this sector and worked closely with European Space Agency in development and deployment of space specific process assessment.

Processes designed to reduce risk include Independent Software Verification and Validation (ISVV), Safety and Dependability Analysis, Information Management (to handle formal communications between large industry contractor groups), Contract Maintenance and the Risk Management process itself. See the Reference book for details of the SPiCE for SPACE process assessment model.

The Risk Management process encompasses additional base practices to manage approval of acceptable/resolved/unresolved risks, communicate risks and risk trends, escalate risks to management and subject residual risks to formal acceptance by management.

Process assessments in the space industry include assessment of several of these processes required by contract (with their additional base practices and work products). Assessment of the Risk Management process is commonly performed for space software projects.

In addition to the SPiCE for SPACE process assessments, an extension to the method called RISK for SPACE is used to provide a means to associate risks with processes and process capability gaps. See the section **Process-oriented risk analysis and capability gaps** in chapter 6 for Target Profiles and Capability Determination for a general overview of the risk analysis method.

The risk analysis is performed after the capability determination process assessment.

First, the potential process risks are identified from a risk-process matrix based using the process capability gap for the assessed processes. The identification provides a list of all the potential risks associated to the processes defined in the assessment scope.

Then the risks are assessed as acceptable or not. This is based on the gap between a desired target capability and the assessed capability. Not all risks need mitigation; some will be acceptable as there will be no capability gap, while others will require further assessment for possible risk mitigation.

Next, (provisional) cumulative risk likelihood is calculated using the capability gap, specifically the Process Attribute gaps – which are summed according to a specific formula. This cumulative likelihood is normalized and scaled (on a scale of 1 to 5) to fit the risk management scale used in the space risk standards [71].

Acceptable risks are submitted to a control and monitoring process. These risks are directly accepted if all the related processes simultaneously are Fully achieved at the target level. If one of the processes is rated below the target level, the acceptance of the associated risk is postponed until the risk has been assessed in a risk workshop.

The risk workshop is run (by the assessors/improvement planners) as a supplement to a process improvement workshop with the assessed organization. The process improvement workshop is normally performed with participants from the organizational units that were assessed, and is based upon the assessment results, containing findings, strengths, weaknesses and opportunities for improvement (see Assessment report template in Annex 3). After the initial process assessment report and recommendations are discussed, the risk workshop is performed. The method is described and the cumulative likelihood results are shown. Each risk with a high or medium cumulative likelihood is described. Depending upon the time allowed, between 20 and 40 of the generic process risks may be described. It is also usual to capture the participants' estimation of the risk likelihood. This allows participants to indicate where organizational factors can influence risk likelihood (for example small teams may have simplified project communication and information sharing regimes that adequately mitigate associated communications risks).

The risk workshop participants act as a 'jury of expert opinion' on the likely consequences (and hence severity) if the risk was assumed to occur. The expert opinion takes into account the types of risk based on the capability gap and the level at which the gap occurs. For example, the risk severity of a risk due to a process capability gap at level 1 (for example a base practice is not performed) is much more likely to be severe than a risk associated with a gap at Capability Level 4 or 5.

The severity ranges from catastrophic to minimal and is normalized (on a scale of 5 to 1).

The risk index is calculated (likelihood times severity) for each risk. This can be calculated for the tool based cumulative likelihood and the participant estimated likelihood. The risks are then ranked based upon the risk index.

**Table 28. Risk Index – Risk Magnitude Likelihood vs. Severity**

| | S=1 | S=2 | S=3 | S=4 | S=5 |
|---|---|---|---|---|---|
| L=5 | A | | | | |
| L=4 | | A | | R4 | |
| L=3 | | A R1 | A | | |
| L=2 | R3 | | A | A | |
| L=1 | | | R2 | | A |
| Cost | S=1 | S=2 | S=3 | S=4 | S=5 |

The risks within the dot patterned magnitude areas with Risk Index $\geq 10$ are used as an additional input to the selection of process improvement actions. Project Managers in particular find this risk supplement to the process assessment improvement suggestions as very useful, as they can:

- select improvement actions that address both current process weaknesses and reduce possible project risks;
- select improvement actions that can significantly change the Capability Level of specific processes, for example to drive improvements to achieve Capability Level four for key processes such as software design or project management;
- use the risk orientation to convince senior management of the need to perform improvement actions, even when no existing specific problem is evident; and
- use the risk list created as an additional monitoring aid to their ongoing project risk management.

Senior managers also find the future oriented aspects associated with this form or risk oriented process assessment to also be useful, not only for monitoring existing projects but also for planning of new projects.

## Consumer Electronics - the Philips experience

Philips NV is based in Eindhoven, Netherlands. Philips NV like most well established technology firms has software development groups that use formalised software development lifecycles with iterative cycles.

Amongst its many businesses and divisions, it runs a large research and development campus where research into new products is performed. Philips research is a very knowledge centric business. Researchers in Information Society Technologies propose concepts, some of which are developed into prototypes and then marketable products.

Within Philips Research, the Software Engineering Services group produces both prototype and working products from these concepts. The SES group may deploy between four and ten teams simultaneously onto a variety of projects. The software development team uses Extreme Programming coupled with SCRUM and ISO9001. The team has been successfully using this composite methodology for over four years.

The author re-interviewed The SES Manager in 2005 to determine the current status of their experience. The SES Manager stated that the role of Software Engineering Services is to:

- Perform software engineering activities for research groups, high technology centre habitants and other organizations (mostly but not exclusively in Philips).
- Knowledge acquisition and anchoring regarding problem domains which are of interest to customers.
- Reuse of knowledge/components across customer boundaries.
- Development of an agile (lightweight) iterative and incremental process, tailored for an organization who wants to facilitate change, and accompanied with state of the art development environment and tools.

Their methods and tools include Visual C++, Eclipse, OO, UML, eXtreme Programming (XP), xUnit, TM SDE, and they develop products for Linux, UNIX and Windows OSes. Their projects are typically small to medium sized, classified as:

- Experimental projects (< 4 months, 1.25 software engineers), project issues are typically speed, feedback, flexible, uncertainty.
- Prototypes (4-9 months, 2-4 software engineers, project issues are typically "agreed" quality, reuse, appealing, proof of concept, which platform.
- King Size (1-1.5 year, > 4 software engineers), project issues are typically quality, control, maintenance, transition.

The group performed a process assessment to show their customers that their approach was compatible with the Philips quality system. The process assessment model and method required adaptation and interpretation to match the agile methods used. The process assessment helped a little to refine the application of Extreme Programming, SCRUM and ISO 9001. More importantly for SES, the process assessment results demonstrated that the group could achieve the customer-desired quality and project performance.

The experience of the group shows that they more often achieve higher customer satisfaction levels than other Philips software development groups using more traditional software development methodologies.

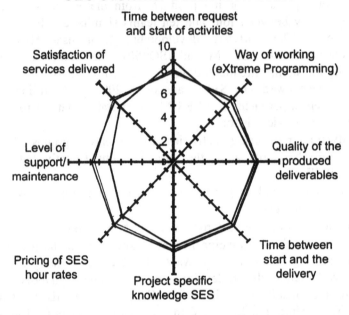

**Fig. 47. Customer satisfaction.**

The group now has grown to 60 software engineers. It has customers in 11 research groups and 3 incubators. From its beginning as a small and experimental software developer, it has grown to cover delivery of market-ready products. The SES Manager indicated that selecting the right personnel (who enjoy the challenge in rapidity of change and volatile customer requirements) is critical to successful teams. Furthermore, he emphasized the need for training and integration of people into the business culture of the group and into the teamwork approach used.

The SES group has evolved several team oriented practices for personnel, starting with the selection and induction of new team members. New team members must have the following qualities:

- High level of discipline (daily stand-up meeting, test-first development, pair programming, daily accurate planning, commitment to planning, incremental delivery to customer every iteration).
- High quality level focus (simple designs, coding guidelines, evolving architecture).
- Able to form self-organizing teams (feedback, coaching, retrospectives).
- Emphasis on verbal communication.

The SES manager emphasized that higher performance in software development requires a people-centric management approach. This people-centric approach is combined with the agile processes and supported by products that automate part of the process (for example, xUnit test tools that facilitate test driven development). The SES group management actively covers people, agile process and product.

### Knowledge-centric innovation teams

The Philips experience highlights several aspects in attaining higher performance in knowledge centric business innovation. The business culture must be understood and actively managed. To understand the business culture requires an instrument to assess the culture, such as Business Culture Survey [27]. When the culture is understood, it is possible to change, adopt and reinforce the desired cultural standards and performance.

- In the case of the SES group in Philips, the group culture differed from the prevalent software development culture and required sheltering, nurturing and adaptation.
- Potential new team members are carefully interviewed to determine their team social behaviour as well as working patterns

A group working within a larger organisation must demonstrate they meet the larger organisation requirements. The SES group adopted and adapted part of the Philips culture to ease their customer concerns. The SES group adopted a cut-down form of the Philips ISO9001 compliant quality system. At the same time, they adapted it to suit agile methodologies and verbal communication orientation (versus the normal Philips documentation approach).

The SES group used process assessment to demonstrate their ability to meet their customer's expectations within Philips. The process assessment required adaptation to the group's culture to produce a valid assessment result. This adaptation may be formalistically or academically open to interpretation or challenge. However, customers are happy to accept the result because the project performance achieves high customer satisfaction, vindicating the assessment result.

- Building a people-centric business culture and teamwork is not automatic.
  - The SES group faced difficulties in its early existence with fostering a new team approach using Extreme Programming and SCRUM.
  - SES recognises that new team members must have a high level of discipline and they need specific team oriented training. The training focuses on the team disciplines used in software development and the general culture within the SES group.
- Knowledge is only useful when shared and understood.
  - The SES group has found that teams comprising customers and developers develop knowledge and products based upon that

knowledge more efficiently and quickly than traditional software teams in Philips.

- Agile methods help build knowledge more rapidly through continual feedback as each small iteration is performed. New team members learn rapidly from experience team members when working together.
- SES and their customers have found that agile methods are very successful in knowledge intensive businesses such as software development.
- Agile methodologies are not hacking.
  - The SES experience is the complete opposite to hacking. The team discipline through small design, test driven development, pair programming, refactoring and team code ownership actively prevents hacking and promotes good practice.
  - Test driven development requires developers to specify tests that are immediately used to test any code. The test suite continually grows and is automatically run (using xUnit) to provide immediate feedback on bugs
  - Agile methods build and support teamwork.

Over the time of operation of SES, teamwork and high quality through agile methods has become part of the group culture. SES has explicitly addressed teamwork issues in building this culture.

Knowledge-centric business teams require a methodology that explicitly addresses team aspects. The Team Based Business Design Improvement and STARS methodologies explicitly do this. This includes aspects such as team synergy, teamwork, authority assignment, individual responsibility and team support actions. The team aspects must support and be supported by the overall culture within the larger group.

The overall business methodology must handle individual, team and enterprise culture aspects. Most enterprises handle through a range of disciplines (for example through human resource management covering individuals) but rarely have a holistic, systematic approach. Such a systematic methodology is described in the author's new book: 'Reach for the STARS' [27].

### Philips NV Experience Conclusions

Developing software is a knowledge intensive business. The European Union sees research into knowledge intensive industries as strategic to future competitiveness. The research focus on team approaches promotes the team concept as the best way to spread knowledge efficiently and quickly. The European Union targets research in information and society technology areas including the software development industry.

Team approaches coupled to agile development methodologies are very effective in developing high quality software in situations of volatile requirements, when properly applied. Fostering a culture that enhances teamwork together with agile methodologies leads to high customer satisfaction.

The existing ISO/IEC 15504 process assessment standard allows adaptation of an assessment to meet the organisation through mapping/translation and the expert judgement of the assessor. This adaptation is very important when performing process assessment in social cultures such as those using agile methodologies. At the moment, the ISO/IEC 15504 standard has no specific guidelines for this adaptation, so assessors use their judgment. The use of assessor judgement makes it more difficult to ascertain that each assessment would produce the same result. Specific extensions or notes to guide assessors in applying ISO/IEC 15504 process assessment to social-networked team organizations using agile methods are needed. The author is working on this subject area.

Understanding an organisation's culture through Business Culture Survey is a starting point for the organisation to define its desired culture and the performance expected from teams and individuals. It is an input to holistic management of an enterprise. Holistic management covers all aspects of business including its people (at individual, team and enterprise levels), processes and products. It uses a systems approach rather than dividing management into a set of individual disciplines. Holistic management provides the ability for a business or a group within a business to set appropriate standards for performance for all business aspects in a variety of cultural settings. The author's new book 'Reach for the STARS' provides a people-centric approach to holistic management [27]. In the future, holistic approaches must guide how specific assessment approaches such as process assessment are adapted to suit the organisational culture. This will help to promote the benefits of process assessment in organizations that are not process centric.

## Public Institutions: verifying process establishment

The Swiss Federal Strategic Committee for Information Technology (*Informatikstrategieorgan Bund*) of the Swiss Federal Government is in the process of upgrading and standardizing the Information Technology services across the 7 departments of the Swiss government and the Federal Chancellery over approximately 5 years.

The description in this section is based upon papers written by Daniel Keller of the Informatikstrategieorgan Bund, Philipp Sutter and Ann Cass, SYNSPACE AG [72].

The Swiss Federal Government had a traditional, strongly functional and hierarchical organization. The management culture was shaped by federalism and a relatively high independence of departments and organizational units. Working together in the sense of a united enterprise named "government" is still uncommon. Process responsibility across organizational borders is new and unfamiliar.

A process model for IT procurement, development, operation, and service provision (called NOVE-IT) was developed in the first phases of a project of the same name. This model is being implemented by more than 70 governmental organizations across the Swiss Federal Government. This IT process model serves as a framework of guidelines for the homogenous but decentralized implementation and the provision of standardized tools. The process documentation is structured uniformly and simply. It is typically produced using normal office tools and published in the Intranet using a Lotus Notes application.

Experiences gained so far show that the cultural change from working in a functional way to process-orientation is the most difficult challenge of the programme.

The performance of process assessments by external parties is a key part of the strategy of independent quality assurance that has been established for the realization phase of the NOVE-IT project.

### Process Comprehension and Modelling

Process concepts and the process methodology have been developed in various process groups, who worked simultaneously on the definitions of their processes, reconciling their results via e-mail. This resulted in a rapid growth of the documents and their versions, which proved difficult to control. Improvements were realized by using the Lotus Notes application for the management of the process documentation.

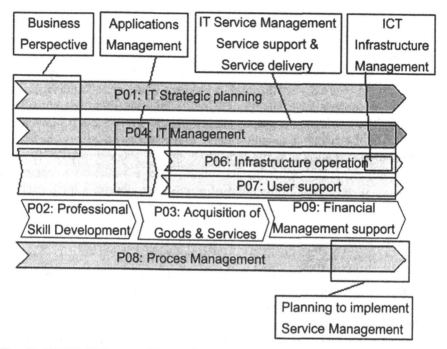

**Fig. 48. NOVE-IT Process Map and comparison with ITIL.**

IT services consumption and IT service provisions in the Swiss Government are defined through 9 IT processes. They link customers (service consumers), internal service providers and external suppliers into common activity chains. The performance of the core processes (P05, P06, and P07) creates the added value for the service provider. The support processes (P02, P03, and P09) are necessary to execute the core processes. The management processes (P01, P04, P08) define guidelines, co-ordinate and secure the process and product quality.

A coarse comparison of the NOVE-IT processes with the current version of the IT Infrastructure Library (ITIL) shows the following differences and similarities:

- The NOVE-IT processes are broader in scope than those described by ITIL.
- ITIL contains only a few clearly defined roles compared to approximately 50 roles in NOVE-IT.
- In some areas ITIL shows detailed task sequences in the form of best practices, while in other areas it just provides general concepts and directions.

- The ITIL processes could not be taken over 1:1 but had to be mapped onto the NOVE-IT processes as end-to-end (from producer to consumer) processes.

The NOVE-IT processes have reached the status of a systematic framework in the Swiss Federal administration, which manages the provision of process instruments and the continuous improvement of the processes. The work of the special interest group "IT Process Improvement Network" of the Swiss association of IT and telecommunication has since then lead to the creation of a similarly structured IT process map. IT Process Improvement Network states as its mission "to advance to a centre of competency of reference in the areas of assessment, design, implementation and improvement of IT processes" and has recently published its own IT process map.

The documentation of the IT processes is stored in a Lotus Notes application that is accessible to all users on the Intranet as a "process portal". From the main page, there are links to the homepages of all processes, each structured in the same way and giving a direct access to all relevant process documents.

The process documentation is structured into several logical levels. A normative process core – spanning all departments – is separated from the rest of the documents. The processes are defined at a sufficiently high level so that they apply to all organizations within all federal departments; the documentation of the organizational management system is not included in the processes.

Levels 0 and 1 comprise the process design and definition, which may include the process description, a graphical diagram (one per process and sub process), role descriptions, and process measurements.

The activity lists of level 2 form the execution-oriented part of the process documentation. They serve as simple and easily understandable descriptions of sequences of actions. They define what each principal role has to do to produce the requested result.

Level 3 defines the "How" and is focused on the details of software solutions and process instruments implemented locally. Therefore, level 3 is available in the central documentation only in small parts, mainly represented through forms and service procedures.

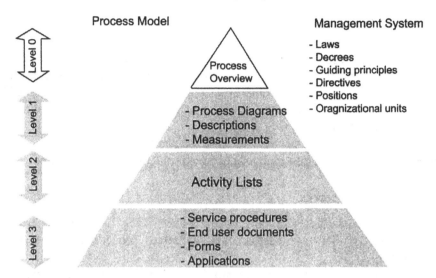

**Fig. 49. Structure of NOVE-IT Process Documentation.**

Each top-level process in the NOVE-IT model consists of the following main elements (figures in parentheses indicate the approximate number of elements in the model):

- Sub-processes (35),
- Sub-sub-processes, optional (60),
- Activities (770),
- Interfaces (540),
- Results (200), some with Supporting Instruments,
- Role descriptions (60), and
- Measurements (95).

## Continuous Process Management

Based on experiences, new requirements or proposals, the processes are continuously improved following the process "Process Maintenance" (P08). P08 comprises measurements, evaluations and continuous process improvement by the process responsible.

Responsibility on the federal level for each process is assigned to a so-called "process group" with the process responsible from all departments. Each department appoints a process responsible per process. A process committee insures inter-process co-ordination.

Improvement suggestions are assessed by the process group, implemented in the process definition and released for departmental introduction in no more than two releases per year. This guarantees a useable balance between stability and change.

The process responsible bears the responsibility for the correct usage and improvement of the processes. Line management is responsible for the process performance of their employees and supports the process responsible in the process improvement. Critical success factors for the continuous process management are:

- A good collaboration between the process and line organizations
- Regular feedback through internal and external process assessments

### Process Assessments

Process assessments are a part of the NOVE-IT process P08 "Process Management". For all assessments, detailed procedures have been elaborated.

- Individual Process Assessment: provide a means for the line manager to discuss the processes and possible improvements in an open meeting with each employee.
- Periodic Process Assessment: the maturity of the process is derived in a structured self-assessment by the process responsible. The result of the evaluation is a quantitative measurement of process maturity. Through direct involvement of an executive manager, decisions on improvement plans can be made as part of the assessment.
- External Process Assessment: using ISO/IEC 15504-like assessments as a means of evaluating both the NOVE-IT processes themselves (as defined in the NOVE-IT process model and supported by various templates and tools) as well as their degree of implementation in the assessed organizational units. The main focus of the assessments is on capability determination. The results however will later on be taken as input into the continuous process improvement cycle.

**Table 29. NOVE-IT Assessment types**

|  | Individual Process Assessment | Periodic Process Assessment | External Process Assessment |
|---|---|---|---|
| Rating Model | Open checklist | Checklists, criteria catalogue, process index | ISO/IEC TR 15504, NOVE-IT process model |
| Size | Approx. 1h | ½ day | 3-5 days, 8-10 group interviews |
| Methods | Interview | Structured self-assessment (review) | Assessment method (group interviews) |
| Roles | Line manager, individual | Process owner, executive management, process team members | Assessor team (internal or external), process users |
| Results | Improvement proposals | Index, measures | Capability level, report |
| Objective | Process improvement | Continuous improvement, fulfilment of middle term objectives, process maturity | Cultural change, determination process maturity, process improvement |

## Assessment method

During the preparation of the first assessments, a custom assessment model was derived from the NOVE-IT process model. The model adopts the structure of the exemplar model in ISO/IEC TR 15504-5:1998, for example regarding the dimensions of the model, its elements and indicators. It consists of a two-dimensional system of processes and ratings.

The process dimension was taken over more or less unchanged from the NOVE-IT process model. Processes and sub-processes become the main elements of this dimension. Indicators are formed as the equivalent of base practices and work products from similar parts of the NOVE-IT process model. Interfaces between the processes in NOVE-IT for example could be used in many cases to represent work products; sub-sub-processes or groups of activities formed the base practices.

The capability dimension was taken over from ISO/IEC TR 15504-2 unchanged. The model therefore has the Capability Levels 0 to 5 with the 9 attributes as defined in ISO/IEC TR 15504-2.

NOVE-IT assessments follow the seven classic steps of Initiation, Planning, Briefing, Data Collection, Process Rating and Reporting. Objective evidence of process performance and capability is collected through interviews with organizational staff and the examination of project documents.

Although originally the project planned to establish the NOVE-IT assessments as conformant with ISO/IEC 15504, the complex relationship between the NOVE-IT processes and the ISO/IEC TR 15504 processes in Part Two made establishing an algorithm for converting ratings difficult and time-consuming. As formal conformity as specified in ISO/IEC 15504 is not a primary requirement for the project, it was decided to abandon this effort. Therefore although clearly the NOVE-IT assessment method follows the requirements of ISO/IEC 15504 "in spirit", no formal proof of conformity was established for the assessment model.

### Assessment performance

The performance of external process assessments has proved difficult, because, among other reasons, the effort needed to perform the full evaluation can be high, both on the side of the organizational unit assessed and for the assessment team. Approximately 25 to 30 assessor days per process (note: a NOVE-IT process is equivalent to a process category in ISO/IEC 15504) have been reported in NOVE-IT. The external process assessments can therefore not be used to evaluate the full extent of all processes in all departments in the Swiss Government; instead, external process assessments are mainly used in focused areas for an in-depth analysis of specifically chosen parts of processes and organizational units.

The large amount of effort required for NOVE-IT assessments may seem surprising at first glance, particularly in comparison with other published results. For example, in a series of ISO/IEC 15504 conformant assessments of space software suppliers sponsored by the European Space Agency, an average effort of 4.5 person-days per process has been reported. However, it must be stressed that these assessments were of individual software development projects. In NOVE-IT, the processes describe organizational activities that in most cases are not project-based. A larger number of interviews with different process roles are necessary to collect sufficient evidence for judging the process performance and capability of an organization. In addition, the granularity of what NOVE-IT calls a "process" is 3 to 10 times larger than the typical ISO/IEC 15504 process. NOVE-IT covers a broader area of activities with 9 processes compared to ISO/IEC 15504 with its 40 processes. META Group concluded that the efforts for NOVE-IT assessments meet or even undercut their benchmark data.

### Benefits and Cost Effectiveness of Process Assessments

The feedback from assessed organizations regarding the benefits and cost effectiveness of external process assessments is mixed. It is however sure that without comparable and standardized assessments the status of implemented processes is not objectively measurable. The performance of assessments that openly evaluate and rate existing processes is a new element in the organizational culture. The effort in relation to the benefits has been specifically analysed for external process assessments. The Swiss Federal Strategy Unit for Information Technology commissioned the consultancy META Group to conduct a study comparing the experiences of performed NOVE-IT external assessments with benchmark data from other organizations [73]. The results of this study can be summarized as follows:

- The basic requirements are fulfilled through a transparent and pragmatic utilization of the standard ISO/IEC TR 15504.
- The cost-value ratio of IT process assessments is directly defined through the productivity gain reached. There are examples in the IT area where substantial yearly increases in productivity have been reported.
- First-time assessments entail higher costs; however costs can be cut down on follow-up assessments through several measures. Proposals include the build-up of internal assessor know-how and the use of mixed assessment teams.
- The study proposes an evaluation over the full area of all NOVE-IT processes based on a simplified evaluation model. The Process Assessment Light method has been developed specifically for this task.

Despite the effort required, the Swiss Federal Strategic Committee for Information Technology of the Swiss Federal Government believes it provides an attractive cost/benefit to have a Process Assessment Model that matches the needs of the 70+ government organizations that will be assessable using the model.

### Process Assessment Light

The purpose of Process Assessment Light is to provide a means, with a minimum of effort, of efficient full-scale process assessment coverage of the Swiss Government IT processes (under the SWISS NOVE-IT initiative). Process Assessment Light consists of two parts:

- A tool, an MS EXCEL-based questionnaire
- A procedure that defines how Process Assessment Light is performed

Process Assessment Light [74] is based on this assessment model of the external process assessment. However to make for a quicker evaluation and to keep the effort needed on both the side of the assessment team and the assessed organization low, Process Assessment Light focuses on the requirements of Capability Level 1 of the assessment model, the process performance as evidenced by its executed base practices and the created work products.

In addition to that, the existence of the primary roles as required in the NOVE-IT process model is evaluated. Roles must be allocated to persons who have the necessary skills and time to perform their tasks. In this aspect, Process Assessment Light also evaluates practices associated with Capability Level 3 of ISO 15504. Some NOVE-IT processes also define so-called scenarios, paths through the process that are typical or that define variants of how the specific process may be instantiated. The existence and use of the scenarios in these cases is also part of the evaluation with a "Process Assessment Light".

### *Process Assessment Light Forms*

Process Assessment Light is based on forms that help the assessment team during the evaluation. For each of the 9 NOVE-IT processes a form consisting of several pages has been developed. The forms are implemented in MS Excel that helps to perform some necessary calculations and allows for an electronic delivery of all questions to the assessed organization before the assessment, as well as the results collected in the evaluation meeting. Detailed information regarding the facts that are evaluated (e.g. a specific work product) is available in tool tips that appear automatically if the mouse is moved over the question. Answers typically are given using the scale as defined in ISO 15504

- Not achieved (0 – 15%)
- Partially achieved (16 – 50%)
- Largely achieved (51 – 85%)
- Fully achieved (86 – 100%)

As a fifth option, "Not relevant" may be chosen under specific circumstances, but a reason must always be given (for example if an element has to be performed on the federal level but is assessed on departmental level, or if some element is ready to be used but has not been performed yet).

The forms have the following structure:

- The front page contains a summary of the information collected for all sub-processes; it also contains information about the conduct of the evaluation meeting (participants, date etc.). The front page also allows tailoring of the rest of the questionnaire. If specific sub-processes will not be evaluated this is noted on the front page, in which case the pages for these sub-processes will automatically become hidden.
- One page for the process itself contains questions regarding
  - Roles
  - Process instruments
  - Interfaces (input and output work products)
- Each process is evaluated on a separate page. They are evaluated for the performance of the specified chain of base activities.

- At the end of the questionnaire a special page gives all participants the possibility to collect problems found and remarks, both regarding the process and the PAL.

Whenever the questionnaire asks for work products, the tool allows one to provide a rating in the usual NPLF scale, and it allows the assessment team to specify if individual examples of a specific work product have been seen.

| Informatikstrategieorgan Bund ISB<br>Swiss federal strategy unit for<br>information technology FSUIT | | Eidgenössisches Finanzdepartement EFD<br>Federal Department of Finance FDF<br>Département fédéral des finances DFF<br>Dipartimento federale delle finanze DFF |
|---|---|---|
| **PROCESS ASSESSMENT LIGHT** | | **QUESTIONNAIRE** |
| NOVE-IT Process Documentation Release 2.01 | | Version 0.9a April 17, 2003 |

**P05.01 Initialise IT projects**

| Base Activities | | | |
|---|---|---|---|
| 1. The **project manager** establishes a project handbook with the IT guidelines, a risk analysis and remedial actions, project description, QA and CM plan, procedure model, project infrastructure and project organisation. | Not Achieved | ▼ | 0% |
| 2. The **project manager** establishes a project plan containing the planning of the efforts, the fixed dates and the working resources (personnel and utilities). | Not Achieved | ▼ | 0% |
| 3. The **project manager** and the **IT security commissioner** decide on the objects to be protected, categorise them and establish the checklists needed. | Not Achieved | ▼ | 0% |
| 4. The **project manager** establishes the PCO report and the project request. The **account manager** establishes an offer for parts or the whole of the project. The **quality assurance person** reviews the request. | Not Achieved | ▼ | 0% |
| 5. The **originator** decides on rejection, abandonment or approval of the project request. If it is approved, the **account manager** establishes a project agreement which has to be signed by the participants. | Not Achieved | ▼ | 0% |
| **Average of BASE ACTIVITIES P05.01:** | **Not Achieved** | | **0%** |

Samples/documents available:

| Interfaces/work products | | | | |
|---|---|---|---|---|
| **Input** | | | | |
| 1. IT guidelines (from P01) | Not Achieved | ▼ | 0% | |
|    IT mission statement | | | ☐ | FALSE |
| 2. Skills information (from P02) | Not Achieved | ▼ | 0% | |
|    Information on available skills | | | ☐ | FALSE |
| 3. Fulfilment of supply (from P03) | Not Achieved | ▼ | 0% | |
|    Delivered goods (incl. note and bill of delivery) | | | ☐ | FALSE |
|    Notification of arrivals (incl. notification of completed installation) | | | ☐ | FALSE |
|    Performed service (incl. documentation) | | | ☐ | FALSE |
|    Report on efforts and costs | | | ☐ | FALSE |
| 4. Purchase information (from P03.06) | Not Achieved | ▼ | 0% | |
|    Status of the ordering and billing transactions | | | ☐ | FALSE |
|    Data on the receipt of goods | | | ☐ | FALSE |
|    General agreements with the contractor | | | ☐ | FALSE |
|    General section specifications of the Federation (GSS) | | | ☐ | FALSE |
|    Ongoing and closed calls for tenders | | | ☐ | FALSE |
|    Comparison of offerings and prices, market studies | | | ☐ | FALSE |
|    Supplier evaluation | | | ☐ | FALSE |
|    Evaluations of the purchasing information system | | | ☐ | FALSE |
| 5. Project registration (from P04.02) | Not Achieved | ▼ | 0% | |
|    Project registration | | | ☐ | FALSE |
| 6. ICO requirements (from P04.02) | Not Achieved | ▼ | 0% | |
|    Controlling calendar | | | ☐ | FALSE |
|    Procedure | | | ☐ | FALSE |
|    Templates | | | ☐ | FALSE |
|    Manuals | | | ☐ | FALSE |
| 7. Change request (from P04, P07) | Not Achieved | ▼ | 0% | |
|    Change request | | | ☐ | FALSE |
| 8. Consolidated change plan (from P05.05) | Not Achieved | ▼ | 0% | |

**Fig. 50. Example PAL Questionnaire.**

### Process Assessment Light Procedure

When the work on the "Process Assessment Light" started, it became obvious from the beginning that simply implementing a form as the basis for the evaluation would not be sufficient. It was also discussed if the form should be distributed for a self-evaluation in the assessed organizational unit, or if it should be filled out in a guided interview. To standardize the process of performing a "Process Assessment Light" a procedure was defined. Key points of this procedure are:

- It is performed as a guided self-assessment with duration of approximately 3 hours per process.
- Several key points for the planning of a Process Assessment Light are specified.
- The performance of Process Assessment Light requires several roles with identified responsibilities. Some of the roles come from the process assessed. The procedure also defines the role of a moderator who is guiding the interview session so that it follows the rules set up for the performance. The moderator will also help to provide a uniform interpretation of the evaluation questions and the ratings.
- It is defined how and where the results of a Process Assessment Light are used.

## Offshore Joint Venture

The off-shoring of software work to China is a fairly recent phenomenon. It is experiencing rapid growth. Japanese companies in general led the way into China, but there are also North American companies with Chinese facilities. The use of Chinese companies follows a common offshore development pattern. In the first stage are cost reduction oriented projects involving restricted coding and testing. The second stage involves more extensive software development, including software unit detail design, where the company fits into the customer software project management and development life cycle. The third stage expands to early life cycle activities including requirements analysis and software design under guidance/cooperation with the customer engineering team. The fourth stage involves the ability to perform complete software projects independently. Most Chinese companies are operating in stages one and two with a few in stage three. Several of the stage three companies are striving to move to stage four.

NEC-CAS is a joint venture company set up by NEC of Japan and the Chinese Academy of Sciences. It holds a privileged offshore software supplier position with NEC, following the Embarkation model. It is moving more into a stage three operation after several quality and process improvement efforts. These include:

- Improve the consistency of software projects to deliver high quality software to the client.
- Establish a unified project management system
- Foster qualified offshore developers, capable of precise communication with the client.

One of the challenges of offshore development is the need to communicate very well with the client. This is harder than it sounds. First NEC-CAS needed to ensure that its personnel can communicate well in Japanese. This requires tested language proficiency. NEC-CAS set a quality improvement goal for language proficiency for its personnel and uses a standard language proficiency test to measure this. Of course, language proficiency is only the first step towards good communication with the client. There also needs to be an understanding of the client business needs, the knowledge and application domains, and the client culture. This requires domain knowledge and development of a common understanding of meaning. This is partially addressed by having developers work in the client's premises, so that they better understand requirements and cultures. It also requires them to understand how the client perceives quality. Related quality goals to better meet client needs included improving productivity and reducing defect rates at delivery.

NEC-CAS has undertaken several improvement programs. The first sought certification to ISO9001. The second sought to improve the overall project management and development processes to achieve the above stated goals. Part of this improvement program included process assessment, with an aim to achieve level 5[38]. NEC used internally qualified assessors to perform process assessment, and trained NEC-CAS personnel as part of the overall assessment program. As a result of assessment and the stated goals, the following areas of improvement were addressed:

- Improved software development processes with tailoring to client needs, and creation of a process infrastructure.
- Improved prediction/analysis of defects and quality/progress control of development processes (quantitative measurement). This includes quantitative targets for quality, productivity, schedule prediction and control for each development cycle phase.
- Introduction of a unified development management system that better controls software project progress, defect management and process management (quantitative process control).

---

[38] NEC-CAS used the CMMI model.

NEC-CAS has used a combination of senior management sponsorship and review, project manager/senior developer training and deployment of tools, explicit client support and a heightened profile for quality improvement to achieve its goals.

During my time at the company, a number of aspects were noteworthy. NEC-CAS delivers over 150 projects per year. Projects typically range from 50 to 100 person-months effort over a duration of 1 to 6 months. NEC-CAS uses a waterfall development model very successfully. Some of the reasons for this success are that the overall development cycle is short (commonly 4 to 16 weeks); they review any project weakness after the first cycle iteration and implement improvements in the next cycle; and the client requirements can be set and achieved within a development cycle (reduced requirements volatility).

NEC-CAS has a strong measurement orientation. They use common improvement measurements and project improvement measurements. Examples of common improvement measurements include the unified management method, standardization of the development process, infrastructure improvement and training of personnel (in processes and tools). Individual project improvement measurements include project goal achievement, review and test methods, client communication, and understanding of specific technologies, maintenance and Japanese capability. For every project, NEC-CAS track progress, quality defects and estimation accuracy. They create a measurement baseline based on the prior year's data. Their aim is to improve compared to baseline each year (process optimization – level 5).

For example, they estimate the effort required and the expected number of bugs for each phase of development activity. Their bug model tracks defects per KLOC, complexity and skill needed to fix bugs. Any problem of significance is entered in the bug model for a project. This includes requirements, design, software, test and even text errors. Bugs can be entered by developers, reviewers and managers. The bug model not only tracks bugs, but is also used to predict the number of bugs for each phase of development. If the bug measures are significantly different from prediction, they perform a review to determine why (for example, design review by additional persons is needed or the testing may need to be expanded). The measurement of bugs is used for judgment of the quality status of a product during development and testing, and whether it is ready for shipment to the client.

In a similar manner, estimation of effort is compared to the actual effort to determine if development is proceeding according to plan. NEC-CAS has well over 90% effort estimation accuracy on its projects and its phases. Their measurement system provides them with a database of baselined project estimates and actuals. They use this to estimate new projects. The use of measurement data provides a significant advantage in estimating new projects. As their database has grown with project actual data, the client has high confidence that estimates are accurate. There is another significant factor that must be taken into account in estimation. As NEC-CAS is a privileged supplier to NEC, their estimates are not subject to the common (bad) practice of downscaling estimates in open competitive bidding, in order to 'win the job'.

Any significant problem that is not resolved in the project raises a Difficulty Record follow-up by the quality assurance team. They may review the process and suggest implementation changes or process changes (process control based upon quantitative data). They collect important issues into a yearly report for senior management, which is an input to the next year's quality improvement program.

NEC-CAS's program to embrace level 5 capability has had significant benefits. Quantitative measurement results indicate that NEC-CAS has reduced delivery defect rates by 5.9 times; its productivity has increased by 2.4 times and Japanese language proficiency by 3.1 times. As significant is their high estimation accuracy for both effort and quality defect rates. These provide significant confidence to the client that software will be delivered with the expected quality, on time and to the agreed cost.

## Automotive

In the automotive sector[39], software production is embedded in an overall environment that shows a complexity comparable to that in aerospace or in telecommunication system construction.

The background however, of a tradition in software development, customer behaviour and use of software is quite different, and it is only recently that process assessment of software development has been considered[40].

Cars have since the beginning been products of highly sophisticated mechanical engineering. Until recently, the basic functionality of cars has been covered by mechanical and electrical parts rather than by electronic devices. Customers - especially those who love cars – have tended to mistrust anything that is more complex than a simple electrical drive, mainly

---

[39] The section on experience in the automotive industry is based upon the contribution of Joachim von Linde, SYNSPACE AG, based upon work with several lower tier suppliers to automotive manufacturers.

[40] By comparison, Bell Canada created Trillium in order to assess their software suppliers in 1991.

because they cannot see how such devices are working, they cannot repair nor assess them, and they are suspicious about the possibility and cost of maintenance. In addition, customers traditionally have been paying for devices rather than for functionality.

While an airbus pilot or the captain of a cruising ship has a technical education and appreciates the benefits he gains of his navigation system, steering by wire, or other elementary features, car drivers may rather pay for additional devices than for a new functionality of a well-known mechanical element.

For these reasons, the development of software driven electronic systems started significantly later in automotive industries than in other comparable sectors, and it has been only very recently that the leading role of software for the further development became apparent. Due to the enormous speed of the evolution of software driven systems the automotive industry is now facing a rapid and fundamental change. New methods and processes have to be integrated into the landscape of traditional construction processes that had been stable and well known for a long time. Obviously, these changes are a great challenge to the organizations, no matter if they are a supplier or an Original Equipment Manufacturer (OEM).

Due to the recent move towards a greater reliance on software for functionality and performance, the average process capability for software development is lower than other industrial sectors with a longer tradition in software development. The process capability also varies widely between the different companies. Software development and integration must also use processes that handle the complexity of developing software for multiple types and variants of hardware.

Software driven systems have to be integrated into the existing development and production processes in the automotive industry. The integration of software development starts in the concept phase with requirements elicitation. It then must be included in the planning and construction of electronic and mechanical production lines to ensure that the software is available when required to be embedded in the electronic control units (ECUs). The software process lifecycle must also integrate with the well established chain of tests of parts, systems and whole cars.

Due to their particular environment and the distribution of work between supplier and OEM (see below), leading European companies founded the work group "HIS" ("Hersteller-Initiative Software in der Automobilindustrie") to adapt ISO/IEC 15504 to their specific needs in the "Automotive SPiCE" standard. Work is ongoing to create the "Automotive SPiCE" standard, and give recommendations on the selection of processes to be assessed at the suppliers' organisations.

In the meantime, the leading OEMs have started assessments of suppliers using a relevant process set from ISO/IEC 15504.

For an assessment team performing software process assessments in the automotive sector, specific conditions have to be faced:

## Technical environment

The system to be constructed consists of the whole car including all hardware, electrical and electronic units, and the software functions. The result is a complex hierarchy of projects, in which software development is only a part. All project planning, testing, configuration management etc. can only be viewed in the framework of the whole development. System life cycle processes for the electronic and software units are closely linked to hardware specific workflows of, for example, cable harnesses. Archiving and versioning of software programs has to be synchronized with the overall versioning of parts in the car.

Electronic control units (ECU) generally consist of a micro controller embedded in an electronic system, which enables the controller to communicate with external electrical and mechanical assemblies. For example, electronic control units may drive a windscreen wiper motor, switch the turn indicator lights on and off, or support the steering and the braking systems.

The functionality of the unit is subdivided into those parts performed by the electronic parts and by the software installed on the micro controller. The software is often providing the increasing sophistication of the functionality required. In the latest generation of top of the line cars, the degree of sophistication reached is becoming quite high.

Due to the many different tasks that are performed by electronic systems and the limited capability of the currently available micro controllers, a luxury car may contain up to 30 or 40 ECUs. These are connected by bus systems and form a network, so that they can be controlled and communicate with each other (actually, cars contain different networks for different groups of functionalities which are connected by gateways).

## Process environment

Software development is split between the Original equipment Manufacturers (OEMs) and suppliers. For this reason the processes to be assessed are different in the complementary organizations. The OEM conceives and plans the system development consisting of the ECUs and associated software. They perform system test and integration of the network of ECUs.

In the supplier organisation, the important processes start with system architecture and include all software and system development processes up to system integration and test on the level of the single system or system part developed by the respective supplier.

In the organisation of the car manufacturers, the processes related to software development typically cover the customer-supplier processes, the requirements elicitation and analysis, system architecture, and the system test and integration.

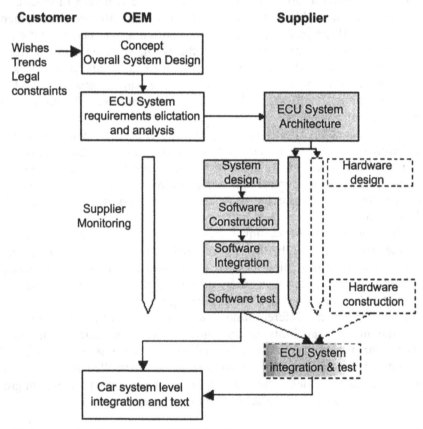

**Fig. 51. Schematic of Automotive ECU development.**

### Cultural environment

Following the arguments given above, electronic system development is still strongly driven by the hardware development tradition. Although this naturally is varying widely between different organisations, a few typical consequences can be found:

- Configuration management and documentation are not yet fully adapted to software development but follow the needs of "classical" hardware development.
- The adaptation of quality assurance is strongly influenced by the "end control" of the production line. The software development specific idea of quality assurance integrated in the development process from the beginning is not obvious to the developers.
- Test processes have to be adapted to software driven systems. Specific methods and knowledge about software testing are presently rapidly evolving. Complex interdependencies of ECUs in the network require an elaborate configuration control as well as an advanced planning of the production flow that is currently being developed.

OEMs currently use software process assessments as a means to raise the quality of the supplied products by motivating their suppliers to improve their development processes. Due to the common subdivision of tasks between supplier and OEM, these assessments focus on the engineering processes and in addition project management and the support processes (configuration management, documentation, and quality assurance).

Process improvement at the OEMs themselves - naturally necessary to keep the same or a higher capability than the supplier - has its main emphasis to processes including project management, supplier monitoring, customer acceptance, requirements elicitation, system requirements analysis/design and the system integration and test. The support processes play the same important role as at the supplier's.

It is apparent that the automotive industry has recognized the challenges involved in the move towards software dependent electronics and is embracing process assessment and improvement in a characteristically comprehensive manner.

The automobile manufacturers have chosen ISO/IEC 15504 as the basis for creation of Automotive SPICE – an industry variant that will provide guidance to suppliers and the car manufacturers. There is a brief overview of the status of development of Automotive SPICE in a section of the Reference book.

## Operational Excellence Initiative - Banking

Credit Suisse has a substantial quality improvement programme under the title of Operational Excellence. Their aim is to create a foster a culture of continuous improvement focussed on delivering excellent customer services leading to profitable and sustainable growth. I met with Jon Theuerkauf the

Global Head of Operational Excellence and Zachery R. Brice Global Head of Execution for Operational Excellence, and discussed their approach.

Credit Suisse is a large global bank with operations in retail, private and investment banking and asset management. Their headquarters are in Zurich, Switzerland. As is usual with many large organisations, it has had in the past a functional organisation basis with the creation of information silos. They have re-organised into a global matrix structure. As the banking environment evolves, Credit Suisse recognises the need to change its way to do business. Initially Credit Suisse embarked upon an improvement program by recruiting many Six Sigma Master Black Belt personnel. They then trained their own Black Belts. All the personnel were trained for situational awareness and analysis, enabling them to recognise and implement opportunity driven improvement.

The management team started an Operational Excellence initiative with the goal to differentiate Credit Suisse from competitors. The aim is to create a business culture focused on excellent customer services, profitable growth, and efficient processes. There is a core operational excellence team that has a training group, a Voice of the Customer team, and communications and human resources responsibilities. They comprise a variety of personnel including trained Lean Sigma trained personnel. Improvement projects are conducted in bank divisions by Black Belts. The Operational Excellence programme is built upon three foundational aspects, namely mindset, methods and management approach (3Ms). Mindset is the way each person looks at what she or he does. It comprises:

- A data driven decision process.
- Active quality prevention, rather than corrective action (Fire prevention versus fire-fighting).
- Improvement is an ongoing and iterative effort.
- Focus on the vital view (critical factors) instead of on many factors.
- Target things that have a bottom line impact by adding value to the customer.
- Challenge the status quo.
- Make speed (process speed) advantageous to the organization.
- Self examination and immediacy in improvement, for example "How can I make something better today?"

The Credit Suisse methods are based upon Lean Sigma. Lean Sigma is a combination of Six Sigma and Lean Manufacturing. Lean manufacturing is derived from the Toyota Production System with its Just In Time and Statistical Control methods.

Credit Suisse have three types of improvement approaches; Quick Wins, Rapid Improvement Process and a Lean Sigma project cycle. The Lean Sigma improvement project cycle consists of five phases: Define

Opportunities, Measure Performance, Analyse Opportunity, Engineer Solution, and Control Performance, commonly referred to as DMAEC. It assumes that there is an existing process to measure.

**Table 30. DMAEC Project Cycle.**

| | Define Opportunity | Measure Performance | Analyze Opportunity | Engineer Solution | Control Performance |
|---|---|---|---|---|---|
| **Activities** | Validate business opportunity | Determine what to measure | Define hypothesis | Generate improvement ideas | Plan and implement solution |
| | Build effective team | Manage measurement | Conduct analysis | Evaluate and select solutions | Process integration |
| | Document and analyze processes | Understand variation | Develop business case | Present recommend-tions | Closure and recognition |
| | Define customer requirement | Determine sigma performance | Establish root causes | | |
| **Key Deliverables** | Project Charter | Baseline performance | Problem statement | Solution report | Implementation plan |
| | Voice of customer | Input, process and output indicators | Data analysis | New process maps | IT requirements |
| | Process maps | Operational definitions | Validated root causes | Process owner committed | New process documentation |
| | Effective team | Data collection plan | | Organization structure impacts | Agreed measures and targets |
| | Stakeholder plan | As-s process maps | | Solutions decided | |
| **Reviews** | Tollgate reviews at the end of each phase. | | | | |

The agreed targets and measures of performance in the fifth phase are customer focussed. Customers see only their individual product or service. Customers focus on (unacceptable) variation in the provision of products and services, rather than assess average performance. Therefore it is important in operational excellence to have customer input (the Voice of the Customer) when measuring performance of existing processes and engineering the solution (i.e. customer needs drive improvement activities).

The third foundation of operational excellence is the management approach. This requires a leadership committed to improvement and based upon strategic alignment of benefit delivery, a customer focus and enabling the appropriate mindset and skills. Creating an appropriate mindset requires training and coaching, knowledge sharing and an emphasis upon fact based decision making.

Strategic alignment and benefit delivery means that improvement projects are aligned with the corporate strategic goals and objectives. Current business performance is measured against the objectives and performance gaps are detected. These gaps are translated into metrics in operational terms such as time, errors and money. This provides a means to identify and prioritise potential improvement projects. Projects need to consider customer, financial, process, employee and risk aspects. This helps to determine the appropriate method to use, whether DMAEC, Rapid Improvement Process, or Quick Wins (Just Do-Its). The benefits are rigorously tracked against these goals. Quick Wins are improvements that can be done without extensive preparation and measurement. They are generally obvious and the benefits are evident. Quick Wins should be completed within one/two days to a couple of weeks.

Rapid Improvement Process (RIP) is a simple concept with an aim to take bureaucracy out of the business. It is a shortened DMAEC cycle time based on General Electrics Workout process. The entire cycle averages one month. The key element to speed up improvement is a workshop lasting up to three days at the end of which there must be commitment to implement an accepted improvement plan. The process consists of four main factors:

1. Decision makers in the organization (for example a region or operating division) define a Business Goal and Objective for rapid improvement. A senior manager becomes the sponsor supporting the process. A core team collect and analyze data and select participants for the workshop.
2. A cross section of people from the organization examines and recommends ways they can implement change to achieve the goals in a workshop, lasting up to 72 hours. Participants form teams and generate ideas why the business goal is not being met and select solutions.
3. A meeting is held where the sponsors are presented with the recommendations, and must immediately approve or reject the recommendations. Rejections may be reworked. The workshop ends with acceptance of solutions.
4. Teams are empowered to implement the recommendations within thirty days. The sponsors and key stakeholders detail time and resources committed to the solution implementation, and then drive the implementation. Reviews are held at 10, 20 and 30 days with a post implementation review at 35 days. This captures lesson learnt including the last approved charter, the process control plan and charts, the key performance indicators, the approved business case and any updates and all actual figures (costs, revenues).

**Table 31. Rapid Improvement Process Project Cycle.**

| | Pepare | | Run | | Implement |
|---|---|---|---|---|---|
| **Activities** | Identify RIP business opportunity. Identify MBB Co-facilitator Sponsor Process experts. | Verify opportunity & business case. Define goals. Determine resources. | Workshop Kick-off by sponsor. Introduce RIP method. Brainstorm root causes. | Detail solution. Pilot solution. Create solution report. | Implement solution Review progress. |
| | Schedule planning sessions. | Complete RIP project charter. | Prioritize & verify root causes. | Create control plan. | Refine solution. |
| | Collect data, VOC, process maps. | Prepare & schedule RIP workshop. | Brainstorm solutions. | Present solution to sponsor. | Track control plan. |
| | Stratify data. Refine project scope with Sponsor. | Define agenda. | Prioritize & select solution. | Approval. | Conduct post implementation review. |
| **Tools** | Project Charter | Cause & Effect diagram (Ishikawa) | Cause & Effect diagram | Brainstorming | GANTT Charts |
| | Voice of customer | Input, process and output indicators | Process Flow Diagram | Scamper | Run Charts |
| | Process maps and Value Stream Model | Value Stream Model | Time Critical Analysis | Failure Modes effect Analysis | Surveys |
| | Suppliers, Input, Process, Output, Customer, Requirements Stakeholder map | Failure Modes Effects Analysis | Spaghetti diagram | Solution report | Final Report |
| **Deliverables** | Project Charter | Baselined process | Identified and verified root causes | Selected solution | Implemented solution |
| | Go/NoGo | | | Town Meeting | Implementation audit |
| | | | | Approved solution | |
| **Time** | 1 – 30 days preparation | | 1 – 3 days workshop | | 2-30 days |
| | Define Opportunity | Measure Performance | Analyze Opportunity | Engineer Solution | Control Performance |

The Rapid Improvement Process has defined roles. These include:

- Sponsor (Project owner) – a senior manager in the business area who has authority to make yes/no decisions on proposed solutions and responsible for follow-up implementation.
- Master Black Belt who builds a relationship with the sponsor and other key leaders throughout the process. This person is the lead facilitator, defines the data requirements and ensures that the sponsor and other key stakeholders support implementation.
- Black Belt, who helps to prepare the workshop, gathers baseline data and helps to facilitate the workshop. She or he collects follow-up data and develops an implementation monitoring process.
- Team members identify and provide data, support analysis of problems, develop and recommend solution ideas and present solutions to sponsors. Team members should come from across the business area so that a wide variety of experience, skills and expertise applicable to the improvement is available.
- Key stakeholder(s) is the person who has a dramatic influence on implementation of ideas that lead to potential solutions. She or he has resources, authority, skills, expertise and technology that assist implementation, and often become the solution owner.
- Experts provide information to resolve technical and functional questions, and verify data integrity. They provide review on feasibility to implement solutions.
- Operational Excellence Controller, who supports the team and its business case, confirms bottom line benefits, and signs off the project charter financial benefits. The controller also assists in implementation review, identifying potential cross area benefits and avoids double counting.
- There may also be on-call resources used by the team to pilot activities, gather additional information and verify its veracity. They may substitute for specific personnel in parts of the process.

The Rapid Improvement Process has many similarities to TBBDI. It is team oriented, focuses on designing a solution to a business issue, empowering a team to make improvements and ensuring they have the resources to do so. The main roles are similar to those in TBBDI. One of the main differences is that TBBDI uses external process assessment standards as an additional input – with an aim to handle Business Process Management aspects. The TBBDI facilitator role is replaced by the Master Black Belt and Black Belt people as facilitators. These people bring a variety of data and statistical techniques into the consideration in the RIP. The preparation time, total time and the approval process reflect its use in a large organization.

Credit Suisse initially recruited many externally trained Six Sigma Master Black Belts and Black Belts. It has recently started its own training courses in its tailored version of Lean Sigma for banking. This consists of several training and application programmes. The Green Belt programme aims to train hundreds of people in lean sigma applied to their specific business area. The programme consists of five days of blended learning (classroom for 2 days, online training for 3 days) and workplace application.

The Black Belt programme focuses on providing people with the ability to work on cross-regional and cross-functional problems of increased process complexity. It consists of twenty days of learning covering lean sigma and improvement concepts (10 days), the DMAEC improvement process model (5 days) and then practical application exercises (5 days). The practical application must address a real business case. Black Belts need to perform three improvement projects providing real business benefit, pass an exam and their competence is reviewed by a panel of Master Black Belts before they can be certified.

The Master Black Belt programme consists of eight training modules. Candidates must choose three modules of initial training. They must have completed or coached a minimum of ten projects, at least one which they run. The projects must be of global reach and importance. Credit Suisse's certification approach for the Master Black Belt includes an interview before a panel of their peers where they 'defend' their certification accomplishments, technical and leadership attributes.

### Improvement examples

Credit Suisse started a DMAEC improvement project to increase the efficiency and productivity of their intermediary channel in private banking. Intermediaries include brokers and investment bankers. Credit Suisse Relationship Managers handle several intermediaries.

In the Define stage they looked at the external and internal pain or challenges that they wished to improve. The project team found that 37% of currently contracted intermediaries were active business partners. They wished to increase this percentage while maintaining profitability. The initial analysis showed that:

- Intermediaries were not serviced proactively enough as partners.
- There was insufficient product information available for intermediaries.
- Intermediary acquisition and relationship management was less than optimal and it was unclear which intermediaries were currently active in acquiring business.
- The selection of intermediaries could be improved to select better business partners.

The improvement project team set several goals covering an increase in mortgage and new asset volumes. The primary metrics were to obtain at least three hundred business deals from inactive intermediaries and an additional three hundred business deals from active intermediaries. The secondary metrics were to maintain business profitability (commission), prioritise the quality of intermediaries (which improves the reputation of Credit Suisse), and maintain a high standard of banking security.

After defining the primary metrics, the team measured them by performing extensive 'Voice of the Customer" (VoC) surveys. They collected 110 responses from active intermediaries and another 72 from inactive intermediaries, as well as 140 responses from the Credit Suisse Relationship Managers. The results were plotted into three segments. The first segment contained intermediaries who generated no business, the second covered intermediaries that created between 1 and 6 business deals, and the third segment covered intermediaries who generated more than 6 business deals per year. The results were subject to a regression analysis to determine whether there were common factors. It was found that the three segments had no significant statistical correlation, so the improvement team performed a cause-effect analysis using an Ishikawa (fish bone) diagram. The main factors included product offering, information, commission, contracts, competition, and image of Credit Suisse.

In the Analyse stage, the team formulated a problem statement and analysed possible causes. The possible causes were subjected to statistical analysis to determine three key root causes. These were the level of proactive contacts, provision of information after a business decision, and provision of information about new products and business changes. The first two causes had a mood median $p=0.00$ indicating a very high correlation to the ability to obtain new intermediary business. New targets were set for each root cause; proactive contacts target a minimum of 4 per year, provision of information after a business decision inside 2 business days, and provision of information about new products and business changes inside 2 business days.

In the Engineer stage, the existing process was improved. A major improvement covered improved client relationship management standards covering contact, cycle time and follow-up. Another improvement covered quality checks on intermediaries. Two other improvements covered intranet and portal improvements for Relationship Managers and Intermediaries.

In the Control stage, the team implemented the proposed solutions and checked that they were effective. Changes included a shift from administration to customer relationship management and marketing, minimum standards for customer relationship management with tracking and reporting, standardised intermediary quality checks, transparent intermediary database, and automatic commission payment and reporting. The result was that there was a 600% increase in the volume of new asset business deals and 5% increase in mortgage deals. This resulted in an overall 64% improvement in the overall business result.

The following Rapid Improvement Process example occurred within a DMAEC improvement project. The improvement team found that there was an opportunity for rapid improvement in the Client ID Establishment Process and decided to run a RIP. The opportunity statement covered Private Equity funds. It found that these funds take too complicated to complete and too long to close. There was a high defect rate resulting in extensive rework and Relationship Managers used other funds in preference.

The RIP group goal was to streamline the process to increase the speed of closing and decrease the defect rate. The project scope would cover direct funds and fund of fund private equity and be cross-divisional. This covers private banking in the USA, Investor Operations, the Client ID team, Fund Management and outside counsel. The group ran a two day RIP workshop to investigate and validate root causes, identify and propose solutions and plan the implementation of the selected solutions.

The participants identified several problems with the current process. They identified four root causes. The team identified fifteen action plans to resolve the issues and selected four potential solutions. These included minimizing defects in one key process; creating standard client documentation, legal roles and responsibilities; and reworking a process to have earlier due diligence. The team redesigned the CFIG process to reduce the process time from thirty days to three days.

Some general observations made about the RIP workshop are that people are highly 'energised' in the workshop by the opportunity to work with people who they normally do not have direct contact with. They are very motivated to find collaborative solutions that help all participants and create better bottom line business results. This is similar to the effect created using Team Based Business Design Improvement.

## Process Improvement Activities in Japan

This section is provided by Katsutoshi Shintani, Process Improvement Task Force, Ministry of Economics, Trade and Industry, and Software Engineering Center, Information-technology Promotion Agency, Japan. In this report, the following is discussed by the task force members.

- Overall perspectives of the Process Improvement Task Force, Katsutoshi Shintani, Software Engineering Center (SEC). The task force was started on an exploratory basis in July, 2005 and after number of meetings, it was officially kicked-off on January 17, 2006. In this section, the outcome from the period of July, 2005 till June, 2006 will be explained.
- Software process improvement models developed in Japan conformant to ISO/IEC 15505, Masa Katahira, Japan Aerospace Exploration Agency (JAXA). Two models have been developed in Japan alongside the participation in SC7/WG10. The 2 models are briefly explained.
- Trial projects of ISO/IEC 15504 Part 5 in Japan, Hiroshi Koizumi, and Microsoft Japan. Japan's long and continuous involvements in SC7/WG10 produced some extensive experience reports in process improvement and its usage in process improvement. These experiences are explained.
- Effective usage of the outcome from the task force, Yasushi Ishigai, Software Engineering Center (SEC). It has been identified that the process improvement is not simply using the assessment results. Enhancing the awareness on process improvement among executives and the line management is considered vital for the success of process improvements.

### *Overall perspectives of the Process Improvement Task Force*

### Background

"Kaizen" is no strange term in Japan. It's been perceived that "kaizen" is one of the strongest characteristics of the Japanese industry as a whole. However, we've been witnessing "system" troubles in a fairly widespread infrastructure, such as security exchange markets, transportation, nationwide banking network, etc. on top of device level embedded software malfunctions. These incidents clearly show that we, in the software development domain, need to look at software development processes in somewhat different perspectives from the past. One is from the perspective of how to deal with non-functional requirement handling, such as considerations on system usage, and another from the system point of view rather than from single software point of view.

## Approaches

After number of meetings since July, 2005, The Process Improvement Taskforce of the Software Engineering Center has come up with plans in the following activity areas:

- Assistance for more challenging process improvement initiatives at companies through:
  - Development and maintenance of a software process improvement framework.
  - Training and following up of software process improvement professionals.
- Assessing and evaluating that process improvement activities at companies are conformant to the framework of ISO/IEC 15504
- Benchmarking Japanese process improvement activities from a global perspective.
- Publicizing Japanese process improvement activities to the world and seeking opportunities for the Japanese activities to be reflected in the international standards.
- Leading Japanese process improvement activities through:
  - Sharing best practices.
  - Sharing results of process improvements.
  - Coordinating process improvement communities.
  - Assisting Japanese companies to become "learning organizations".

## Working groups, the current outcome and following ups

Within the above activity areas, the process improvement task force is chartered to complete the following action items within the three year time frame forming 4 working groups.

- WG1: Developing and utilizing process assessment models conformant to ISO/IEC 5504.
- WG2: Collecting and analyzing best practices for process improvements.
- WG3: Enhancing awareness of process improvements to a wider audience (e.g. executive managers and groups not normally working in software engineering).
- WG4: Positioning Japanese process improvement activities in the global standards.

At the time of writing this report, the following deliverables are at their final draft stage with completion planned before the second quarter of 2007.

- Guide to utilize process assessment models. This guide covers the following topics:

- Principles of process assessment.
- How to develop a process assessment model or to have through knowledge of the nature of a process assessment model.
- Considerations of conformity to ISO/IEC 15504.
- Making use of process assessment results.
• Guide to navigate process improvement activities. This guide covers the following topics:
  - Why process improvement?
  - Styles of process improvement.
  - Considerations on implementing process improvement.
• References to process improvement best practices. The references will be covering the following cases:
  - How CMMI level 5 (Staged and Continuous) has been achieved as a result of consolidation of previous and various process improvement activities.
  - Incorporating testing processes at design stage by designers to discover possible defects.
  - Independent Verification & Validation process.
  - Implementing the "Toyota Method" in software development.
  - And a proposal for a reference scheme to process improvement activities.

This task force is not only publishing technical reports and guides to process improvements. It will assist a limited number of companies in utilizing the deliverables for their process improvements, and train process improvement professionals. The training will enable them to enhance their process improvement activities as well as validating effectiveness of the guides and revising them accordingly. Some mechanisms to promote process improvement activities will be developed. These will foster enhanced communities for process improvement professionals and simpler and more effective sharing of experiences.

## Task force members

This task force has 25 members in the following areas:
• Developer of SPEAK, an ISO/IEC 15504 conformant process assessment model.
• Developer of SPINACH, also an ISO/IEC 15504 conformant process assessment model.
• CMMI lead appraisers.
• ISO/IEC 15504 assessors.
• Process assessment and improvement professionals from industry.
• Managers and software development professionals.

- SEC researchers.
- SC7/WG10 members with experiences in ISO/IEC 15504, software and system engineering and process improvement.
- A university researcher on process and process improvements.

### Software process assessment and improvement models

The models described in this section are developed in Japan and are conformant to ISO/IEC 15504.

### SPINACH

The Japan Information Technology Services Industry Association (JISA) has a Software Process Assessment subcommittee in their Software Process Improvement committee. The subcommittee found in the lessons learned from performing SPICE trial phase 3 that the application of Part 5 model caused a heavy burden on assessment and improvement participants. It concluded that the documentation and assessment method should be upgraded and tailored for Japanese use. In 2002, the subcommittee decided to develop their own assessment model. This would include extensive modifications to the Part 5 model to improve usability. The subcommittee formally announced the SPINACH model in 2003.

There are two models, called Type A and Type B. The Type A model is a simplified staged model. The Type A model uses the capability scale of ISO/IEC TR 15504-5 and the process entities of ISO/IEC 12207. The model introduces the staged approach, which is similar to the maturity levels, as used in the SEI SW-CMM®. The processes/process areas to be targeted and improved are staged according to the level of predefined stages (maturity). As the result of this concept, the number of processes to be targeted and improved in the first (lower) stage of the maturity level can be minimized. In the higher stages, the assessment of particular process attributes which are already achieved at a lower level can be skipped. The aim of the model is to reduce assessment effort (lightweight assessment). Therefore the tools (predefined forms etc.) are developed to support this form of lightweight assessment.

The Type B model is basically developed using ISO/IEC TR 15504-5. It uses selected processes, and is simplified from the viewpoint of capability perspective. The explanation was rewritten to make it easier to read and to improve utilization. The concept of this model is to focus on the pre-selected processes based on the company's unique business model for process assessment and improvement. Several business models can be considered. The normal target business model is "A development organization which develops software based on requirements for various domains, with specified maturity levels within system development". In other words, the software is not intended for special specific domains. This is typically of small-middle range software house business models. In addition, the development of the Type B model is preparing extensions according to business models as needed. It is not only simplifying the overall process model, but also focusing on key processes that could cause or mitigate problems. In addition, the measurement method guideline was further strengthened from that in ISO/IEC 15504 because of the importance of measurement during Software Process Assessment. The following 11 processes, out of all 40 processes defined in ISO15504-5 [new Process Identifier follows] are adopted as being particularly important:

- CUS. 3   Requirements Elicitation [ENG.1]
- ENG1.2   Software Requirements Analysis [ENG.2]
- ENG1.3   Software Design [ENG.5]
- ENG1.4   Software Construction [ENG.6]
- ENG1.5   Software Integration [ENG.9]
- ENG1.6   Software Testing [ENG.8]
- ENG1.7   System Integration and Testing [ENG.7]
- ENG.2    System and Software maintenance [ENG.12]
- SUP.1    Documentation [SUP.7]
- SUP.2    Configuration Management [SUP.8]
- MAN.2    Project Management [MAN.3]

The models have been used in trials. One result is a shortened timescale for assessments with the lightweight model. There is no restricted requirement for the assessment team organization. Questionnaire checklists and input support tools were developed for assessment with Type A model, and it can be also used for Type B model

## SPEAK

When core members, who later have become key role players in SPEAK model development, attended assessor training course, they recognized that their own model could be developed. It is the derivation of EFRAME, a development methodology conformant to ISO/IEC 12207 at ENICOM, a subsidiary company of Nippon Steel Corporation. It did not directly refer to the SEI CMMI®, but referred to SCAMPI as an assessment method. The aim of the SPEAK model developers was to address several issues:

- Reorganization of software process improvement, especially CMMI, inside and outside of Japan.
- Increase in the number of cases that objective proof of development capability is required from the customer as a contract condition.

- Common understanding that better process capability/maturity results in better quality products.
- NS Solutions Corporation, also a subsidiary company of Nippon Steel Corporation, reinforces the company wide improvement activity.

In 2002, the team released the first version of SPEAK. They released a modified version in 2003. The SPEAK model has not been made available to the public yet. It will be released to the public as part of the Process Improvement Task Force activities. As of now, SPEAK is conformant to ISO/IEC IS version of 15504. The Process Improvement Task Force will release SPEAK after some necessary modifications for the public release. As a result, some of the technical contents may be different from what is presented by NS Solutions Corporation. The structure of SPEAK model consists of the followings:

- Part 1: Introduction of usage
- Part 2: Assessment Procedures (Implementation Plan, Report Template)
- Part 3 Requirement of Assessor capability
- Part 4: Checklist for simplified assessment
- Part 5: Assessment model (Detail Explanation with Assessment Sheet)
- Part 6: Terminology
- Appendix ISO/IEC 15504

The capability scale is currently based on ISO/IEC TR 15504-5. The task force will investigate changes required for the issued version of the standard. The model can be used for:

- Self Assessment Results based on CMMI reference model (Capability Level 1-2).
- Improvement of Basic Processes for development.
- To aim improvement to level 2 and 3 (and later 4 and 5).
- Establishment of development process which is the main part of system construction.
- The processes targeted in SPEAK are as follows:
  - 7 Engineering processes.
  - 4 Support processes deeply related to ENG from the view of quality.
  - 1 Management process.
  - 2 Organisation processes.

The assessment procedure is basically the same as that defined in the ISO/IEC 15504 standard. The Policies of Assessment are:

- An assessed organization needs to study the assessment model in advance.
- Meaningful assessment can be done only by understanding terminology and goals.

- The assessor performs interviews and helps the assessed organization understand the purpose.
- The Assessor's questions and evaluation should not be ceremonious, and should be substantive.
- The evaluation mechanism is explained to the assessment participants before performing assessment.

### Trials of ISO/IEC 15504 in Japan

In course of developing ISO/IEC 15504, ISO/IEC JTC1 SC7 WG10, the SPICE (Software Process Improvement and Capability determination) project conducted a few trials as a world wide activity. Through these trials, they performed process assessments based on TR or draft version of the standard for several organization, collected and analyzed the assessment result data, and validated and modified the TR or draft. The objectives of the trial were two fold;

- To judge suitability of the document for international standard.
- To study for benchmark the data and effectiveness of transforming the results of different models.

Several Japanese companies and Japan national body of ISO/IEC JTC1 SC7 WG10 made significant contributions to this trial, under leadership of Dr. Kiyoshi Ogawa, who has been the head delegate for the Japan national body of ISO/IEC JTC1 SC7 WG10 for over 10 years. He was the SPICE North Asia Pacific Regional Trial Coordinator (China, Korea and Japan). The following governmental organizations and industrial associations supported the trial;

- Japan Standard Association.
- Information Technology Standards Commission of Japan/ Information Processing Society Japan.
- Japan Information Technology Services Industry Association.
- Union of Japanese Scientists and Engineers.

The trials were performed three time and the lessons learned were captured.

- 1st stage: SPICE project internal trials on selected documents.
- 2nd stage: SPICE project internal trials on all documents.
- 3rd stage: public trials on the published Technical Report (ISO/IEC TR 15504).

Seventeen (17) companies in Japan participated at the 3rd stage trials. The characteristics of the participants vary from some different perspectives:

- Size: from very small team to large enterprise.
  - One development organization of 1~11 members.
  - Three development organization of 11~25 members.

- Two development organization of 26~50 members.
- Two development organization of 51~100 members.
- Four development organization of 101~500 members.
- Four development organization of over 500 members.
- Industries: 1 government office, 1 public sector, 1 manufacturer, 1 communications, and 13 IT services or software industry, 2 internal ITs, 14 commercials developers.
- Eight ISO 9001 certified organizations, 8 ISO 9001 uncertified.

Through these experiences, many important findings were found in Japan and reported to the trials coordinator. .

- First, following preconditions should be satisfied to ensure the assessment effective;
  - To assess organizations and projects, assessors must be selected properly.
  - To use assessment results for process improvement, motivation and basic engineering skills must be established proactively.
  - To utilize assessment results for process improvement, action plans should be focused on engineering staff's productivity or motivation. And elimination of what is known as '3-mu' in Japan in management needs to be done. '3-mu' refers to 'MURI', 'MUDA', and 'MURA', which means excessiveness, waste, and unevenness or irregularity.
- Second, assessors frequently encountered challenges or difficulties, for example;
  - Front line and engineering teams' understanding of process assessment was inadequate.
  - Decision on what to focus in improvement, improve areas of process weakness or focus on increasing strong processes.
  - Lack of clear and effective guidance for leveraging assessment results into process improvement.
  - How to deal with 2nd party or 3rd party assessment in procurement, improvement, or mixed contexts.

Third, the following points were identified in the use of assessment in procurement context;

  - A well known general assessment model, like ISO/IEC 15504, is fairly valid for large scale project.
  - Assessors should have experience in small projects to effectively assess small projects.
  - Assessors should have experience in large projects to effectively assess large projects.

- Domain knowledge needs to be organized and documented, given that processes do not work alone (i.e. they require to be applied in a product domain context).
- To assess both sides of contract is critical. It is important to assess the acquirer as well as the (potential) supplier(s).

The Japanese national body of ISO/IEC JTC1 SC7 WG10 contributed significantly to improve ISO/IEC 15504, based on these trial experiences. The main areas of the contribution are;

- Practices of assessment.
- What makes assessment better.
- What must be done at any conformant assessment, and why.
- The need for assessment results to be comparable even based on different assessment models.
- Series of continual assessments of the same organization by the same assessor are reasonably comparable.
- There are difficulties to compare assessment result for different domain or different processes.
- What are the key attributes to distinguish capable assessors from candidates?

The process assessment and improvement community in Japan has been actively developing knowledge around process assessment and improvement and contributing international activities.

### Effective usage of the outcome from the Task Force

The importance of the role of executives is well known in achieving successful Software Process Improvement. However there have been too many cases, where lack of commitment by executives resulted in failure of process improvement. Therefore, the third working group (WG3) of the Process Improvement Task Force has been considering how to focus on sending the right messages/motivation to executives, as well as methods and practices of process improvement. The following is the working group summary of how executives of both IT suppliers and IT acquirers need to consider assessment and improvement.

There is a need for a paradigm shift regarding business and IT systems. In the last century, almost all the industries in Japan have achieved business improvement to some extent by way of Information Technologies (IT). During this time, IT customers focused on what parts of businesses they should support with IT systems. Although the level of QCD (Quality, Cost, and Delivery) of business activities were raised by the incorporation of IT systems, IT systems still handled only a small part of businesses until the 1990's. In the past decade, the business world has evolved and now many businesses are highly dependent on IT systems. In other words, the success of businesses is totally reliant on the Quality, Cost and Delivery of IT systems. This in turn means they are reliant upon the Quality, Cost and Delivery of the system and software development.

Time to market, for example, is directly linked to the speed of delivery of IT systems. Nowadays delivery of services is equivalent to that of IT systems. At the same time, failures of IT systems mean failures in the business. Quality of IT systems is now playing a much more important role. Accelerated proliferation of IT around almost all the daily activities of ordinary people as well as enterprises emphasizes the situation.

Without quality IT systems, most of attractive and high quality businesses could not be achieved. It is the case especially in the banking, insurance, and financial areas for the past decade. Recently it has come to be also the case in the cutting-edge areas such as cellular phones, digital electrical appliances, and automobiles.

This requires executives in most industries to realize that IT systems are an essential core for businesses. They must raise the Quality, Cost and Delivery of business through the Quality, Cost and Delivery of IT systems. Executives of IT customers need to align the development of businesses with the development of IT systems. They need to invest resources to improve the capabilities of acquiring IT systems as much to plan business themselves.

Executives of IT suppliers, of course, realize the important role of IT systems in the customers' businesses and support them through high quality IT systems and eventually succeed in improving development of IT systems.

## Process improvement as capability and accountability

Since the success of a business is highly dependent upon IT systems, the capability of IT system development including acquisition need to be improved. This has a direct influence upon hardware makers in Japan. Japanese hardware makers are famous for high quality. They are now required to be competitive in hardware and software. The leading companies realise that the functionality of products is becoming increasingly implemented by software. Hence they also realise that minimizing time to market and maximizing quality within budget is achieved mainly by software. The competitiveness of Japanese companies is now dependent on capabilities of development and acquisition of quality software.

This requires them to improve the quality of the software processes. Process improvement covers every spectrum of the system life cycle processes with ways to enhance activities and eventually achieve high Quality, Cost and Delivery of IT systems and businesses. In Japanese industries, process improvement was always present as a foundation for high quality.

Turning to IT systems, we are now somewhat behind the global trends. Continual process improvement is required to be competitive in the global market. It is therefore important for company executives to realize the role of process improvement, not only as a way to implement high capability but also as a way to account for the capability.

In 21st century IT customers should be capable acquirers armed with high capability in systems acquisition and development. Similarly IT suppliers should be much more capable developers if they are to be the best business partners with IT customers. Entering into 21st century most businesses are deployed globally. Players in the global scenes are now required to demonstrate their capabilities of system development and businesses based on IT systems. Process improvement now becomes not only the way to improve the capabilities of IT systems development but also the way to demonstrate the capabilities.

We could describe that the process improvement in 20th century mainly focused on how to prevent problems and avoid risks. The goals of most companies were limited to activities up to level 3 of Capability Maturity Model, which is "defensive" process improvement. In the 21st century ambitious executives focus on higher quality services in shorter time to market with high Return on Investment (ROI) through IT systems. To achieve the goal, excess weight of processes must be removed and organizations must embrace continual improvement, which is "offensive" (pro-active) process improvement. The highest capability level must be the only goal for the companies in the 21st century to survive in the fast moving, changeable global environment.

While this report is written by the WG4 members, our activities are based on the efforts being carried out by other working group members. Without their dedicated efforts, this report could not be completed. We wish to acknowledge the members of the SPINACH and SPEAK development teams, the Japan WG10 members and our sponsors, Ministry of Economy, Trade and Industry and Software Engineering Center of Information-technology Promotion Agency, Japan.

# Annex 1

## Templates and Examples

In this chapter, I provide some templates and examples for use in assessments. This chapter will be of interest to assessors and assessment sponsors (part).

---

### Assessment Plan

#### Introduction

This document defines the assessment input, assessment teams, responsibilities, constraints, risks, schedule and logistics for the assessment to be undertaken at the *Organizational Unit*. It also provides a summary of the approach to the performance of the assessment.

An authority designated by Sponsor shall approve the Assessment Plan.

#### Sponsor

The sponsor of the assessments is:

**Name**
**Organisation/Company**
**Address**
**Phone/Fax**
**Email**
**The sponsor is the *Position* in the *Organisational Unit*. (*Specify sponsor's relationship to the OU being assessed.*)**

#### Purpose

The primary purposes (and the business goals) of the assessment are:
- Primary Purpose One

The secondary purposes of the assessments are

- Secondary Purpose One

Include how the assessment is aligned with the business goals of the OU.

## Organizational Unit

For the purposes of this assessment, the *Organizational Unit* is defined to be (*the Y Business Unit, Project X, etc.*).

## Scope

The project(s) to be assessed at *Organizational Unit(s)* is (are):

- 

The scope of assessment for the project(s) is given below:

| Organizational Unit | Project One | Project Two | Department A | |
|---|---|---|---|---|
| Processes | | | | |
| Capability level | | | | |
| Assessment focus | | | | |

In addition, during the performance of the assessment, the following additional information will be collected:

- 

## Context

The context of the four projects to be assessed is:

| Organizational Unit | Project One | Project Two | Unit A | Unit B |
|---|---|---|---|---|
| Size (number of staff) | | | | |
| Duration (months) | | | | |
| Project size. *Small, medium, or large, see PAQ-Project for definitions* | | | | |
| Location | | | | |
| Business Unit | | | | |
| Demographics | | | | |
| Application domain. *IT, commercial software, space software, hardware interface, support* | | | | |
| Current project phase | | | | |
| Standards | | | | |

## Schedule

For a complete schedule of the assessment activities, see Assessment Schedule.

## Local Assessment Coordinator

The Local Assessment Coordinator is:
**Name**
**Organisation/Company**
**Address**
**Phone/Fax**
**Email**

## Assessment Teams

The assessment team is:

Name, Function (Assessment Team Leader or Assessment Team member), Organization, Email,

Name, Function (Assessment Team Leader or Assessment Team member), Organization, Email

## Participants

The following staff will participate in the assessment(s):

Project One

| Name | Role in Project | Process |
|------|-----------------|---------|
|      |                 |         |
|      |                 |         |
|      |                 |         |

Project Two

| Name | Role in Project | Process |
|------|-----------------|---------|
|      |                 |         |
|      |                 |         |
|      |                 |         |

## Responsibilities

Sponsor responsibilities:
- Ensure availability of resources.
- verify that the assessors who are to take responsibility for and oversee the assessment (the Assessment Team Leader) have the necessary competence and skills
- review and approve the assessment plan (with Local Assessment Coordinator)
- review and approve the progress of the assessment team at defined milestones defined in the assessment plan
- sign assessor logs

- accept or designate another actor to accept the assessment report and record

Assessment Team Leader responsibilities:

- planning the assessment
- confirming the sponsor's commitment
- production and submission of the assessment plan
- representing and managing the assessment team
- ensuring that each member of the assessment team has the knowledge and skills necessary for his allocated responsibility
- briefing the assessment team
- leading the assessment kick-off meeting and the feedback meeting
- production and submission of the assessment report
- quality assurance of the assessment team's performance and work products
- verification that the assessment is planned and performed according to the process assessment method and specified requirements
- verification, that all requirements for a ISO/IEC 15504 conformant assessment are met
- ensuring confidentiality agreements are effected before assessments take place
- submission of Pre-Assessment Questionnaires to the Local Assessment Coordinator for completion and subsequent checking for completeness
- producing tailored Organizational Unit briefing materials
- ensuring participants in assessment are briefed on the purpose, scope and approach of the assessment
- interfacing with the Local Assessment Coordinator on logistics for assessment
- ensuring assessors have access to appropriate documentation on how to perform the defined assessment activities and the necessary competence to use any instruments or tools to support the assessment
- identify mandatory practices for processes within scope of assessment (with support of Local Assessment Coordinator ).

Assessor responsibilities:

- assessing the processes assigned to them
- rating the Process Attributes

- ensuring that the participants understand the purpose and outcome of each of the processes to be assessed
- collecting data in a sensitive, clear and non-threatening way with reference to the Assessment Instrument
- working within schedule to exercise judgment on the adequacy of the baseline practices within their processes in line with the Organizational Unit's characteristics
- documenting supporting observations and references to evidence that emerges during the interviews
- completing assessor logs

Local Assessment Co-ordinator responsibilities:

- ensure the required assessment logistics (e.g. rooms for discussions, presentations, appropriate audio-visual equipment, word processing facilities, escort requirements, and access to facilities)
- be available on-site when assessments are performed
- act as a liaison with Organizational Unit and Assessment Team Leader in assessment planning
- completion of Pre-Assessment Questionnaires (organization and organizational unit/project)
- review and approve Assessment Plan (with Sponsor)
- help Assessment Team Leader identify mandatory practices for processes within scope of assessment

Participant responsibilities:

- Testify to process performance and capability in interviews
- Provide project documentation upon request

## Confidentiality Arrangements

Confidentiality arrangements will be covered by the signed confidentiality agreements before the performance of the assessment takes place.
*Specify any special arrangements concerning confidentiality of assessment results and ownership of assessment outputs.*
- 

## Constraints

Possible constraints may include:

- availability of key resources,
- the maximum amount of time to be used for the assessment,
- specific processes or organization al units to be excluded from the assessment,
- the minimum, maximum or specific sample size or coverage that is desired for the assessment,
- the ownership of the assessment outputs and any restrictions on their use, or
- controls on information resulting from a confidentiality agreement.
  General

- 

  Project-Specific

- 

## Risks

General

| Risk | Mitigation strategy |
|------|---------------------|
|      |                     |
|      |                     |

Project-specific

| Risk | Mitigation strategy |
|------|---------------------|
|      |                     |
|      |                     |

## Logistics

The following resources are required at the *Site One* assessment site:
- *List required resource and designated provider*

The following resources are required at the *Site Two* assessment site:

- *List required resource and designated provider*

## Assessment Performance

The following activities will be performed as part of the assessment at *Organization:*
- Assessment Initiation
- Planning
- Briefing
- Data Acquisition

- Data Validation
- Process Rating
- Reporting

## Briefings

Specify when and how briefings for both the Assessment Team and the Organizational Unit will take place.

## Data Acquisition

Specify how the assessment data will be collected, recorded, stored, analysed and presented.

## Assessment Tool

Specify any tools used for the assessment and how a permanent record of the assessment is captured, to produce capability profiles and to aid production of the assessment report.

## Data Validation

Completeness of data for the assessment purpose and scope will be reviewed in assessment team meetings following completion of interviews and assessment. If necessary, the assessment team may require additional interviews or access to further information if some data is found lacking.

The relationship of indicators to attributes is defined within the process assessment method. The process of relating evidence to indicators will be done during the interview sessions by the assessment team and consolidated during assessment team meetings following interview sessions.

The assessment team members will confer about evidence collected and ensure that there is sufficient data to make a judgment about rating. Where this is lacking or some clarifications are necessary, they will consult with the Local Assessment Coordinator to obtain or validate such data. Ratings will be assigned by assessment team group negotiation and consensus.

## Rating

After each interview (or interviews), the assessment team will rate the processes attributes of the processes assessed by round table negotiation and consensus *or specified means.*

*Capability level ratings will be automatically calculated by the assessment tool, according to the defined formula in the process assessment method.*

## Reporting the results

Provisional assessment report findings will be produced on-site by the assessment team, discussed with the Local Assessment Coordinator and presented to the participants. Feedback from all parties will then be incorporated into the report on- or off-site. The Assessment Team Leader will submit the final assessment report to the Local Assessment Coordinator. The assessment report will be forwarded to the *designated recipient*.

The assessment report will be produced using the template.

## Verifying Conformance

At the end of the assessment, the Assessment Team Leader will verify that all activities required for conformance to ISO 15504 have been followed. The assessment record described below will be established so that conformance can be verified at a later date.

## Assessment Record

The assessment record will contain as a minimum those items defined in the template. The assessment record will consist of:

- Assessment tool data record
- Assessment plan
- Assessment report

The assessment record will be provided to *agreed recipient*.

The Assessment Team Leader will verify that assessment records are complete as part of checking conformance of the assessment to ISO/IEC 15504 requirements

## Assessor Logs

Following the assessment, the assessors will prepare logs for signature by the sponsor.

## Assessment Schedule

| Date | Activity | Assessors | Participants | Project One | Project Two |
|---|---|---|---|---|---|
| **Day One** | | | | | |
| 09:00 - 09:30 | Assessment Team Briefing | | | | |
| 09:30 - 10:00 | Welcome and Company Presentation | | | | |
| 10:00 - 10:30 | Organizational Briefing | | | | |
| *10:30 - 10:45* | *Coffee Break* | | | | |
| 10:45 - 11:15 | Project One Briefing | | | | |
| 11:15 - 12:30 | Documentation Examination | | | | |
| *12:30 - 13:30* | *Lunch* | | | | |
| 13:30 - 14:00 | Assessment Team Meeting | | | | |
| 14:00 - 15:00 | Process One | | | | |
| *15:00 - 15:15* | *Coffee Break* | | | | |
| 15:15 - 16:15 | Process Two | | | | |
| 16:15 - 17:15 | Process Three | | | | |
| 17:15 - 17:45 | Assessment Team Meeting: Debriefing | | | | |
| **Day Two** | | | | | |
| 09:00 - 09:30 | Assessment Team Meeting | | | | |
| 09:30 - 11:00 | Process Four | | | | |
| *11:00 - 11:15* | *Coffee Break* | | | | |
| 11:15 - 12:30 | Assessment Team Meeting: Rating | | | | |
| *12:30 - 13:30* | *Lunch* | | | | |
| 13:30 - 14:30 | Process Five | | | | |
| 14:30 - 15:30 | Process Six | | | | |
| *15:30 - 15:45* | *Coffee Break* | | | | |
| 15:45 - 17:00 | Process Seven | | | | |

| Date | Activity | Assessors | Participants | Project One | Project Two |
|------|----------|-----------|--------------|-------------|-------------|
| 17:00 - 17:30 | Assessment Team Meeting: Debriefing | | | | |
| Final Day | | | | | |
| 09:00 - 12:30 | Assessment Team Session - Report Preparation | | | | |
| 12:30 - 13:30 | Lunch | | | | |
| 13:30 - 14:30 | Assessment Team Session - Feedback Preparation | | | | |
| 14:30 - 15:45 | Project One Report Presentation | | | | |
| 15:45 - 16:00 | Coffee Break | | | | |
| 16:00 - 17:00 | Project Two Report Presentation | | | | |

**Sample Assessment Schedule template**

## Assessment Report

### Executive Summary
The assessment was based on the specified process assessment method (provide details).

The purpose of the assessment was assessment purpose.

The (number of) processes were selected for assessment against a target capability profile. The majority of the processes were found to be well established.

The excellent preparation and co-operation of the project team enabled a very efficient and effective performance of the assessment (or other statement).

Assessment Input

### Assessment Sponsor.
Name

### Organisation/Company
Address
Phone/Fax
Email

### Assessment Purpose
The primary purpose of the assessment is:
- 

The secondary purpose of the assessment is:
- 

### Assessment Scope

The focus for the assessment is the XXX project currently at the XXX Phase. The assessment covers the following processes:

| Process to be assessed | Maximum capability to be assessed |
|---|---|
| ACQ.1 Acquisition Preparation | 3 |
| | |
| | |

**Local Assessment Co-ordinator**

The Local Assessment Co-ordinator for the assessment is:

**Name  Organisation/Company  Address  Phone/Fax  Email**

**Assessment Team**

The assessment team comprised:

Name, Function (Assessment Team Leader or Assessment Team member), Organization, Email,

Name, Function (Assessment Team Leader or Assessment Team member), Organization, Email

**Assessment Performance**

**Assessment Schedule**

The schedule for the assessment is:

1    Pre-site assessment planning (date from-date to)

2    Organisational unit briefing (date)

3    Assessment performance (date from-date to)

4    Delivery of draft assessment report and presentation of results (date)

5    Final assessment report (date)

**Project Participants**

The following personnel from the projects were interviewed during the assessment:

| Name | Position | Interviewed for |
|---|---|---|
| | | *CUS.1.1, ..* |
| | | |

**Confidentiality**

All members of the assessment have signed confidentiality agreements with *assessed organization regarding* the assessment.

**Briefings**

Assessment team briefings were held prior to the on-site phase and at regular meetings during performance of the on-site assessment.

An organization al unit presentation was made to relevant *assessed organization* staff on the first day of the on-site phase.

### Data Acquisition and Verification

Evidence of process capability was collected and established through

- Completion of Pre-Assessment Questionnaires providing general information about the organization and the project to be assessed.
- Interviews using prepared checklists and questions based on the indicators provided by the *process assessment model*.
- Feedback of findings to the interviewees at the end of each interview
- Verification and validation of collected data against documents during and after the interviews.

Reference to evidence was recorded in assessor notes.

The relationship of indicators to Process Attributes is defined within the *process assessment model*. The relationship of collected evidence to the *process assessment model* indicators was done during the interview sessions by the assessment team and consolidated in assessment team meetings.

### Assessment Tool

The *SPICE 1-2-1 assessment tool (specify)* was used in performance of the assessment. The assessment tool is used to provide a permanent data record of the assessment and to produce capability profiles as an aid to production of the assessment report.

### Data Validation

Completeness of data was reviewed in assessment team meetings following completion of assessment interviews. The assessment team followed up with additional interviews or requested access to further information when some data was lacking.

The assessment team members ensured that sufficient data was available for rating the Process Attributes.

### Rating

Process attributes were rated for each of the processes assessed through round table negotiation and consensus.

Process Attributes are rated on a percentage scale 0 - 100% which relate to the following four point achievement scale:

0 - 15% N; Not achieved: There is little or no evidence of achievement of the defined attribute.

16 - 50% P; Partially achieved: There is evidence of a sound systematic approach to the achievement of the defined attribute.

51 - 85% L; Largely achieved: There is evidence of a sound systematic approach to and significant achievement of the defined attribute.

86 - 100% F; Fully achieved: There is evidence of a complete and systematic approach to and full achievement of the defined attribute.

### Reporting

A draft assessment report was presented and discussed with assessment participants on-site. A final report is distributed to *recipient(s)* within three weeks.

## Assessment Output
The assessment output consists of:

| Output | Owner | Distribution |
|---|---|---|
| Completed Pre-Assessment Questionnaires | Assessment sponsor, | Assessment team members |
| Assessment plan | Assessment sponsor, | Local Assessment Coordinator Assessment team members |
| Statement(s) of Confidentiality | Local Assessment Coordinator AT members | Assessment sponsor |
| Assessor notes | Assessment team members | |
| Assessment report | Assessment sponsor | Local Assessment Coordinator Assessment team members |
| Assessment record | Assessment Sponsor | Assessment team members |
| Assessor logs | Assessment team members | |

## Additional Information Collected
Summary of additional information collected during the assessment as specified in assessment plan.

## Process Profiles

## Assumptions
For the rating of the Process Attributes, the assessment team used the following interpretation of the Process Attributes:
Examples:
- *Process attribute 3.2 about process resource, is evaluated only with respect to the definition/standardisation of the process, not as whether the resources were assigned and defined for that specific Organizational Unit.*

- *Generic practice 2.1.2 about the planning of the performance of the process is evaluated considering that it is not necessary to have a formal plan.*

**Process Attribute Ratings for all Processes**

Ratings of Process Attribute profiles are presented using the following scale:

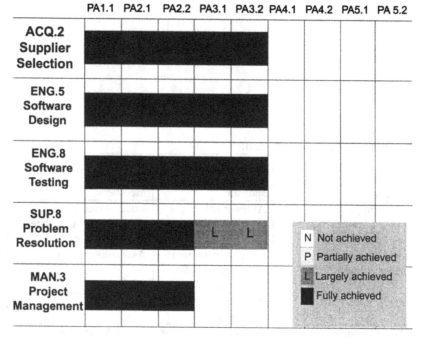

Fig. 52. Capability Levels for all Processes.

**Key Findings**

**ACQ.2 Acquisition Preparation**
   *Summary statement (e.g. "The acquisition preparation process was found to be well managed, but not formally established.")*
   *Objective evidence based on assessor notes*

**ENG.5 Supplier Selection**
   ...

**Observed Strength and Weaknesses**
   The assessed processes seem to be *well performed and managed (modify accordingly)* by the *Organizational Unit*. The processes seem to be based on *solid practices and correspond to the department's business goals (modify accordingly)*. The Capability Levels of the assessed processes may be considered *adequate (modify accordingly)* for the criticality of the product.
   The processes could be improved as indicated to reach higher Capability Levels. Those improvement opportunities take into account the following findings.

**Strength One**

**Strength Two**

**Weakness One**

**Weakness Two**

**Identified Risk Factors**
This section applies if a risk assessment (to be developed in future) has been performed together with the assessment. Delete if not applicable.

**Improvement Opportunities**
List between two and six major opportunities.

**Opportunity One**
. . . . . . . . . .

**Opportunity Two**
. . . . . . . . . .

-----------------End of Report ------------------

## Improvement Opportunity

| | |
|---|---|
| Date: _____ | |
| Improvement Number: _____ | |
| Company/person suggesting the improvement<br><br>Contact information and details<br> Phone<br> Fax<br> email | |
| System/Site information:<br><br>Affected systems, projects, processes:<br><br>Impact to operations of existing systems, projects, processes: | |
| Criticality of request (1 = lowest, 5 = highest) | |
| What is the suggestion/improvement?<br>Reason for suggestion/improvement opportunity?<br>Suggested actions to implement the suggestion/improvement?<br>What is the value (expected benefit) in performing the improvement?<br>What is the penalty for not making the improvement?<br>What are the expected customer response/closure requirements | |

## Meeting register

Organization Unit          Assessment Number:

| ASSESSMENT | NAME | ROLE | ENTRY | EXIT |
|---|---|---|---|---|
| | | | | |
| | | | | |

COMMENTS

## Observation record

Supplementary Observation Record

    Page    of

| Number | REFERENCE | OBSERVATION |
|---|---|---|
| | | |
| | | |
| | | |

## Example Process and Capability checklists[41]

### Process Checklist

Organizational alignment process ORG.1
Organization _____Unit _____
Representative _____
Assessment ID _____ Assessment Reference _____.

### Process Indicator Record

> MAN.1       Organizational alignment process
> The purpose of the *Organizational alignment process* is to ensure that the
> individuals in the organization share a common vision and culture ......

#### MAN.1.BP1: Establish strategic vision.

Has a strategic vision for the organization been established to identify what
business the (software producing part of) the organization is in?

Existence                                          _____

    Adequacy_____

No  ☐ Yes  ☐ Not  ☐ Partially  ☐ Largely  ☐  Fully  ☐

| Work Products | Ref# | Completed | N/A | Notes |
|---|---|---|---|---|
| 13) Vision statement | | | | |
| 50) Commitments / agreements | | | | |

#### MAN.1.BP2: Deploy vision.

Has the organisation strategic vision been deployed to all individuals
working for the organisation, using appropriate management and
communication mechanisms?

Existence                                          _____

    Adequacy_____

No  ☐ Yes  ☐ Not  ☐ Partially  ☐ Largely  ☐  Fully  ☐

| Work Products | Ref# | Completed | N/A | Notes |
|---|---|---|---|---|
| 87)    Communication mechanism | | | | |
| 14) Policies | | | | |

Associated Work Products:

| Input | | Output | |
|---|---|---|---|
| 12) | Business goals | 3) | Process description |
| 13) | Vision statement | 12) | Team goals |
| 17) | Project plan | 50) | Commitments / agreements |

---

[41] This is an illustrative example and not complete. Refer to the exemplar
ISO/IEC TR 15504-5 for the complete text.

## Level 1 Capability Dimension checklist

Practice performance characteristics, resources and infrastructure characteristics and associated processes, listed here, may be used when assessing management practices for a particular process implementation. These characteristics and associated processes provide guidance to find objective evidence supporting the effective implementation of the management practice. A methodology and assessor judgment is needed to ensure that the process context (application domain, business purpose, development methodology, size of the organization, etc.) is considered when using this information. The tables should not be considered as checklists of what every organization must do or have, but rather as a starting point for considering whether, given the context, management practices are effectively performed, thus contributing to the achievement of the related Process Attribute.

Level 1: Performed process (based on ISO/IEC 15504)

The base practices that are associated with the performance of the process have to be considered, unless they are not relevant in the context of this process. Any other practices that are essential to the achievement of the process purpose in the context of this process may also be considered.

NOTE 1 To help evaluate the Level 1 management practices, use the indicators of process performance defined in clause 5 (Base practices), Annex A (Work products associated to processes) and Annex C (Work product characteristics).

Process Attribute 1.1    Process performance attribute.

The extent to which the process achieves the defined process outcomes by ………..

**Generic Practice 1.1.1**
Identify ……

| Practice performance characteristics for GP 1.1.1 | Y | N | N/A | Notes |
|---|---|---|---|---|
| For each process assessed, the input work products are identified | ☐ | ☐ | ☐ | |
| For each process assessed, the output work products are identified | ☐ | ☐ | ☐ | |
| For each process assessed: Associated work products exist, among those defined in annex A of the standard that are applicable according to the process context, | ☐ | ☐ | ☐ | |
| Input and output work products have characteristics to indicate an adequate implementation (see the applicable characteristics among those included in the | | | | |

annex C) □ □ □

---

The identified work products satisfy the purpose of the process □ □ □

---

A mechanism exists to distribute the work products □ □ □

---

Work products are delivered to users on a need to know basis □ □ □

---

**Generic Resources for GP 1.1.1**
- Resources for process performance are available
- See Process dimension

**Related Processes for GP 1.1.1**
This practice applies to each process within the scope of the assessment.

For each process, the scope of work in performing the process is identified
□ □ □

**Record of Participation**

This form is used to record an assessor's participation as a provisional assessor or as an observer in assessments conducted according to the provisions of Part 6 of the Technical Report. A qualified assessor or the assessment team leader verifies the involvement in assessments. Each assessment is recorded on this form and is completed by a qualified assessor or an assessment team leader.

Name of the person: _____

Date:                                                                                    /

No. of days for the assessment:          ☐

Scope of the assessment:          Process categories/areas assessed by the person:

Organization/Organizational unit:

Effective Communications:

| | |
|---|---|
| Were the discussions with the customer reasonable? | Yes/no |
| Was a satisfactory understanding of this Technical Report shown? | Yes/no |
| Was the inter team relationship satisfactory? | Yes/no |

Judgment and Leadership:

| | |
|---|---|
| Were the assessment activities completed in a timely manner? | Yes/no |
| Were the interviews conducted satisfactorily? | Yes/no |

Integrity:

| | |
|---|---|
| Reasonable sample taken? | Yes/no |
| Range of activity satisfactory? | Yes/no |
| Depth of questioning satisfactory? | Yes/no |
| Review of results consistent? | Yes/no |

Rapport :

| | |
|---|---|
| Communication - telling the good and bad news: | satisfactory/unsatisfactory |
| Review of the programme: | satisfactory/unsatisfactory |
| Conduct: | satisfactory/unsatisfactory |
| Team Management: | satisfactory/unsatisfactory |

Comments: (on Diplomacy, Discretion, Persistence and Resistance handling ability)

Performance:          Acceptable/More Experience Required/Not acceptable

**Name and signature of qualified assessor/ team leader:**

.........................................

# Annex 2

## Assessment Tools

In this chapter, I look at assessment tools. This chapter will be of interest to assessors and tool developers. There are several types of tools available to support process assessments. The most common tools are document templates and checklists. Document templates include:

- Assessment Plan
- Assessment Schedule
- Assessment Report
- Pre Assessment Questionnaire
- Meeting Register
- Observation Record
- Process checklist
- Process Capability Dimension checklist
- Improvement Opportunity
- Record of Participation

These templates are useful, help present a uniform appearance, and capture the general information required in the planning and reporting stages of a process assessment. The templates are manually filled in during an assessment, and the assessors then use them as an 'aide-memoir' to analyse the assessment finding and produce the assessment result.

The checklists record the detailed assessment results. While these are adequate to begin with, they do not provide assistance with rating processes and plotting assessment results (Process Attribute achievement and Capability Levels per process).

The next level of tool assistance normally consists of some minor form of automation, for example provided by an EXCEL spreadsheet. The most common automation provided by these tools is in the rating of processes, where the management practices that are assessed as being satisfied are accumulated for each Process Attribute.

Some assessment methods, for example NOVE-IT are investigating the use of EXCEL to translate scores in a NOVE-IT into an ISO/IEC 15504 conformant rating. This requires two dimensions of interaction, the first mapping the NOVE-IT processes to the ISO/IEC 15504 Process Assessment Model and the second mapping to the Capability Dimension. The first mapping in this case is more difficult due to the scope and granularity differences between the definitions of processes.

EXCEL has also been used for a series of tools providing extensions such as Risk for SPACE where it provides risk to process matrices combined with scoring mechanisms.

The third type of tool is one purposely designed for process assessment.

In this category, exist SPICE 1-2-1 and a set of variants such as S4S, PULSE, and CMM-QUEST. SPICE-121 [75] allows users to select process they wish to assess.

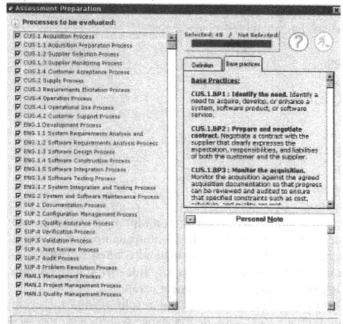

**Fig. 53. Rate the process on the Not/Partial/Largely/Fully scale.**

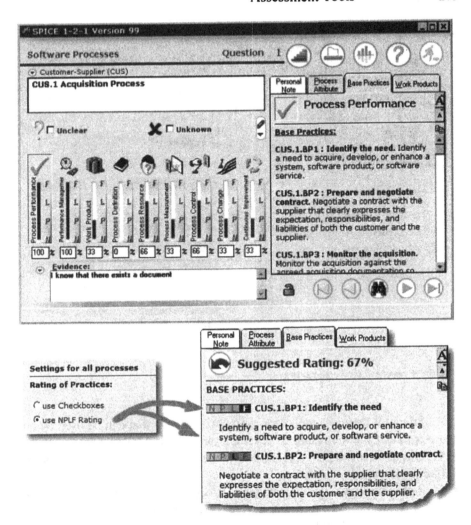

**Fig. 54. Process Attribute rating and Capability Level rating.**

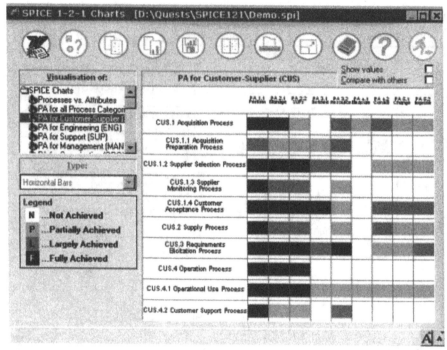

**Fig. 55. Process Attribute rating.**

Additionally there are tools (for example SynEval) that can be used by an assessor to analyse the results of several interviews and assessments.

- Several assessments (interviews) of an assessment week are consolidated (put together)
- Multiple interviews can be categorised to groups and than analysed. The grouping can be done from several viewpoints, e.g. you can group together small, medium and big projects, or compare Host/PC/Web projects, or projects from different departments or business areas or in chronological order (useful for re-assessments).

  This additional level of evaluation allows an assessor to:

- Distinguish global strengths and weaknesses from single highlights/lowlights.
- Characterize each group.
- Identify trends.

  The Evaluation Screen displays the evaluator's desired combination of results.

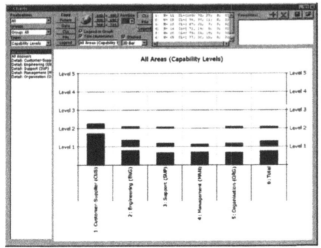

...and additional samples for the evaluations:

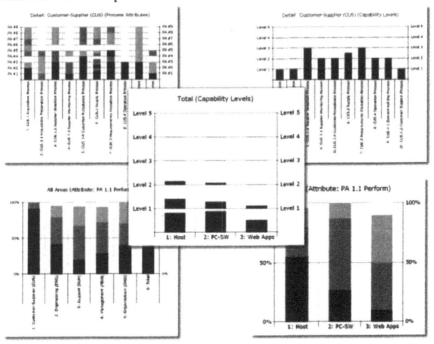

**Fig. 56. Sample rating screens.**

Finally, tools can prove a capability to define specific processes (for example SynEdit).

Other process assessment tools that include a part of this functionality include Process Professional Assessor for ISO 15504 [76] and SEAL.

# Annex 3

## Supplementary Improvement Information

In this chapter, I provide some supplementary information supporting the Business Case - Process Improvement section. This chapter will be of interest to customers, managers, assessors, assessment sponsors, and improvement sponsors.

---

A Business Case for Software Process Improvement Revised [77.] This State Of the Art Report from the US Department of Defence Information Analysis Center describes the benefits of software process improvements including secondary benefits.

The report looks at total development costs, total rework costs, average schedule length and post release defects (delivered defects). It also looks at secondary benefits including the effect of project sales, penalties and bonuses, yearly turnover costs (staff, etc.), repeat business, risks and the cost of improvements.

The report also looks at the risk perspective (risk when performing SPI, and risk of not performing SPI). The two Software Process Improvement risk types are summarised in the following two tables. The risks tables are provided here and support the overall comparison of process improvement metrics table in the Business Case - Process Improvement.

**Table 32. Risks involved in performing software process improvement.**

| Risk No. | Risk Description | Potential Loss | Likelihood | Weighted Cost |
|---|---|---|---|---|
| 2 | Poor training in new methods | $ 1,000,000 | Low | $ 50,000 |
| 6 | Not able to achieve rework reductions | $ 900,000 | Low | $ 45,000 |
| 4 | Inability to achieve productivity goals | $ 750,000 | Low | $ 37,500 |
| 5 | Not able to achieve cycle time improvements | $ 500,000 | Low | $ 25,000 |
| 3 | Inability of staff to change | $ 250,000 | Low | $ 12,500 |
| 1 | Inability to get management support | $ 100,000 | Low | $ 5,000 |

**Table 33. Risks of not performing software process improvement.**

| Risk No. | Risk Description | Potential Cost | Likelihood | Weighted Cost |
|---|---|---|---|---|
| 1 | Loss of key person #2 | $ 700,000 | Medium | $ 175,000 |
| 2 | Loss of key person #1 | $ 1,000,000 | Medium | $ 250,000 |
| 3 | Higher turnover | $ 512,500 | Medium | $ 128,000 |
| 6 | Loss of market Leadership | $ 500,000 | Medium | $ 152,000 |
| 7 | Loss of Repeat Business | $ 4,000,000 | Medium | $ 1,000,000 |
| 4 | Cost Overruns | $ 500,000 | High | $ 375,000 |
| 5 | No award fees | $ 50,000 | High | $ 37,500 |

The two SPI risk types (risk when performing SPI and risk of not performing SPI are combined and compared in the table of process improvement metrics.

**Table 34. Comparison of process improvement metrics.**

| Metric | Without Improvement | With Software Process Improvement | Benefit |
|---|---|---|---|
| Primary Benefits | | | |
| Total Development Costs | $ 2,886,543 | $ 780, 174 | $ 2,106,370 |
| Total Rework costs | $ 619, 369 | $ 26,080 | $ 593,288 |
| Average Schedule length | 27 calendar months | 17 claendar months | 10 months |
| Post Release Defects | 15% of Total Defects | < 5% of Total Defects | 80% |
| Secondary Benefits | | | |
| Projected sales | $ 10,000,000 | $ 10,500,000 | $ 500,000 |
| Penalties/Bonuses | ($ 50,000) | $ 50,000 | $ 100,000 |
| Yearly Turnover Costs | $ 615,000 | $102, 500 | $ 512,000 |
| Repeat Business | $ 1,000,000 | $ 5,000,000 | $ 4,000,000 |
| Cost of the Improvement | | $ 373,000 | ($ 373,000) |
| Weighted Risks | | | |
| High | $ 412,500 | $ 0 | $ 412,500 |
| Medium | $ 1,678, 125 | $ 0 | $ 1,678,125 |
| Low | $ 0 | $ 175,000 | ($ 175,000) |

The report concludes that it is clear from the data presented that SPI can have a significant bottom line cost savings to a software development organization (as much as a 67% reduction in development and rework costs).

The following graphs come from a report [78], which describes the process improvement activities performed at Advanced Information Systems Inc. The paper characterises the pre-1992 completion of projects as based upon individual ability and 'herculean' efforts of the project managers and engineers (typical capability level 0 processes). The organization introduced software process improvement (following the CMM) and in a second step introduced the Personal Software Process.

Carnegie Mellon University
Software Engineering Institute

## The AIS Transformation – Reduction in Effort Deviation

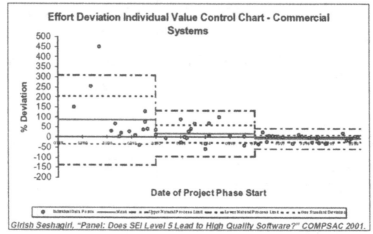

*Girish Seshagiri, "Panel: Does SEI Level 5 Lead to High Quality Software?" COMPSAC 2001.*

## The AIS Transformation – Reduction in Schedule Deviation

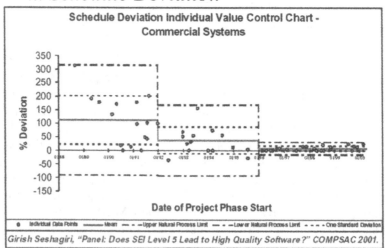

*Girish Seshagiri, "Panel: Does SEI Level 5 Lead to High Quality Software?" COMPSAC 2001.*

**Fig. 57. Effect of Software Process Improvement on effort and schedule.**

The graphs above show that effects of process based improvements in the middle data group (1992 to 1995) and then the effect of introduction of Personal Software Process (1996 onwards). It is evident that the improvements not only improves estimation accuracy but also the ability to work against the planned estimates.

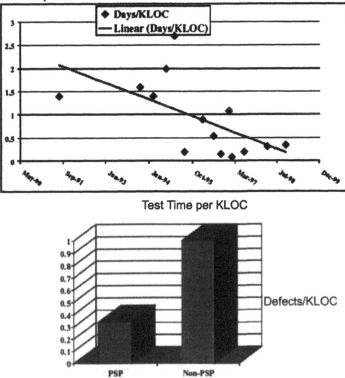

Fig. 58. Effect of Software Process Improvement on Test time and Defects.

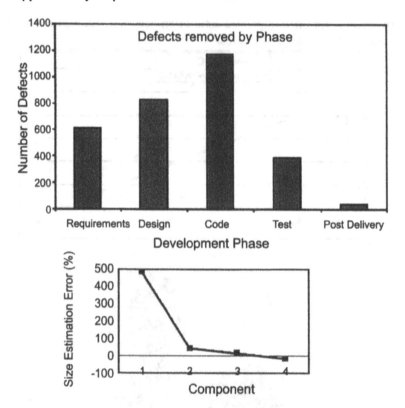

**Fig. 59. Defect removal by phases and size estimating accuracy.**

The report concludes:

- The organizational change has been towards a process culture with an emphasis upon high process capability (CMM assessed), coupled to financial, customer and employee improvement (through Personal Software Process).

- The results of this high capability process culture has been better project effort (cost) and schedule performance (hence lower risk to not performing the planned activities), improved test times and acceptance test defect rates, better software component sizing and more defects removed in earlier development phases.

- The ability to remove defects sooner leads to software entering acceptance tests with less defects, and hence less repetition of acceptance tests (after a test failure and software error correction, it is normal practice to rerun the relevant acceptance tests).

- The shift in defect removal to earlier phases results in lowered defect rates requiring removal in delivered products and hence a lower risk that defects will cause failures of various criticalities.

# Index

# Bibliography

[1] Han van Loon. Getting the Best from People, Process and Product. 1994. www.lc-stars.com

[2] Hammer, M. (1990, July/August). Reengineering Work: Don't Automate, Obliterate. See also Harvard Business Review, 104–112. and Hammer, M., & Champy, J. (1993). Reengineering the Corporation: A Manifesto for Business Revolution. New York: Harper Business Press.

[3] NATO Conference on Software Engineering 1968.

[4] Standish Group. Chaos Chronicles. www.standishgroup.com

[5] National Institute of Standards and Technology, The Economic Impact of Inadequate Infrastructure for Software Testing, May 2002.

[6] Andersson. M. and J. Bergstrand. 1995 "Formalizing Use Cases with Message Sequence Charts." Masters Thesis. Lund University of Technology.

[7] Death March. Edward Yourdon. 2nd Ed. Prentice Hall. ISBN 0-13-143635-X

[8] National Institute of Standards and Technology, The Economic Impact of Inadequate Infrastructure for Software Testing, May 2002

[9] A Business Case for Software Process Improvement Revised. Thomas McGibbon. The Department of Defence Information Analysis Center. ITT Industries, Advanced Engineering and Science Division. Rome, NY.

[10] Investing in Software Process Improvement. An Executive Perspective. Mark C. Paulk. © 2002 SEI. CMU Pittsburgh, PA 15213-3890. Trends in Software Process and Quality. Mark C. Paulk. © 2002 SEI. CMU Pittsburgh, PA 15213-3890.

[11] Demonstrating the Impact and Benefits of CMMI: An Update and Preliminary Results. Dennis Goldenson, Diane Gibbon. October 2003. Special report CMU/SEI-2003-SR-009. Process Maturity Profile CMMI V1.1 SCAMPI v1.1 Appraisal Results. September 2003.

[12] Quantifying the effects of process improvement upon effort. Bradford K. Clark. IEEE Software Nov/Dec 2000.

[13] 'An Empirical Review of Software Process Assessments' by Khaled El Emam and Dennis R. Goldenson (National Research Council Canada) November 1999.

[14] ISO/IEC TR 15504-8:1998 Information Technology - Software Process Assessment Part 8: Guide For Use In Determining Supplier Process Capability.

[15] See ISO/IEC TR 15504-8:1998 Information Technology - Software Process Assessment Part 8: Guide For Use In Determining Supplier Process Capability.

[16] Safety and Security Extensions for Integrated Capability Maturity Models. Linda Ibrahim et al. United States Federal Aviation Administration. September 2004.

[17] Processes for software in safety critical systems, O. Benediktsson, R.B. Hunter, A.D. McGettrick, published in Software Process Improvement and Practice Volume 6 No 1 March 2001 pages 47-62 SPIPFL 6 (1) 1-64 (2001) ISSN 1077

[18] ISO/IEC 61508: 1998-2000, Functional Safety of electrical/ electronic/programmable electronic safety related systems. Parts 1 – 7

[19] EADS Astrium SAS. QML.NT.SA.7134.02 on 15/10/2002, v1.0 "Astrium SAS: Rapport d'étude de tailorisation des activités qualité logiciels bord"

[20] See ISO/IEC TR 15504-8:1998 Information Technology - Software Process Assessment Part 8: Guide For Use In Determining Supplier Process Capability.

[21] See: IDEAL: A guide to software process improvement; Bob McFeeley; CMU/SEI-96-HB-001.

[22] ISO 9004: 2000 Quality Management Systems – Guidelines to performance improvements.

[23] John Micklethwait, Adrian Wooldridge. The Witch Doctors. Heinemann. London 1996. ISBN 0-434-00426-X

[24] C. Völcker and A. Cass, SYNSPACE, Yves Tréhin, Objectif Technologie. Guidelines for Software process Improvement. ESA/ESTEC Study Contract No. 10662/93/NL/NB WO6-CCN2. Analysis, Specification and Verification/Validation of Software Product Assurance Process and Product Metrics for Reliability and Safety Critical Software.

[25] R. Ouared, C. Völcker, H van Loon, SYNSPACE. L. Poulin, Grafp. Risk Management based on S4S Assessment ESA/ESTEC Study Contract No. 10662/93/NL/NB WO6-CCN5

[26] Taxonomy based risk identification. Marvin J. Carr, Konda, Monarch, Ulrich, Walker. June 1993 CMU/SEI-93-TR-6 ESC-TR-93-183 Software Engineering Institute.

[27] STARS © 1997-2006 Han van Loon. STARS of Quality Management. Quality Progress. American Society for Quality. September 2000. www.lc-stars.com

[28] Han van Loon, Reach for the STARS. Leadership and management in the new millennium. LC Publishing. 2006 ISBN 0-9758325-0-6. http://www.lc-stars.com

[29] SPICE Project. Phase 2 Trials Final Report. Version 1.01. January 2003. Vol 1. Executive Summary and detailed reports. Vol 2. Findings from Phase 2 of the SPICE Trials. Ho-Won Jung, Robin Hunter, Dennis Goldenson, Khaled El-Emam. www.csi.strath.ac.uk/research/spice/

[30] Process maturity Profile. CMMI ® v1.1. SCAMPISM v1.1 Appraisal Results. First Look. CMU/SEI September 2003.

[31] M. Paulk. CMU/SEI. Trends in Software Process and Quality. October 2002.

[32] CMU/SEI. CMM-Time_to_Move_up slide in online results for SW CMM based improvement. http://seir.sei.cmu.eud/seir/domains/CMMspi/Benefit/IMP/

[33] SPICE Project. Phase 2 Trials Final Report. Version 1.01. January 2003. Vol 1. Executive Summary and detailed reports.

[34] Cambridge Advanced Learner's dictionary

[35] Merriam-Webster Online Dictionary 10th Edition

[36] Han van Loon, Reach for the STARS. Leadership and management in the new millennium. LC Publishing. 2006 ISBN 0-9758325-0-6. http://www.lc-stars.com

[37] ICT and eWork in European SMEs. Patrizio di Nicola. Han van Loon. Proceeding of the 10th International Conference on Concurrent Engineering: Research and Applications. Advanced Design, Production and Management Systems. A.A. BALKEMA Publishers.

[38] Alistair Cockburn. Agile Software Development. Addison Wesley. Pearson Education. ISBN 0-201-69969-9

[39] CMU/SEI-98-TR-012. People CMM® - Based Assessment Method Description. V 1.0. William E. Hefley, Bill Curtis. August 1998

[40] Fons Trompenaar, Charles Hampden-Turner. Riding the Waves of Culture. Understanding Diversity in Global Business - 2nd edition. 1998. McGraw-Hill

[41] Kent Beck, eXtreme Programming Explained: Embrace Change, Addison Wesley, Reading, Massachusetts, 1999. ISBN 0-201-61641-6

[42] Fons Trompenaar, Charles Hampden-Turner. Riding the Waves of Culture. Understanding Diversity in Global Business - 2nd edition. 1998. McGraw-Hill

[43] Michael Hammer and James Champy. Reengineering the Corporation – A Manifesto for Business revolution. Harper Collins Business publishing. 1995. Revised 2001

[44] Han van Loon. 'From Formality to Agility – Applying ISO 15504 Agilely' June 2000. Business Process Mapping © Han van Loon. 1997-2004.

[45] Alistair Cockburn. Agile Software Development. 2002 Addison-Wesley, Pearson Education Inc. ISBN 0-201-69969-9

[46] Alistair Cockburn. Agile Software Development. 2002 Addison-Wesley, Pearson Education Inc. ISBN 0-201-69969-9.

[47] Kent Beck, First Class Software, Embracing Change with eXtreme Programming. IEEE Computer October 1999.

[48] Kent Beck, eXtreme Programming Explained: Embrace Change, Addison Wesley, Reading, Massachusetts, 1999. ISBN 0-201-61641-6

[49] Kent Beck, Test Driven Development – By Example. Addison Wesley, Reading, Massachusetts, 2003. ISBN 0-321-14653-0

[50] Kent Beck, Martin Fowler. Planning Extreme Programming. Addison Wesley, Reading, Massachusetts, 2000. ISBN 0-201-71091-9

[51] Hugh Robinson, Helen Sharp, Centre for Empirical Studies of Software Development, Open University, Milton Keynes, UK. XP Culture: Why the twelve practices are and are not the most significant thing. IEEE Proceedings of the Agile Development Conference 2003.

[52] Mark C. Paulk. eXtreme Programming from a CMM Perspective. IEEE Software vol.18 No. 6 November/December 2001.

[53] Michale K Spayd, QWEST Communications Inc, Evolving Agile in the Enterprise: Implementing XP on a grand scale. IEEE. Proceedings of the Agile Development Conference 2003.

[54] Donald J Reifer, XP and the CMM. IEEE Software May/June 2003

[55] Michele Marchesi, DIEE - University of Cagliari. Agile Methodologies and Quality Certification. 4th International Conference on extreme Programming and Agile processes in Software Engineering. www.xp2003.org.

[56] Control Chaos from ADM Inc, which is part of the Agile Alliance. www.controlchaos.com

[57] Christ Vriens, Philips Research – Software Engineering Services. Certifying for CMM Level 2 and ISO 9001 with XP@Scrum. IEEE Proceedings of the Agile Development Conference 2003.

[58] XP2003, 4th International Conference on extreme Programming and Agile processes in Software Engineering. www.xp2003.org.

[59] J. Nawrocki, B. Walter, A. Wojciechowski. Poznan University of Technology. Towards Maturity Model for extreme Programming.

[60] Takeuchi and Nonaka, The New Product Development Game. Harvard Business Review, Jan-Feb 1986

[61] Alistair Cockburn, Agile Software Development. Addison Wesley. ISBN 0-201-69969-9

[62] ESA/ESTEC Study Contract No. 10662/93/NL/NB WO6-CCN5 PASCON/WO6-CCN5/TN7BISO/IEC TR 15504 Conformant Method for the Assessment of Space Software Processes, Part B: SPiCE for SPACE Method.

[63] Quick Scan © 1999-2004 H. van Loon. www.lc-stars.com

[64] T. Rout, A. Tuffley, B. Hodgen. Software Quality Institute. RAPID: Method for RAPID Assessment of Process Capability, Griffith University, Brisbane, Australia, 30 August 1999

[65] SYNSPiCE © 2000 H.Stienen. SYNSPACE AG/SYNSPACE GmbH. Basel Switzerland. www.synspace.com

[66] See ISO/IEC TR 15504-8:1998 Information Technology - Software Process Assessment Part 8: Guide For Use In Determining Supplier Process Capability.

[67] SPICE Project. Phase 1 Trails Report. Version 1.00, 15th July 1998.

[68] SPICE Project. Phase 2 Trials Final Report. Version 1.01. January 2003. Vol 1. Executive Summary and detailed reports. Vol 2. Findings from Phase 2 of the SPICE Trials. Ho-Won Jung, Robin Hunter, Dennis Goldenson, Khaled El-Emam. Vol 3. Annotated Bibliography. www.csi.strath.ac.uk/research/spice/

[69] Han van Loon. "The audit is dead, long live assessment!'. June 1998. The Quality Magazine. The Australian Organisation for Quality. Han van Loon. 'An early SPICE Experience'. February 2000. Quality Progress. American Society for Quality.

[70] ESA/ESTEC Study Contract No. 10662/93/NL/NB WO6-CCN5 PASCON/WO6-CCN5/TN7BISO/IEC TR 15504 Conformant Method for the Assessment of Space Software Processes, Part B: SPiCE for SPACE Method.

[71] ECSS-M-00-03A: Space Product Management – Risk Management. ESA-ESTEC Requirements & Standards Division, Noordwijk, 25.04.2001.

[72] Daniel Keller, Ann Cass, Philipp Sutter, Questionnaire based process evaluation in NOVE-IT. EuroSPI Conference 2003.

[73] Beurteilung der externen Prozess-Assessments (nach ISO 15504) des Informatikstrategieorgnas Bund ISB durch die META Group Schweiz AG, part of the information pages of the FSUIT [ISB]

[74] Daniel Keller, Ann Cass, Philipp Sutter, Questionnaire based process evaluation in NOVE-IT. EuroSPI Conference 2003.

[75] www.hms.org

[76] www.processprof.com

[77] A Business Case for Software Process Improvement Revised. Thomas McGibbon. The Department of Defence Information Analysis Center. ITT Industries, Advanced Engineering and Science Division. Rome, NY.

[78] Software Process Improvement Works. Advanced Information Systems Inc. Pat Ferguson et al. Technical Report CMU/SEI-99-TR-027. ESC-TR-99-026.

## About the Author

### Han van Loon

Han van Loon is a practicing consultant in the management field as well as Visiting Professor at Nottingham Trent University in the UK and the University of Business and International Studies in Switzerland. He is the copyright owner of this work. Han has published articles on quality management topics over a period of two decades, and worked with the ISO/IEC 15504 standard since 1994. He has successfully led organizations to the highest levels of process capability. Han is an accomplished international speaker and teacher. He has presented at conferences, led seminars and workshops and conducted training in Australia, Asia, Europe and North America.

Han consults to companies and organisations wishing to improve their enterprise results through holistic improvement facilitation, including the use of process assessments and human centred improvement. He specialises in helping clients wishing to achieve business enterprise excellence and world class performance.

Han may be contacted via email: welcome@lc-stars.com or via his web site: http://www.lc-stars.com. His web site provides more details of his holistic management and improvement methodologies and publications.

### About the cover

The cover is a combination of the symbol for Yin and Yang, the symbol for Infinity ∞ and the Team Based Business Design Improvement cycle. It symbolizes the balance and tension between process performance and process change, the continuity required for quality and change implied in improvement, and a holistic balance between people and process. The symbol is copyright of Han van Loon and is used as his corporate trademark.